T0385199

He Said, She Said

He Said, She Said

Truth, Trauma and the Struggle
for Justice in Family Court

CHARLOTTE PROUDMAN

WEIDENFELD & NICOLSON

First published in Great Britain in 2025 by Weidenfeld & Nicolson,
an imprint of The Orion Publishing Group Ltd
Carmelite House, 50 Victoria Embankment
London EC4Y 0DZ

An Hachette UK Company

The authorised representative in the EEA is Hachette Ireland,
8 Castlecourt Centre, Dublin 15, D15 XTP3, Ireland (email: info@hbgi.ie)

3 5 7 9 10 8 6 4 2

A CIP catalogue record for this book is
available from the British Library.

ISBN (Hardback) 978 1 3996 1244 9
ISBN (Ebook) 978 1 3996 1246 3
ISBN (Audio) 978 3996 1247 0

Typeset by Input Data Services Ltd, Bridgwater, Somerset

Printed in Great Britain by Clays Ltd, Elcograf, S.p.A.

www.weidenfeldandnicolson.co.uk

www.orionbooks.co.uk

To every woman who has fought to protect her child from domestic abuse, know that your courage and resilience are truly heroic.

This book is for you.

In the face of silence, I promise to continue raising my voice.

Contents

Author's note

This book is not intended as an academic text or legal publication. It is written for a general audience, and I have sought to make the stories accessible. The purpose is to reveal some of the inner workings of the family justice system, and the difficult experiences many vulnerable women and children have had within it. That presents an inherent challenge, for private family law cases have strict measures to protect the anonymity of parties, and as a barrister I must also safeguard the privacy of my clients. Every case described in this book is factual, and wherever possible I have referred to published judgments. However, almost all names have been changed, some locations have been altered, and other details amended where necessary to maintain the anonymity of those concerned. The descriptions of individuals have been changed, and my conversations with clients do not specifically represent what passed between me and that individual client. Wherever possible, I have sought and received permission from former clients to write about their cases.

Introduction

What happens in family court? Most people will be lucky enough never to find out. Even some of those who want to know – journalists and academics – find their efforts frustrated by strict procedures that throw a privacy net around many cases. But a few people know all too well what can and does go on. Because family court happened to them. First, their life was torn apart by a relationship that failed, often as a result of abuse. Then, contact arrangements for the children broke down. And finally, they ended up in court, having every detail of what went on in their marriage, their home and their bedroom scrutinised by lawyers and judges. Every year in England and Wales, over 50,000 applications are made for such cases to be heard.[1]

They are rarely simple, easy or pleasant proceedings: there is more than an element of truth to the idea that nobody wins in family court. But even with no winners, there can be losers. The more of these cases I worked on, and the more I was exposed to the agony of people having to relive the worst traumas of their lives, the more I came to see that the losers in family court are so often women and children.

It is women who make up almost three-quarters of domestic violence victims in the UK,[2] and who will more often be asked to recall the painful details of how their partner verbally abused, coercively controlled, physically assaulted or raped them. It is women who are mostly bringing forward the most serious allegations and who must prove what they are saying, while male respondents can sit back, poke holes in their arguments and cast doubt. And it is women who must face judges who are predominantly male, relying on their understanding of the nuances of domestic abuse and coercive control. As of 2024, 62 per cent of court judges in the UK were men, rising to 69 per cent in the High Court and 75 per cent in the Court of Appeal.[3]

Let me illustrate with a few examples what can and does happen in family court.

Pauline (who I later represented) was forced to participate in a hearing from her hospital bed when she collapsed in court after testifying – a result of stress and an existing medical condition. Although she was taken to hospital, the hearing simply carried on via video link, and she listened to her alleged rapist give evidence.

Mary's allegation of being raped and strangled during sex by her husband was disbelieved by a judge, who deemed her (in part) too 'intelligent' to have allowed it to happen or to be unable to recall the exact date of the rape.[4]

Isla's claim that she was raped by her ex-partner was disbelieved by a judge because she had not attempted to physically resist. Hannah was told that she had imagined being raped, and Matilda that she had not been raped, even though the court acknowledged that she had not wanted sex on the occasion in question.

Denise, who had made allegations of assault and rape against her ex-partner, was threatened with having her child taken into care and adopted if she continued to make allegations of violence.

Daniella, who had terminal cancer and was trying to protect the interests of her children during a divorce proceeding, had to sit and hear her husband's lawyer argue that she should be awarded a modest financial settlement because she was going to be dead soon.

Melody, who was accused by her ex-partner of alienating their children against him, and telling them to fabricate allegations, decided to go back and live with a man who had abused her because the court had supported his allegations and granted him contact. She chose to put herself at risk rather than allow this man unsupervised time with the children.

And Kate was just one of a number of women who was forced to pay for the man who raped her to have supervised contact with her child – until we won an appeal that changed the law on this point.[5]

Many of these stories and more like them are covered in this book. Almost all are cases I have worked on, just one family law barrister among hundreds. And still, when I talk about how the family court fails women and children, many of my colleagues tell me that I shouldn't. They complain that highlighting the worst of what goes on in family court undermines our judicial system. They say it spreads false ideas and ruins public confidence in the system that is supposed to protect them. They make complaints to my professional body and to my chambers about the things I say and write in public.

I speak up because in my experience the family justice system has a fundamental problem with how it treats women and children. Routinely in my working life, I see survivors of sexual and physical violence accused of not telling the truth because their story is somehow inconsistent or because they lack the evidence to prove what happened to them. I see professionals in the family justice system who struggle to recognise women as victims of abuse because those women are articulate, professional and have their own money. And I see them try to support their stance with arguments that betray a pub bore's interpretation of domestic abuse: why didn't she leave, why didn't she tell someone, why didn't she report him, why didn't she fight him off? By contrast, there is often an apparently generous interpretation of how men behave: he was sexually inexperienced and couldn't read the signals, he has a naturally loud voice and enjoys arguments, he was lashing out in frustration and didn't mean to hit her.

Where women suffer in the family justice system, their children frequently suffer with them. So many of my clients have been women who were desperate to prevent the father having unsupervised contact with their children, knowing from experience the kind of dangerous and abusive behaviour he was capable of.

This puts children at the heart of these proceedings – many of them victims of domestic abuse by virtue of living in a frightening household under the threat of violence or control.[6] They too are punished by a system that does not pay sufficient regard to their needs, and which often condemns them to months or years of uncertainty about who they are going to live with, or whether they have to spend time with a parent who they say scares them.

Florence, just a teenager, and the youngest client I have represented, had been fighting for years to try and overturn a court order which compelled her to live with her father against her wishes. Chloe's son had routinely told his school that he was afraid of his dad, who would stand on his fingers and pull hairs from his arms and legs, but was having court-ordered contact with him until we mounted a successful appeal. Gemma's children, who had said they wanted no contact with a controlling father who had been physically abusive and patrolled the house with a GoPro camera recording everything that went on, were about to be subjected to court-ordered assessments by a psychologist at the father's request before we appealed against it.

Most judges and lawyers never meet the children whose future rests in their hands and many children report feeling disbelieved, unheard and lost in a system that denies them a voice.[7] In 2016, Women's Aid – the charity that campaigns against domestic abuse – published a report showing nineteen children had been killed over a ten-year period during formal or informal contact with an abusive parent, twelve of them during contact that had been ordered by the court.[8]

These stories are personal to me, because I know a little of what it is like to grow up with a violent and alcoholic father. When I read court documents detailing the abuse children have suffered and their fears about spending time with one of their parents, I remember the small child within me. I think back to one of my earliest memories in nursery. I knew something was happening because the nursery staff kept looking at me with concern on their faces. After a while, I was taken outside and told to sit with my father. I saw that his face was a strange yellow colour, and his teeth were rotten. Later, I would learn that these were indicators of his alcoholism. The way he looked, and the things I had seen at home, made him a frightening figure to me. I wanted to leave, but my feet were frozen. I said almost nothing, hoping it would be over soon. All I knew was that I was scared and didn't want to be left with him. I looked back at the staff, my eyes begging them to rescue me, but they turned their backs on me. Eventually, he left. I think this was the last time I saw him before he died in a road traffic accident when he was driving drunk. I was lucky not to be in the car with him.

The impact of going through family court can be profound. Many of the women involved in these cases have already endured deeply traumatic experiences: abused by a violent partner, accused of abducting or alienating their own child, coerced into continuing with or terminating a pregnancy. The tragedy is that this ordeal may only be the beginning. Often, they have been brought to court by their abusive ex-partner, who is seeking to change or expand the terms of their court-ordered contact with the children. If the mother wishes to prevent this to safeguard her child, she must present her allegations of what the ex-partner or husband did to her to the court, recounting every excruciating detail of the alleged abuse. During this proceeding she may be questioned about how she chose to act in the aftermath of a rape or serious assault: why did she not report it, or if she did, why is her account now slightly different from the one she told to the police or a women's centre years before? If the judge ultimately finds against her, saying the allegations are not proved as facts, the written judgment that follows can never be expunged. It will always say that she was not, in fact, raped, beaten up or verbally abused and humiliated to the point of despair – or even worse that she fabricated the allegations. It will follow the woman, and her children, around for a lifetime.

Frequently, this feels like a game that women cannot win: one will be told that they don't have enough evidence for their claims, and another that their story feels too manufactured to be believed. One will not be considered a victim because they appear insufficiently emotional, another not taken seriously as a witness because they naturally become upset or struggle to express themselves when describing horrifying experiences.[9] Traumatised women who I represent are often held to the highest imaginable standard of demeanour, evidence and consistency. They are asked to walk an impossible tightrope and then blamed for falling from it.

And that may be just the first set of proceedings. For some, the agony is prolonged for months or even years as hearings are delayed and more applications are made by the litigant – a father who may be complaining that he needs more time with his children, that the mother is poisoning them against him, or that financial arrangements need to be reviewed. They are dragged through hearing after hearing, required to relive the worst moments of their lives on an endless loop. The family court, which should serve to liberate victims of abuse from terrible circumstances, instead risks locking women into a secondary relationship with their abuser, which may go on for longer than they were together in the first place.

The results of these cases can range from frustrating to horrifying. Rosie wept as she told me that she felt she had no option but to go back to her abusive partner, who had been granted unsupervised contact with the children. She knew the risks he posed and believed that only by endangering herself could she protect them. Lydia begged me that there must surely, *surely* be something we could do to prohibit her child from having contact with a father who had allegedly threatened to kill both her and her unborn foetus during her pregnancy. Lisa crumpled into a heap on the floor outside the courtroom after she was told that her appeal had been rejected, and that her young child must return immediately to the country from which they had fled to escape an abusive household months earlier. She had got out, and now the court was sending her and her child back into the clutches of their abuser. It is hard not to feel hopeless when you must tell a desperate woman that no, there is nothing more you can do for them. They are out of time, out of appeals, out of hope.

The urge to avoid uttering those words is the motivation for my work. Many of the women I represent want not just to be heard by the court, to have their concerns addressed and their children safeguarded, but also to try and help others in the same position. We use their cases to present arguments that have established important precedents to protect women and children from dangerous men.*

As a result of cases I have argued, women's refuges are no longer required to disclose their addresses for the purposes of delivering court orders, whereas before, these confidential and highly sensitive addresses were at risk of falling into the

---

* In court, you may use the result of one case to help you argue another, and part of a barrister's job is to present the most relevant historic cases to the judge for them to consider when determining the one in front of them.

hands of perpetrators and their lawyers, putting residents in harm's way. Thanks to another, victims are no longer required to help pay for their abusers to have supervised contact with their children.[10] And judges are encouraged to consider whether, when a perpetrator of abuse works in a regulated profession, such as a social worker or doctor, their professional body should be informed of the findings against them.[11] I have also secured judgments that recognised gaslighting as a form of domestic abuse,[12] defined DARVO (deny, attack, reverse victim and offender) as a form of abuse,[13] recognised coercive and controlling behaviour as an insidious pattern of domestic abuse,[14] reinforced the need for victims to receive special measures while giving evidence – such as protective screens and separate waiting areas so they do not need to look at their alleged abuser[15] – and established that there should be strict limits to introducing a victim's sexual history into evidence so this cannot be used to portray them in a negative light.[16]

Laws are applied and interpreted in court, but they are made in Parliament, so in parallel to my work as a barrister, I have campaigned alongside other lawyers and victims' groups for changes in the law around domestic abuse, rape, coercive control, virginity testing, child marriage, forced marriage and female genital mutilation (FGM). We helped to draft amendments that have given the court new powers to protect girls at risk of FGM from being taken out of England and Wales, to raise the legal marriage age in England and Wales from sixteen to eighteen, and to criminalise virginity testing, hymenoplasty and child marriage.[17] I worked on the Domestic Abuse Bill that introduced the first statutory definition of domestic abuse, defined children as victims in their own right, recognised coercive and controlling behaviour as a distinctive form of abuse, and banned perpetrators from being able to cross-examine their victims in court.

In the fifteen years since I was called to the bar, some strides have been made to improve how both the law and the family court treats women and children. Yet there remain gaping holes in the law through which vulnerable women frequently fall. In family law there is no statutory definition to tell a judge what is and isn't rape. There is no law to prevent a victim's medical records from being disclosed to their abuser during proceedings. And if a couple was ever married, there is no legal means to terminate the father's parental responsibility, not even if he had raped the mother. There is no way of holding judges personally accountable for their decisions, even if they have caused harm, nor are there sufficient protections for women against being dragged through one case after another by abusers who use the court as an extension of their controlling behaviour post-separation.*

Then, of course, there are attitudes. The law on paper is one thing – a constellation of primary legislation, advice set out to judges (in what are known as practice directions) and precedents that provide a thread for others to pick up. Much of a barrister's job is to wrestle all this material into a written 'skeleton' argument that supports your client's case, which both sides will submit to the judge before any major hearing.

Parallel to this is the law in practice – how the judge

---

* Judges are protected by judicial immunity for everything they say, do or decide in court. No legal action can be brought against them pertaining to this.

who hears a case chooses to interpret and apply all of this. In family court, there is no jury. There are no charges or convictions. There are simply applications (such as for a divorce or contact with children), allegations which one or both sides bring against the other to support their case, and findings made by the judge, usually communicated in a written or oral judgment that sets out their reasoning. The judge upholds or dismisses allegations on the balance of probabilities – whether it is more likely than not to be true, i.e. at least 51 per cent likely – and makes orders that amount either to a final decision or a referral to another hearing.

The upshot is that the judge is a figure of overwhelming power. Their view of a case and the validity of witness testimony will go a long way to determining the outcome. That is why we should all be concerned by certain comments of family court judges: one described an incident of strangulation as a prank, another told a woman that 'it's not like you were beaten', and a third that 'you could not have been raped because you did not fight him off'.[18] Such dismissive attitudes are not just deeply traumatising for the women who are subjected to them. They can also underpin life-changing decisions for children in cases where the evidence often amounts to little more than his version of events, her version, and a judge who must decide which one they prefer.

I write, talk and campaign on these issues because I simply refuse to watch so many vulnerable women and children be so badly treated by a system that they expect to provide justice. My experience tells me that only by fighting back in court, and raising awareness beyond it, can you make a difference – one case, one precedent, one amendment to parliamentary legislation at a time.

I never knew that this was the cause I would dedicate my career to: growing up in a working-class, single-parent household in the Midlands, I had no idea what working in the law would be like. But once I had joined the bar, it did not take long to realise that the law was failing women, not to recognise the misogyny – ingrained prejudice against women – that affects both young women seeking to become barristers and the vulnerable clients we represent. After that, there was no question about what I wanted to do and to achieve, and of my desire to make the law fairer and more just for women.

That purpose continues to motivate me because there are so many women and girls for whom we must do better. Women who only wish to protect their children from men they know to be dangerous. Women who are trying to escape abusive relationships and often become locked in legal proceedings that drag on for years, sometimes bankrupting them. Women who were raped and sexually assaulted and are still living with the trauma of that experience years later, only to be interrogated about why they did not behave more 'logically' in the aftermath. Women from marginalised backgrounds who are suffering intersectional inequalities stemming from classism, language barriers, transphobia, lack of access to legal aid, ableism, or outright racism and cultural and religious prejudice.* We cannot achieve fairer outcomes without critically examining the current system

---

* The Ministry of Justice's Harm Report highlighted evidence citing 'the vulnerabilities and sense of powerlessness' felt by BAME domestic abuse survivors, relating to everything from community and social pressure to insecure immigration status, language barriers, and the feeling they were not perceived as reliable witnesses in court.[19]

and its failings, however uncomfortable that may be for those working within it.

In turn, we must do better for children, who often become like hostages traded between two households when a court orders a forced transfer of residence because it accepts a parent's, often father's, allegations that the mother has 'alienated' them from him. We must do better for girls who may need someone to fight in court to protect them from being sent abroad to a place where their family intends to perform FGM.

Family court is where people who have suffered unimaginably, with no other place to turn, end up. We owe these people understanding, fairness and, above all, justice. None of that will be achieved until we can have an honest reckoning about sexist attitudes, victim-blaming tendencies and a too-common lack of understanding about the complex dynamics of abuse and control within intimate relationships.

I have written this book because I believe that, like any institution, the family justice system can only evolve through honest reflection and a willingness to confront its flaws. I am an admirer of the objectives of our justice system as well as a critic and a participant: I respect the dedicated work of solicitors, barristers and judges who strive to uphold justice and improve our system, often in circumstances that are far from easy or ideal. The stories in this book reflect moments where the system has both succeeded and failed, especially in its treatment of women and children who have suffered the horrors of domestic abuse. I wish to emphasise that, while the content is often unavoidably critical, the intention is to reflect on systemic failings, using individual cases and judgments to cast light on these, not to try to challenge their outcome. Ultimately, I believe the system is robust enough to withstand constructive criticism, and that scrutiny of this kind should be seen as beneficial to creating change. That is a belief I ended up having to fight for in a professional tribunal, when my regulatory body prosecuted me for things I had written about a case on social media.

I also believe that more people need to understand how the family court works. They should know what happens when parents fight in court, and who is responsible for deciding whether a man accused of physical and sexual violence gets to see and look after his children. A broken relationship and a family court case can happen to anyone, and almost no one is prepared for what that is like. Nor is there nearly enough recognition of when and how the family court gets it wrong, and the shocking consequences of those decisions on the lives of women and children.

What goes on in family court affects us all – as my clients often tell me, it is the kind of experience that you think only happens to other people until it is happening to you.

I

'Where Are You From?':
Becoming a Barrister

'Oh, I don't think this is for you, Charlotte.'

My teacher lifted her head from the giant, Yellow Pages-style book she had been consulting, raising her huge dome of curly grey hair. We were sitting alone in her box room office for a careers advice session. I had just told her that I wanted to be a lawyer. Her smile was gentle, and she intended no harm. But the meaning, the same one that had been transmitted by laughter in the classroom when I said, aged fourteen, that I wanted to be a solicitor, was clear enough. I had set my sights too high. My teacher returned her attention to the jobs bible in front of her. 'Maybe you should try and become a clerk.'

The idea of the law had taken root in me before I really knew what it was or what the job entailed. Growing up in the small market town of Leek, a career in law simply represented what it meant to be successful. My mum encouraged me to aspire to it because she thought it would mean achieving a better standard of living than she had. I adopted the dream because I thought it would give me the one thing I wanted most in life: freedom and a new beginning.

As I discovered when training to be a lawyer in London, not everyone has heard of Leek. 'Where are you from?' I would be asked at the interminable dinners we had to attend to become a member of one of the Inns of Court. My answer was rarely met with anything less than a bemused look, which often lingered when I explained that Leek was in Staffordshire. When I confirmed that it was near Stoke, bemusement would give way to a kind of sympathetic horror. It didn't occur to me to say it was on the fringes of the Peak District: my childhood weekends had fondly been spent far more in the Potteries Shopping Centre than the National Park.

Those who do venture ten miles north and east of Stoke will find a market town like so many others, complete with mock Tudor trappings, red-brick storefronts and pubs proclaiming their long history. Leek may be a very pleasant place to be at certain stages in life, but the second half of childhood is not one of them. By my late teens, I already felt tired of the sight of the same streets, buildings, walls and faces. Everything had its place, everyone seemed to know you, and no part of it ever seemed to change. I could have drawn every inch of the town from memory. While some people found this familiarity reassuring and even comforting, to me it was oppressive.

At sixteen, I started working at the Co-op supermarket to support myself through college and then my degree at Keele University. For five years, week after week, I could almost predict who would be filing through my checkout at what times, the items I would be scanning, the chit-chat we would have, and even the way people would count out their money. Leek felt like the town that change forgot: I was desperate to escape to the city, and clung to law as my life raft.

At this time in my life, knowing so little about my future career, being a lawyer meant becoming a solicitor. All the lawyers in and around Leek were solicitors. But when I did work experience during my law degree at a few local firms in Stoke, it felt like more of the same – the market town transplanted to the office. It wasn't until one of the lawyers I was shadowing took me to court that I found what I was really looking for. All day my eye was drawn to a woman perhaps ten years older than me. She had marched into court wearing a pale pink and grey pinstripe suit, a Louis Vuitton bag on one arm, papers bound with pink ribbon under the other, and blond hair visible under her horsehair wig. Watching her cross-examine a witness, with precise and challenging questions, I knew this was not just another day like all the others. There was a tension that seemed to cloak the entire room, holding people in place. She was defending a teenage boy who had never had a chance in life, thrown out by his parents and enmeshed in a life of crime. In a world where I was used to everything seeming mundane, this felt different and exciting. I went home that day knowing that now I had found something I really wanted to be. It was no longer an abstract idea but a concrete goal.

Soon, this slightly idealistic notion took me to London for the first time and to bar school at the age of twenty-one. The work was challenging enough on its own: a crash course in the law, in preparation for trying to gain a pupillage (traineeship) at a barristers' chambers, an application process with a success rate of around 8 per cent.[1] It turned out the

3

studying was the easy part. Far more difficult was getting used to the atmosphere that prevailed in this new world and the people who seemed to thrive in it, effortlessly gliding through the networking and the flummery while I was gulping at air that felt thin. There were cliques of people who seemed to have known each other all their lives, whose fathers were barristers or judges and who already had a pupillage in their pocket before we had sat our first exam.

'What did your father do?' This was another of the questions that came around and around at the mandatory dinners, after we had got Leek out of the way, and established that I'd been to university at Keele (which they hadn't heard of either). I always avoided this one, though the answer might have helped to explain why I was in those opulent dining halls with people so different from me, who made little attempt to hide their belief that I had no place being there.

The truth was that I hardly knew my dad, who had died when I was four. Nor would I have wanted to know him, an alcoholic and a violent man, a story I pieced together over the years from what various relatives and family friends told me. Although I have few memories of my father, he did leave one important legacy in the form of his will. In a final act of control, he wrote my mum and me out of it, instead giving everything he had – which was also everything we had – to charity. I watched my mum spend years contesting the will on my behalf: an unconscious early education in how abusive relationships can leave a legal long tail that stretches over time, creating stress and anxiety that compounds the trauma of the abuse itself. My mum's regular lectures about the need to be independent and have

4

a career of your own, stemming from these experiences, were another thing that had helped to push me towards the unlikely destination of the law.

Having worked to get this far, I was not going to give up easily. But I kept running into a wall of cheerful faces, pinstriped accents and ever-so-polite disdain. Early on in my time at bar school, I had lunch with the barrister who had been assigned as my mentor. We sat together in the Great Hall at Lincoln's Inn, at one of the long trestle tables, surrounded by dark wooden panelling. Above us loomed paintings of long-ago judges in their wigs and flowing robes, and completing the picture was a gargantuan fresco depicting figures such as Moses and Muhammad, Pythagoras, Alfred the Great and Charlemagne.

It was a long way from my grandparents' living room in Newcastle-under-Lyme, where I would sit on the settee with my granddad – a retired railway worker and trade unionist, as well as a talented pianist – reading Marx. My nanna would sit in her armchair watching the world go by from the front window, balancing a book about Ancient Egypt on her knee. By contrast, a room like the Great Hall still felt bizarre and overawing even after multiple visits. To many of my peers who had been to centuries-old private schools and Oxbridge, it was just a dining room.

Our lunch finished and my would-be mentor surprised me by suggesting we should go for a walk so we could chat about how I was getting on. The real news, it seemed, was not for nineteenth-century judges to overhear. The lunch had been our first proper conversation, and he was still quizzing me about my background. Then he stopped, turned to me with a sad smile that reminded me of my teacher from years before, and spilled out words he had clearly been storing up.

'You've done really well to get here and get this far, but you'll never make it.'

It was so cruel, so fleeting, such a snap judgement from a person who barely knew me that I was shocked into silence. I didn't argue with him or ask why he had said it. How he had decided, based on such minimal information, that I would never pass the incredibly fine sieve through which the bar filters its wannabes. I just took in his words and internalised them, chewing them over and over as I answered his remaining questions on autopilot.

We parted, and he gave me a sheepish grin – I really think he believed he was doing me a favour, saving me from so much time and money spent in an apparently wasted effort. But in the days and weeks that followed, disbelief hardened into anger and resolve. Knowing what some people thought of me having the nerve to try and enter their world made me more determined than ever. The message was clear from the very beginning. I wanted the bar, but the bar – or at least parts of it – did not want me. In the years that followed, it would become a familiar feeling.

'This kid: she's going to be as thick as her father and as ugly as her mother.'

It was my brutal yet truthful induction into how the family court can be during one of the very first hearings I attended as a baby barrister. The local authority had brought a case against the two parents, one of whom was autistic while the other had learning difficulties. These parents, who needed help and support to care for a baby they obviously loved deeply, were instead being threatened with an adoption order for their child.

The man I overheard during a break in proceedings was flicking through a photo album that the mother had brought along, showing pictures of the family together. It would have been bad enough if he had no influence in the case. Unbelievably, he was in fact the voice of the child – the lawyer representing the guardian *ad litem*, who is the social worker appointed by the court as the child's independent representative. They would make recommendations to the judge about how the child should be cared for. This little girl's life chances were being brushed aside with callous indifference by a man who was meant to be her advocate. Meanwhile, the social worker from the local authority had allegedly said to the mother, 'Don't worry, you can always have another one. They might let you keep that one.'

I was shocked, even more so when I shared my concerns with a senior lawyer, who responded with laughter. Almost from the moment I started working at the bar, I realised that some of my new colleagues were people for whom the extremes of suffering had become normalised. They would represent clients facing desperate circumstances in the morning, have jocular conversations about it over lunch in an expensive restaurant (or if needs must a dingy court café), and then move on to another case the next day without a second thought. People were cases. Victims were witnesses. Wrongdoing was a matter of technical debate and should never be viewed through the lens of fairness or justice. Who was the judge, who were we against, and whether we would win were accepted topics of conversation. Less so questions about whether the truth had been established, whether people had been treated fairly, and if justice had been done.

By doing this, barristers are not subverting the system but working as it intends them to. From the beginning of your training, you are told that it is desirable to keep a professional distance from your clients. Yes, you are bound to represent them to the best of your ability and act in their best interests (core duty 2 of the Bar Standards Board code of conduct), but you are also meant to remain independent (core duty 4). Getting too friendly with the client and identifying too closely with their interests could compromise that independence. If there is ever any conflict between these two requirements, the code of conduct makes clear on which side you should fall: 'Your duty to act in the best interests of each client is subject to your duty to the court.'[2] In other words, the court must come first and the client – the person who needs help – second.

As I took my first steps into this world, I realised I was entering not one unfamiliar sphere but two. Many of my colleagues at the bar had come from much more privileged backgrounds than I had – they spoke and behaved a certain way, expecting that their voice would be heard because experience had told them it always would be. But my upbringing, while hardly gilded, was far from suffering. Leek may have been dull to my teenage mind, but it was also safe. My mum and I lived comfortably. The same was not true of some of my clients. I will never forget a horrible case I observed while doing a mini-pupillage (work experience) at a set of chambers that specialised in criminal law. I was shadowing a barrister who was prosecuting a teenage boy for the sexual assault of another, younger boy.

Among the evidence was a picture of the room where the defendant had been living: a completely bare room with nothing in it except an old, stained mattress. No carpet, no pictures or posters on the wall, no possessions, no curtains, no bedclothes even. It conveyed a squalor and despair that no child should be exposed to. Now, one damaged life had broken into another.

Joining the bar brought me up close to stories like this – of deprivation and trauma that I could not have imagined. From the top rung of the ladder, the bottom one was apparently far enough away that its realities could be shrugged off. But I kept thinking about those two boys and their two ruined lives: how poverty and abuse can spread like a crack in plaster, snaking up a wall or across a ceiling. I kept encountering cases that shocked me either because of the details of trauma and abuse they contained or by how lightly these seemed to be worn by the barristers I was working with. I knew I could not tiptoe through my career, chewing up and spitting out these cases, shrugging my shoulders at the worst of what I saw and heard. But it would take a few years, and several shoves in the right direction, until I worked out what I could do about it.

In these early days at the bar, trying to find my place in a world that was in every way unfamiliar, I soon realised another novelty. This was, by some distance, the most male environment I had ever encountered. Perhaps it felt so jarring because of my own background – an all-female household, a university where over 60 per cent of the students are female, and five years on the shop floor of a supermarket, another place where women are in the clear majority.[3] It was not that women were absent at the bar: we represented 37 per cent of the profession in 2011, the year after I was called, a figure which remained almost unchanged a dozen years later.[4] But the environment and culture felt overwhelmingly male: deep voices rumbling through the cavernous dining halls, and the courtroom often featuring two male lawyers before a male judge. Almost every barrister I shadowed while doing mini-pupillages was a man.

It was during one of those weeks that I saw what the predominance of men and male attitudes can lead to. We were in a taxi to court. The barrister I was with had papers spread across his knees and we were discussing the case. Then, as if it was the natural next point in the evidence we were discussing, his hand was on my leg. He groped me the same way he talked, calmly and confidently, a statement and not a question. The hand moved up and down my thigh as he spoke.

'You know there are a lot of things someone in your position will do to get a place.' He paused, and the hand remained, for two or three endless seconds. My mouth was open but I didn't speak. The taxi continued its smooth progress towards the court. Realising that there would be no response, the hand withdrew. It straightened the file in front of him and he resumed our discussion about the case.

I might have dismissed this as an isolated incident – a phrase so beloved by those who wish to downplay problems with our profession and legal system – if it was the first time. I had been no less shocked a year or two before when applying for work experience at a firm of solicitors. Don't send a CV, one of the partners said to me. What about a bikini picture instead? Then there were the stories some of my peers would tell me or which were sent to me after I gained a public profile for speaking out about sexism at the bar. One of these women said she had approached a judge about mentoring her while she was a law student. Over lunch, he had propositioned her to become his mistress.

Surveys suggest that around 40 per cent of women lawyers in the UK have experienced sexual harassment in some form.[5] These are not isolated incidents or rogue individuals. The problem is endemic and it is getting worse. A Bar Council survey in 2023 found that 44 per cent of barristers have experienced or witnessed bullying, harassment or discrimination in the prior two years. The figure for 2021 had been 38 per cent and in 2017 it was 31 per cent. Perhaps needless to say, such behaviours disproportionately affect barristers who are women, those who come from an ethnic minority background, who are LGBTQ+, who have a disability or who went to state school.[6]

Right at the beginning of my career, I had seen and experienced for myself what it means to be sexually harassed as a young woman trying to break into the profession. Those experiences meant that, when a jarring message landed in my LinkedIn inbox in 2015, I was not overly surprised. It was far from the first, although it would turn out to be the most significant. From a male solicitor more than twice my age, it read:

Charlotte, delighted to connect, I appreciate this is probably horrendously politically incorrect but that is a stunning picture !!! You definitely win the prize for the best Linked in [sic] picture I have ever seen. Always interest to understant [sic] people's skills and how we might work together. Alex.

I replied, telling him that I found his message offensive, that I was using LinkedIn for professional reasons, 'not to be approached about my physical appearance or to be objectified by sexist men'. Then I posted a screenshot of our messages on Twitter, asking if other female lawyers were receiving similar approaches. In the weeks and months that followed, as I became the focus of an onslaught of media attention, many assumed that this had been my intention from the start. That I had set out to make myself famous and used a message to stoke controversy.

Anybody who knows what it is like to have your face on the front page of a tabloid newspaper and be branded a feminazi, to have the way you look debated in public, and your family and friends harassed by journalists, would immediately understand what an absurd proposition this is. All I had wanted to do was tell a man why I found his behaviour unacceptable and to start a conversation with my small social media audience about how women are treated online (since this was not the first message of its kind I had received, nor the first example of sexual harassment). I knew that the only approaches my partner received on LinkedIn were to offer him a job. Whereas I was being messaged, first and foremost, so that men could comment on my appearance.

The message may not have been the worst thing on its own, but it did not exist in isolation. Low-level sexism never does. It was the thin end of a wedge of misogyny and sexual harassment in the legal profession. One that slopes up to much more serious incidents. To a barrister's hand rubbing up and down my thigh when I was a law student. To Kevin Barry, an equal opportunities officer at his chambers, who in 2019 was fined £3,000 for 'unwanted sexual conduct' towards a woman in a bar five years earlier, where he had told her she was beautiful, tried to kiss her, put his hand down her skirt and squeezed her bottom.[7] To Dominic Woolard, a barrister who over the course of one evening at a social function grabbed a young woman around the neck, smacked her hard on the bottom and pulled her onto his knee – he was fined £6,000.[8] And to Robert Kearney, who had told a woman undertaking a mini-pupillage at his chambers that he 'kept his nails short because you can't finger women with long nails', sniffed her neck in a lift, told her to 'wear skirts and heels instead of trousers' and asked her about her bra size, what perfume she was wearing and whether she had ever had sex in her parents' house. For that, he was suspended in 2021. He was not disbarred until a separate disciplinary tribunal in 2023 found that he had told another mini-pupil at his chambers: 'You need to have sex with senior members of the Bar, then you will be successful.' And another young woman that she was 'frigid' and needed to 'go and have fucking sex'. With both these women, the tribunal found that he 'had inappropriate contact and hand placement'.[9] At the time of writing, Kearney's disbarment was set for review after he was granted the right to appeal.[10]

These incidents of misogyny stem from a common root of male entitlement, sexist attitudes and lack of accountability. What begins with comments that many men consider harmless does not end there. An unwanted remark may receive a neutral response in an attempt to defuse the situation. Taking encouragement from that, a man may soon move on to propositions, demands, a hand up your skirt or his lips pressed onto yours. Every woman knows this is how it can be. And yet so many men deny it. The power dynamics of the bar, with a disproportionate number of men in senior positions, exacerbates the likelihood that an entitled older man will seek to exploit his power over a young woman who has none, who knows there are ten other highly qualified peers who could easily take her place. The nature of career progression also means that the senior barrister who sees fit to put his hand up a young woman's skirt may soon (or may already) be the judge who gets to decide what does and does not constitute sexual abuse. If we have a warped view of what constitutes sexual misconduct in the legal profession, there is a real risk that then seeps through into the judicial system. How can the judiciary be insulated from sexist and misogynistic attitudes when it must recruit from the bar, where a troubling culture of sexual harassment and bullying has been widely recognised?

I believe, now as I did then, that you cannot eliminate sexual harassment until you confront the attitudes that underpin it. That is why I published the LinkedIn message I had received, to start a discussion that, perhaps naively, I expected to remain within my small circle of followers. I anticipated a little push-back from men online, but was in no way prepared for it to reach such a wide audience, or what this would involve.

When I received the initial message, I was not even working at the bar. I had taken a career break to pursue a PhD and was about to leave for a semester at Harvard as a visiting researcher. My flight to Boston was in a few days, and I had only just responded to the solicitor's message. Within twenty-four hours or so, newspapers were reporting the story, and soon my face was on the front of the *Daily Mail* alongside a banner that blared: 'A glam lawyer and the Feminazis who hate men who praise their looks'. It previewed an article from the columnist Sarah Vine, featuring lines about me such as 'heaven help the poor man who actually tries to ask her out on a date, let alone try to get her into his bed. He'd have better luck propositioning a porcupine.' And: 'this is not really about helping women overcome sexism, is it? It's about Ms Proudman making sure she's the absolute centre of everyone's attentions.'[11]

In fairness to Sarah Vine, her piece was a masterclass of its kind, a perfect example of how our society demonises women who speak up about misogyny, sexual harassment and worse. First comes the blame: why not have used a different picture or none at all? Then, the insults and the typecasting: frigid, touchy, self-righteous, humourless. Next, the minimisation and whataboutery: 'it's not as if he sidled up to her in a bar and pinched her bum, or thrust his unwanted attentions on her on the bus', Vine wrote. And finally the gaslighting, telling you that your concerns aren't real and asking you to disbelieve what you know to be true. It's all a big joke, and you don't get it. This is how the world works, love. Dare to question men's right to leer at you, whether in person or online, and soon red tops and red faces are screaming at you with lines that would not have been out of place in a Bernard Manning routine.

The column accused me of having brought about 'a state of war' by posting the messages on Twitter. In reality, this was what the *Mail* had achieved. Having my face on its front cover – on two consecutive days – set me up as target practice for the media. Soon I had a reporter following me to Harvard and contacting new colleagues I had barely met to dig for dirt. Back in Staffordshire, the same was happening with any family member they could find. The stories that resulted included one that inaccurately attacked my relationship with my paternal grandmother, who had died the previous year. What she had to do with a story about sexism in the law, I will never understand. Invasion of privacy barely begins to describe what this was like.

In parallel, and incited by the absurd and overblown international media coverage, I was receiving a deluge of fan mail on social media. Much of it was the mindless abuse of internet trolls, who spat out every insult under the sun, told me I should kill myself, and went out of their way to assure me that they were not, in fact, attracted to me.[12] After receiving an email threatening to find me, kill me, chop me up and put my head in a plastic bag, I struggled to sleep. As I lay awake in my flat at Harvard, I could hear rustling outside; fearful that the author of the death threat might actually have hunted me down, I telephoned the police. Little in the way of help followed: the local cops in Boston even suggested that I go on a self-defence course.

Concerning in a different way were messages from other lawyers, including solicitors. 'Nomorebriefs4u', tweeted one, a reference to the fact that barristers rely for work on their relationships with solicitors who instruct them with cases. In subsequent media interviews, a male solicitor confirmed that he would never consider giving me work.[13]

This had all begun days earlier when I sent the fateful tweet, attaching a screenshot of the message, which read: 'How many women @LinkedIn are contacted re physical appearance rather than prof skills?' Now, I was being subjected to the kind of media scrutiny usually reserved for serial killers, accompanied by a deluge of hate online and plenty of signals from within my profession that I had seriously damaged my career. At the time, I felt overwhelmed as this tide washed over me, even from over 3,000 miles away. Now, I have come to recognise it as the characteristic response of the Establishment in defence mode: closing ranks to punish, threaten and humiliate a woman who dares to speak out. It is disproportionate by design, eviscerating one dissenter in the hope of discouraging the next.

Nor was the initial flare of media and public attention the last word on the matter. That came several months later, when I returned from Harvard and to chambers, reasoning that with my career in question, I couldn't afford to wait to re-establish myself. I continued with my PhD in parallel, and it fed into much of my subsequent legal work campaigning for women and girls at risk of FGM.

At this point, I was an associate tenant at Mansfield Chambers, the set of the legendary barrister Michael Mansfield KC, whose campaigning work for people who had suffered miscarriages of justice – including the Birmingham Six, the families of Bloody Sunday victims, and later the relatives of those unlawfully killed in the Hillsborough disaster – was a model of advocacy I one day hoped to emulate. I was initially concerned by how he might respond to the media coverage, but he dismissed it as rubbish before I could even raise the subject. In the unmistakable voice that matches his appearance – big, booming and flamboyant – he declaimed in typical Michael manner, 'Good on you.' I felt at home.

But it was a home on whose door my critics were now

hammering. On my first day back, I went straight to my pigeonhole to see what I had missed. One letter immediately caught my eye. Printed on its envelope was the crest of the judiciary of England and Wales. I opened it while standing in the mailroom and took out several sheets of similarly headed paper. In blue ink and a slanting hand with looping, fountain pen flourishes, my correspondent took aim. I had brought the profession into disrepute. Should not be allowed to practise. Needed to be disbarred. On and on it went, quoting from interviews I'd given and citing details that suggested the author had read every single article published about me. It was personal, accusatory and did not even seek to conceal its threatening and mocking tone. Unsigned, it concluded with a PS: 'I'll tell Mike to give your bottom a good slap the next time he sees you!!'

This came after months of enduring deeply unpleasant things written about and sent to me. I thought that, in the process, I had grown a thick skin. But this letter, written from the highest echelon of my profession and delivered directly to my workplace, inflicted a different kind of wound. It told me that among the people who apparently now hated me was at least one who wanted to destroy my career and might have the power to do so. At the bar, a small world of overlapping networks, having one influential person against you can quickly bring more.

'What is it?'

My senior clerk must have noticed that the colour had disappeared from my face, my hands were shaking, and tears were in my eyes. I felt like I could only breathe in and not out. Only when he spoke did I lift my eyes from the page and realise he was standing in front of me. Without a word, I handed the letter to him, and he began to read. He scanned the first page and looked back at me.

'Don't worry about that. I'll see to it.'

I knew that he meant it. Officially, the clerks – the career that had once been suggested to me – manage the administration of the chambers and are responsible for facilitating contact with solicitors and negotiating fees. Unofficially, and no less importantly, they are the bar's power brokers and information mongers, working as connectors, fixers and, when necessary, enforcers. If you want something done in this world, you ask a clerk for help. I watched as he returned the pages to their envelope, opened the top drawer of his desk and placed it inside.

In the event, we didn't speak about it again until years later at a colleague's party, long after we had both moved to different sets. The judge who wielded the poison pen had eluded discovery. But the message, even under cover of anonymity, was unmistakable. Just a few years into my career I was a marked woman. Now, everything I did or said would be scrutinised by people who were desperate for me to fail.

If there was any doubt that being labelled a feminazi might affect my career, it was dispelled when I sought a new job the following year. One set of chambers, which was advertising open roles on its website, told me when I contacted them that they weren't accepting applications. Another said that they didn't want to recruit someone known as a 'troublemaker', while several others turned me down without offering feedback.

When I did secure a tenancy in family law at Goldsmith

Chambers, I began to realise the damage had not been so bad. I had a steady stream of instructions, many of them from female solicitors. I began to carve out my practice area, specialising in fields such as FGM and child abduction cases. I had quit social media to insulate myself from the hatred that had been spewing in my direction since the LinkedIn drama. For the first time, I began to feel comfortable in a world that had hitherto felt alien.

Equally, I could never quite dispel a sense of unease. The more work I did, the more clearly I began to see the patterns of the family court. Representing victims and perpetrators, I both heard and made the arguments that seemed to undermine women's allegations of domestic abuse. Did she really look like a credible victim? Where was her evidence? Why had her story changed? And could he really be blamed for what had happened?

I saw how easy it is to be lulled into acquiescence by the rhythms of the system: another case, another face and on to the next one without a backwards glance. You are often briefed at the last minute, working into the night to digest thick stacks of paperwork and prepare lengthy arguments. You may only meet your client on the steps of the courtroom for a rushed conference to explain their options before going in front of the judge minutes later. There is barely time to think about what is directly in front of you, let alone the wider questions it throws up. That twinge of doubt is soon buried under yet another stack of files.

For a few years, I worked like this. But I could not keep my head down forever. We were living through a collective awakening of the sheer prevalence of sexual violence against women and how deeply enmeshed this was with the power structures of professions and the workplace. The #MeToo movement took flight in October 2017 after the arrest of the sexual predator and movie producer Harvey Weinstein. In 2018, the University of Cambridge, where I had been doing my PhD and later became a junior research fellow, acknowledged a 'significant problem involving sexual misconduct'.[14] Some of my female students told me that they had been raped and sexually assaulted by other students.

The knowledge that society was coming to terms with sexual violence against women, however imperfectly, made the situation in family court even more jarring. Here, we still seemed to live in a world that was anything but awake when it came to the dynamics of power and control that underpin a man's choice to rape, assault or otherwise coerce a woman. A world that in some places still seemed to believe that women should be made to account for what their abusive partners had done to them. Certainly, there was little recognition of the fundamental plight uniting many women in the family court – the need to spend money they cannot afford, and relive the trauma of an abusive relationship, in the simple hope that the court will help them to protect their children from a man they know to be dangerous.

In 2019, a series of events, both inside and outside court, helped to push me to a realisation that I could no longer be a passenger in this system. The first came when I was invited onto the BBC's *Victoria Derbyshire Show*, which had produced a segment about women who had tried and failed to prevent abusive ex-partners from having contact with their children. One told the programme that her ex, who she said had assaulted her while she was pregnant, was later granted unsupervised contact. 'Unless he's beaten you black and blue, he'll be deemed a good enough father,' she recalled her solicitor having advised her.[15] She said her children would wake up crying on the day they had to go and stay with their father.

Her story was one of many told that day, both during the programme and in conversations outside the studio with the women who had come forward. I was not surprised by anything I heard, but I was moved in a way I hadn't expected to be. Something about listening to these women outside the courtroom, several grouped together and without the need to filter their experiences through a legal prism, affected me. It broke the trance that a barrister's existence can hold you in, with each case considered in isolation and soon left behind.

This push had come at the right time. In the aftermath of #MeToo, there was a movement forming of survivors, lawyers, politicians, academics and policymakers who wanted to change the family justice system, ensuring it would better safeguard vulnerable women and children. I watched them speak out and felt drawn to this cause. I wanted to use my voice to help make the law work better for women and children who were most in need of its protection.

As a result of the show and my returning to social media, more women in similar predicaments contacted me, and I began to do more work on domestic abuse and child contact cases. It confirmed all my worst impressions about how the family court treats women in this acutely vulnerable situation – trying at once to escape an abusive man and to stand between him and their children.

Daisy had been so badly abused that she fled the family home with her son. She had applied for a non-molestation order, the legal mechanism for preventing an ex-partner from coming within a specified distance of the applicant, typically used to protect domestic abuse victims. The court had already limited her ex-partner's contact and ordered that it should be supervised in a contact centre, an acknowledgement that he posed a risk to the child. But her application for a non-molestation order was simply never heard. For months, it went unlisted – not scheduled by the court – as Daisy had to seek extra security at home to make sure she was safe, including a panic alarm. To make it worse, under the existing court order, she had to cooperate with her ex-partner about parenting decisions. It seemed to sum up everything wrong with how women and children were and are treated in family court. Two victims were being punished and an alleged perpetrator seemingly protected.

Around the same time, another case brought me uncomfortably close to the kind of man the court frequently fails to protect vulnerable women from. I took up Louise's case after she contacted me directly. She had already been through a fact-finding hearing, where her allegations of rape against her ex-partner had been ruled a fabrication by the judge, who stated that she had made it up. Now I represented her at a final hearing that would determine contact arrangements for the children.

During a recess in the hearing, I was standing outside the courtroom when I realised the father was approaching me. I don't remember the words he shouted at me because of what happened next: his hand grabbing my shoulder, pulling me towards him, so close that I could smell his aftershave. I'm not sure how many people were near us, but no one intervened. Just minutes later, we were back in court, and I told the judge what had happened. He questioned the father, who at first denied it before equivocating when it was suggested CCTV might be sourced. His explanation – that it had been a heated discussion, and whatever he had done, he hadn't meant to – was deemed satisfactory. I will never forget the dismissive way in which the judge brushed off what had just happened, describing it as something from which we needed to move forward. I have never forgotten that day in court, nor have I forgotten his words. It was the moment I knew that I needed and wanted to fight. Not to let men like that father win. Of course, in court, he had won, securing an order that he should have regular contact with the children and that Louise should meet half the cost of facilitating this.

The final radicalising event that year was a case I had no involvement in but which every family lawyer soon became aware of. Judge Robin Tolson KC, then one of the most senior family law judges in London, heard a contested child contact case in which the mother alleged that the father had raped her. Judge Tolson's finding against her and the explanatory arguments in his judgment sparked controversy and soon led to a remarkable appeal. Of one of the incidents of alleged rape, Tolson had written: 'My concern about this occasion centres on the idea that the mother did nothing physically to stop the father . . . the mother was not in any sense pinned down on this occasion, but could easily, physically, have made life harder for the father.'* In other

---

* Tolson continued: 'I do not find that the father was in any way on this occasion so physically forcing her as to cause her not to be able to take preventative measures, nor, in fact, is that case alleged. Following

words, she didn't fight him off, so it couldn't have been rape. Not yet done, he commented that because the mother had said she had difficulties enjoying sex, it would have been 'nothing unusual' if she was 'upset afterwards'. So, it was her fault for not being able to communicate more clearly?

This judgment was rightly subject to a swift appeal, where Ms Justice Alison Russell, a highly regarded judge, repudiated it forcefully. As well as highlighting numerous problems with how Tolson had handled the case, she criticised his comments and attitudes about rape, writing: 'it is clear that the judge's approach towards the issue of consent is manifestly at odds with current jurisprudence, concomitant sexual behaviour, and what is currently acceptable socio-sexual conduct'. His judgment had been 'so flawed as to require a retrial' and 'unjust because of serious procedural irregularity and multiple errors of law'.* As she pointed out, these attitudes and misapplications of the law had come from someone at the very top of the family court: 'a senior judge, a Designated Family Judge, a leadership judge in the Family Court'.[16]

Often I had read judgments that I could hardly believe,

the event, as I have already said, the mother took no immediate action to report the matter to the police, or indeed to anyone else. Her description, of course, does not indicate that the circumstances were such that she might in any way have been thought wise to seek medical advice.' *JF v. MF* [2020] EWHC 86 (Fam) Section 36.

* 'For the reasons set out above the judgment was so flawed as to require a retrial; his decision was unjust because of serious procedural irregularity and multiple errors of law. The case is to be remitted for retrial by a High Court Judge or Deputy High Court Judge at the Royal Courts of Justice.' Ibid. [58].

but this appeal judgment was the first time that I felt shocked because I agreed with what I was reading. After so many examples of prehistoric attitudes towards women and about domestic abuse, here finally was evidence that someone was willing to push back. A judge who had so manifestly failed to handle a rape allegation with due sensitivity and understanding of the law had been put firmly in his place by someone of equivalent, in fact senior standing. At a re-trial ordered by Ms Justice Russell, a High Court judge upheld most of the mother's allegations, including that the father had twice had sex with her without her consent.[17]

It was the spur that I didn't know I had been waiting for – a sign that there was some willingness for the system to change, some energy that could be harnessed towards progress. Soon I was involved, along with the charity Rights of Women and two other lawyers, in co-authoring an open letter to the Justice Secretary and President of the Family Division – the most senior family court judge in the country – that highlighted the 'systemic issues' foregrounded by the Tolson judgment, and argued that training for judges alone would not be sufficient to fix the problem.[18]

The urge to campaign for change had taken hold, both in and out of court. It meant that when the next outrageous case crossed my desk, a woman alleging rape who was threatened by a judge with having her children taken into care, I was ready to fight. By the time I met Denise, I had been representing women in court for close to a decade. But her case felt like the moment my career as a barrister truly began.

2

The Flip of a Coin:
Meet the Judge

If I had not been looking for Denise, I might easily have missed her, a frail figure almost swallowed up by the vast stone edifice. Perhaps dozens of men and women in suits had hurried past as she sat outside the Royal Courts of Justice, hunched over against the freezing cold January morning. Had any of them noticed that she was in tears? Certainly, none of them could have realised how much it had cost her to reach this point: the trauma that even stepping over the threshold of this building would represent.

I had already been representing Denise for several months, but this was the first time we had met in person. The sight of her face on the screen, and the measured tones of her voice on the phone, had masked the reality: this was a woman who appeared utterly overwhelmed – as much by the situation facing her as by the building that loomed behind her. Like many clients I represent, who have been worrying about this day in court for months if not years, knowing that their future is at stake, Denise was a walking portrait of anxiety and fatigue, dark hair framing her pale face. She looked defeated by the prospect of the hearing even before it had begun.

Denise was already a veteran of the family court and a victim of some of its worst tendencies. By the time we came to work together, she had been fighting for more than two years to protect her daughter from her ex-partner, a man she had made serious allegations of physical and sexual violence against.

Her treatment by the court was so extreme that it achieved something I no longer believed possible after a decade of hearing harrowing tales of relationships turned violent. It actually shocked me. When Denise's mother first contacted me, asking if I would help with an appeal, I struggled to credit her story. Even knowing what I knew, I could not quite accept what was supposed to have happened during prior proceedings before I heard it for myself on the court tape.

This audio recording from her original hearing in 2019 left no room for doubt or disbelief. Denise was contesting her former partner's application to have their three-year-old daughter live with him. The evidence her lawyers submitted alleged that this man had verbally, physically and sexually assaulted Denise throughout their two-year relationship, that he had raped her, convinced her that she had a serious mental disorder, forced her to take drugs, and been controlling. Her ex-partner denied the allegations.

In response, Denise faced questioning from a judge that was demanding and confrontational. He firstly asked if she had used drugs and whether it was fair to call her an addict. Then he said he would have to inform social services when it was confirmed she had. When her lawyer intervened to point out that Denise said she had only used drugs while under coercion from her partner, she began crying and saying out loud that she was not an addict.[1]

But the judge was just getting started. Having focused in detail on the question of whether Denise had taken drugs, he appeared to be dismissive of her allegations of rape and domestic abuse. 'Well how's that going to affect contact?' he snapped.[2] He went on to underline that he considered it a fait accompli that Denise's serially abusive partner would spend time with their daughter in an unsupervised environment (outside a contact centre).[3] He even came close to blaming her for having brought such serious allegations, describing hearings like the one they were in as 'often a complete waste of time', because Denise's ex-partner was going to get some form of contact with their child anyway.[4]

I was staggered to hear a judge speaking like this to a vulnerable woman simply because he was having a bad day and was unhappy at how preparations for the hearing had been carried out, which he called a 'shambles' (papers had been submitted to him late and the barrister for the father was not present).[5]

The real problem was how His Honour Judge Richard Scarratt appeared to take out his frustration at these procedural issues on Denise. First, he made clear his view that the case should be resolved by an agreement between the parties – effectively telling a woman she should be willing to negotiate with a man she said had raped and been serially violent towards her, and who was already prohibited from having contact with her by an existing court order. Worse still, the judge then went a step further and directly threatened

Denise: 'if this goes on, the child will be taken into care and adopted'.[6] He also complained, in an apparent reference to both Denise and the ex-partner, that 'you should have had the riot act read to you months ago'.[7]

Consider what it would have been like to be Denise in that situation. You have endured a horrendous relationship, suffering every form of cruelty imaginable. Your (in your eyes) abusive ex-partner has taken you to court, where he intends to get custody of your daughter. Next, a judge criticises you for the allegations you have made and suggests that you may be a drug addict. And then he threatens you with having your child taken into care if you fail to reach an agreement over contact with the man you say raped and tormented you.

Judge Scarratt's words had to be seen, read and heard in the official court record to be believed. The judges who oversaw the subsequent appeal made clear their opinion of this behaviour: 'the judge, no doubt when under pressure and at a moment of intense irritation, said a number of ill-judged things', they wrote, also noting that there was 'no justification' for him to threaten adoption or to report the case to social services.[8] As they concluded: 'It is hard to imagine a more serious and frightening prospect for any mother, let alone a young, single mother, than that of having her child taken off her and placed for adoption.'[9]

In the deliberately dry language of a court judgment, and considering that justices are not in the habit of criticising their peers, these were notably strong rebukes. Yet, this was the closest thing to a sanction the judge received for how he had treated Denise. She was left traumatised while there were no repercussions for him. Her life had been changed forever, and his career continued unaffected.

Denise's case, and my involvement with it, was typical of the legal maze that women often become trapped in as they try to escape from harmful relationships and protect their children from men whom they know to be violent abusers. By the time I first spoke to her, she had already been fighting her case for more than two years. After her ex-partner first tried to gain custody of their child and Denise opposed it, the matter went into limbo for eight months, with hearings cancelled on no fewer than five occasions due to a succession of procedural issues. Then, after the disastrous initial proceeding in March 2019 at which the judge threatened her with the removal of her child, five more months passed until she ended up before the same judge again – an unacceptable state of affairs that her lawyers, somehow, decided not to contest. It was during this hearing that an agreement was reached between Denise and her ex-partner over child contact arrangements. The validity of this agreement became the basis for our appeal, given she had acquiesced to it following traumatic court proceedings that left her feeling like she had no choice.[10]

Family court cases so often proceed on this bumpy treadmill, with hearing after hearing spread out over the course of months or years. When two parents are in dispute over child contact arrangements, both invariably make allegations about the other. The court must first determine which of these issues are most relevant and will be considered, and then make what are called 'findings of fact' around them. Additional hearings may be required to establish ground rules for how the case will be heard, any special measures that may be required to protect vulnerable individuals, and to secure the disclosure of evidence from third parties such as the police or medical professionals. Between all these stages, delays can be added if there are issues over legal aid and disclosure of evidence, or when new allegations are made. Only then might a decision be reached about where and with whom the child is going to live – which, of course, could itself be subject to an appeal that may involve many more months of waiting.

It is all too easy for vulnerable people and basic human needs to be trampled under this slow-moving steamroller. For abuse survivors, it means an afterlife for the relationship that haunts them, as they are forced to relive its events and submit their stories to the meat grinder of our adversarial system, in which every detail will be scrutinised, held up to the light and challenged. For children, it means confusion and uncertainty as the facts of their day-to-day lives change, and they watch a parent deal with the trauma and anxiety that a court battle brings.

By the time I first heard about it in early 2021, Denise's case had reached what seemed to be the end of this painful road. She was well past the twenty-one-day limit to lodge an appeal, which meant that special permission would need to be granted by the court. She had previously been told she didn't stand a chance with an appeal – after all, she had signed the agreement. The obvious response would have been for me to tell her mother that, unfortunately, there was nothing I or any other barrister could do.

But when I spoke to Denise, I soon saw that hers was a case I could not walk away from. A case on paper is one thing, but when you are speaking to a desperate mother, showing you pictures of her child, telling you how afraid she is of what might happen to them, it becomes almost impossible to turn away. While reading long court documents, I sometimes find myself looking at a photo a client has sent me with their smiling child. And then I hear their words in my head, always some version of what a woman once said to me about her son, and what it was like handing him over for contact with his father: 'Every time I say goodbye, I wonder if I'll ever see him again.'

I was determined that Denise's case was not going to be another of those where I would have to tell a woman that this was the way of the world, and that her legal options were exhausted. I thought of Louise, forced to pay for her children to go and spend time with the man she alleged had abused her. I thought of the women I had sat with in the BBC studio and how the abuse perpetrated against them had not been bad enough to convince lawyers to argue the fathers should be denied contact. Where does this end if we accept, time after time, the rights of women and children being put aside and their safety jeopardised?

I read the papers again, looking for the argument on which to build a case. As a lawyer, you are hunting for needles, searching for details of evidence and case law with which to construct a solid argument. There were plenty of these in Denise's case, from the judge's conduct towards her to the pressure that had been on her when she signed the agreement concerning contact. Yet the bar to have an appeal granted 'out of time' – after the twenty-one-day window had closed – was high and I questioned if what we had would be enough. We needed more than a hill of details.

Thinking about those other cases provided the spark. This went far beyond Denise. Her story of being mistreated by her partner, and having her case mishandled by the court, was also the story of so many other women. That was the argument that needed to be heard – the flawed approach of the family justice system to managing the cases of vulnerable domestic abuse survivors.*[11] It was the first time I saw the opportunity to make a difference by doing more than fighting the case in front of me.

While I was reviewing Denise's options, I was also instructed on another appeal, on behalf of a woman whose allegations that her partner (later her husband) had raped her on two occasions, and that he had 'banged her head against a cupboard' when she tried to tell a friend about it on the phone, were dismissed by the court, which ruled they 'were not proven and did not happen'.[12] There was also a third appeal that resembled the others in many respects. So similar were the problems in these cases that I started to wonder if there was a way of getting the court to consider them together. We were well overdue a definitive case in this field. It was more than twenty years since the Court of

---

* The previous year, the 'Assessing Risk of Harm' report commissioned by the Ministry of Justice, which received widespread submissions of evidence from women and children who had been through family court as well as professionals, highlighted 'deep-seated and systemic problems with how the family courts identify, assess and manage risk to children and adults'. It pointed to submissions which suggested 'court proceedings had not provided protection from further harm for children or adult victims of abuse, but had made things worse, with abuse being continued through court-ordered contact arrangements'.

Appeal had set out guidance on domestic violence, in which time understanding of abusive relationships and coercive and controlling behaviour had advanced significantly.[13]

I didn't know how to link the appeals together, and by law I couldn't share the details of one client's case with another. Not knowing any better, I wrote a letter to the court asking if they could be heard in parallel. I received no reply and assumed that it had come to nothing. Then, without warning, an order arrived in my inbox. Four appeals would be heard by Sir Andrew McFarlane, the President of the Family Division, and two Court of Appeal judges: the three I had put forward and one I assumed the court had added itself. This was exactly what I had hoped for: the appeals to go before the most senior family judge in the country, providing the chance to argue points not just about the individual cases but concerning the family court's overall approach to allegations of rape, domestic abuse and coercive control.[*14]

Soon, the idea that had started in my head had sprouted into a cluster of activity, with lawyers being instructed across the different cases and evidence gathered.[15] I watched the email thread get longer and longer: suddenly this was real.

One of the four appeals was Denise's. Another was the case of a woman who, among other allegations, said her ex-partner had put a plastic bag over her head from behind

---

* The offence of coercive or controlling behaviour, sometimes abbreviated as coercive control, was codified by the 2015 Serious Crime Act and further defined by the 2021 Domestic Abuse Act. Coercive behaviour is defined as 'an act or pattern of acts . . . used to harm, punish or frighten the victim' and controlling behaviour as 'an act or pattern of acts designed to make a person subordinate and/or dependent'.

while she was sitting on the floor playing with their child and told her, 'this is how you are going to die'.[16] Judge Jane Evans-Gordon, in the original fact-finding, had downplayed this as 'some sort of prank'.[17] She also referred to the mother as 'no shrinking violet' in the context of rape allegations.[18] The other two cases were ones which had been heard by Judge Tolson,[19] the judge who had been criticised for wondering why a woman did not attempt to fight off her rapist.

It was not my first time taking a case to the Court of Appeal, but it was by far the biggest and most significant. It was an open hearing, and it felt like working in a goldfish bowl as prominent politicians commented on the case and journalists filed daily reports. Stranger still was that, in court itself, I did not speak a word. Even though I had been the instigator of these unusual proceedings, and was doing the legwork on two of the four appeals, I was still the junior barrister. My primary role was to assist in drafting the skeleton arguments and help to prepare the cases in advance. In court itself, I sat and took notes during the hearing, occasionally prompting my senior colleague, Amanda Weston KC, with suggested points to advocate. I watched as she skilfully answered the judges' questions and made our arguments.

The combined appeal did not achieve everything I had hoped for – the judges declined to set out a clear definition of rape and consent in family law cases or to tackle the issue of how women's sexual histories and medical records are routinely used against them during cross-examination. However, they did issue general guidance for family judges to pay more attention to the issue of coercive and controlling behaviour in relationships and emphasised the need, already set out in a practice direction,* for domestic abuse and coercive control to be considered as a potential pattern of behaviour, rather than arising only from specific incidents. In other words, a perpetrator's lawyer should not be able to take a 'gotcha' approach of discrediting the evidence around certain allegations and using this to claim that no domestic abuse occurred: abuse had to be considered in its totality. As a lawyer representing victims, often one of the hardest parts of my job is to convince the court that a woman felt powerless because she had been groomed, gaslighted and controlled by her abuser – made to feel useless and doubting her own judgement and ability to be independent. This guidance, emphasising the pattern of abuse as much as the most egregious examples, was an important development.

Finally, the judges' comment that the 'principal relevance' of a fact-finding hearing was to determine whether or not such a pattern had existed was significant: it felt like a subtle rebuke to the judge in Denise's original hearing, who had described such proceedings as often being a waste of time.[20]

Having set out this guidance, the panel of judges turned their attention to the cases. In three of the four, including Denise's, they granted the appeals. Denise would get her chance to fight back after all. This meant another fact-finding hearing, which brought us to that cold January morning in 2021, when I met her sitting in front of the Royal Courts: one vulnerable woman against the system. After more than two years slogging through the legal system, Denise was back

---

* A practice direction is a document that gives guidance to judges about how they should apply the law and manage cases, usually focusing on issues of procedure and interpretation of law.

where she had started, hoping this time that her allegations would be heard with the respect and understanding that they warranted.

It should have taken me about a week to prepare her case: reading through the two-thousand-page bundle of documents, drafting my skeleton argument to submit to the judge, and preparing my statements and questions for cross-examining witnesses. But the law is the law, and few barristers ever get close to the time they need to do this work. In the event, I was in court on another case for a full week before Denise's fact-finding, and the bundle – exceeding 1,000 pages – was not finally sent to me until the Friday afternoon. I got home around 6 p.m., changed into comfortable clothes and knew that I had three nights and two days to complete a full week of work.

At this point, there is no option but to compartmentalise: I would have to prepare the case in sections, doing as much as I could in advance and then relying on the standardised order of the hearing – Denise, who was bringing the allegations, would give evidence first – to read and rehearse only what I needed for the next day's proceeding. I was already exhausted from the week just finished, beginning to come down with a heavy cold, and knew that I would not be able to rest properly until a week from now.

Still, come Monday morning, I donned my war paint: a bright slash of red lipstick and a colourful pair of earrings to remind me that I am more than another anonymous robe and wig. I was ready to go to court, but not fully prepared for the sight of Denise, pale and unsteady as she sat outside on a cold stone slab.

Things quickly got worse once we had made our way into

the Gothic hallways. We were not even through the security checks when she started saying, 'I can't do it. I can't do it.' She was shaking, and I could see that she was having a panic attack. She had been so frightened by her earlier experiences in court that just the thought of standing in the witness box was proving too much for her.

In our earlier conversations, Denise had insisted that she wanted to go ahead despite her fears, but on seeing her that morning, I thought it would be doing more harm than good to proceed. I took her aside and said that we didn't have to go on; we could go to the judge and say she was too traumatised to give evidence, and ask for another way to be found. But somehow, even in a state of extreme distress, she resolved to carry on. 'I have to do it for my daughter,' she said through the tears. 'I've got to protect her.'

It had been hard enough for Denise to get this far, to the door of the courtroom, when she was faced with another cruelty, yet another example of how the justice system so routinely gets it wrong. As we rounded a dimly lit corner, she saw him, sitting on a bench across the wooden panelled hall. Even though a hearing had been held to establish robust special measures for the case, including an agreement that she would not have any contact with her former partner in court, there he was. Denise had dragged herself through panic and anxiety to make it here and put on record her evidence about the man who had raped, emotionally abused and gaslighted her. And now she found him sitting across the hallway from her, a shockingly vivid reminder of everything she had endured. She immediately retreated and was crouched on the floor, another panic attack washing over her as I went to confront opposing counsel and have the ex-partner removed. He quickly complied, but the damage had been done, pushing an already vulnerable Denise to an even greater peak of distress.

We were about to step into a hearing that would be highly revealing about how family court can work, demonstrating the impact of these proceedings on the people involved in them. Denise's case wasn't just symptomatic of a system that puts women through so much in their struggle for justice and to safeguard their children. It also showed how abusers like her ex-partner can try to exploit gendered stereotypes, presenting themselves as reasonable and their victims as irrational. And it brought to the fore the question of truth and memory: in how much detail can a traumatised woman be expected to remember the hideous abuse they have spent so much time trying to forget?

Viewed in retrospect and from a distance, Denise's relationship had been draped in what her grandmother described at the hearing as 'red flags' from the very beginning.[21] She had been twenty when it began, working as an apprentice and only recently having moved to London. Her partner was seven years older than her and had been in multiple relationships, including with a woman in his home country of Uganda, with whom he maintained ambiguous links that would become a source of contention. He was Denise's first serious boyfriend. Like many abusers, he was far from the stereotypical wife-beater, presenting in a three-piece suit as charming, well spoken and a responsible professional who worked as a mental health assistant. He looked every bit as comfortable in the court environment as she seemed out of place, as confident about the outcome as she was nervous.

'He was an articulate and ostensibly self-disciplined man, whose evidence was polished and clear,' Mr Justice Cobb, who oversaw this hearing, wrote in his judgment. 'It was easy to see how the impressionable young woman, newly arrived in London, could fall for his apparent charm and how easily she could become infatuated with him.'[22]

That infatuation had led Denise into what soon became an abusive and harmful relationship. She testified how he had taken her phone, house keys and credit card away from her, that he would not use her name but only refer to her as 'woman',* and that he had told her she was rubbish in bed. She told the court how he had sexually assaulted and raped her, allegations which were ultimately upheld.[23] Perhaps most insidiously, he exploited Denise's vulnerable mental health and his own professional credibility to make allegations against her and to intimate that she was an unfit mother.[24] This had become particularly apparent when the father reported Denise to the police, telling them that she was suffering from bipolar disorder, had previously abused cocaine, and 'has an issue with alcohol in general'.[25] He had also made the claim about bipolar disorder to Denise's mother.[26]

While most of this was found by the judge to be untrue – Denise neither had a cocaine addiction nor had she been diagnosed with bipolar disorder – her partner had been trying to convince Denise, and those around her, that she

---

* In my time as a barrister, I have seen examples of men degrading female partners through abusive naming. In another such case, a man called his partner 'whore', even entering it into the contact book on his mobile.

was indeed suffering from bipolar disorder. His allegation of this 'in an attempt to characterise her to third parties as mentally unstable and/or unreliable . . . was immensely disparaging and undermining of the mother, damaging to the mother's self-confidence and self-esteem, and caused her to doubt her own mental health', the judge concluded.[27] This is a classic gaslighting tactic used by abusers: they convince their victim that there is something wrong with them and that they are always responsible for problems, making them question their own understanding of what has happened. Denise's evidence demonstrated what a profound impact this kind of abuse can have on a person's mental health. She described herself as 'often terrified and deeply confused by constant contradictions, not able to speak my mind or think clearly. I was controlled through fear, intimidation and bullying.'[28] Her GP later diagnosed her as suffering from depression, which he believed was directly related to the abusive relationship.[29]

I was determined that the court recognise the very specific pattern of abuse Denise's ex-partner had perpetrated against her: the way he had sought to control and undermine her by convincing Denise, her close family members and authorities with power over her that she was suffering from a serious mental health disorder. I made a point of accusing him of having engaged in gaslighting tactics.[30]

The upshot was that Mr Justice Cobb's judgment became notable for being one of the first to use the term gaslighting in the context of domestic abuse, a description he termed 'apposite', also commenting that 'the father's conduct represented a form of insidious abuse designed to cause the mother to question her own mental well-being, indeed her sanity'.[31] As welcome a development as this was, in its own way it symbolised how slow the law is to adapt: the term gaslighting was coined as far back as 1938 and was being widely used in psychological circles for at least fifteen years before this judgment helped to bring it into case law.[32]

In Denise's case, the gaslighting did not just cause harm to her and to the couple's daughter, who showed 'unsettled' behaviour at her nursery after a particularly volatile incident between the parents, which had led to the police being called.[33] It also shaped perceptions of both her and her ex-partner in the eyes of the law and legal system. Denise was falling victim not just to a violent and manipulative abuser, but to one of society's oldest stereotypes: the irrational woman whose behaviour cannot be explained and whose word cannot be trusted. Like many abusers, her ex-partner played the part of the confused and concerned man, framing the situation for the benefit of other men in positions of authority, using the classic DARVO playbook (deny, attack, reverse victim and offender). According to this narrative, he was behaving reasonably out of concern for his daughter; Denise was a drunk, a drug user and mentally ill. The father's labelling of the mother as bipolar, which was written into the police log,[34] illustrates how such false premises can quickly become part of the official record. It shows how abusers can groom the system into accepting their version of events, condemning the victim they have already gaslighted to the secondary trauma of being deemed untrustworthy and a risk to their children. Denise's treatment by the family court, where the first judge she encountered demanded to know if she considered herself a drug addict and threatened to have her daughter adopted, simply underlined the point.

Now she was about to find out how challenging the experience of being cross-examined in court can be. In rape and domestic abuse cases, it can be commonplace for opposing counsel to pursue lines of argument, no doubt under their client's instructions, that demonstrate victim blaming. So it was here. On the allegations of sexual assault, the ex-partner contended that Denise herself had instigated 'rough sex' between the two, referring to text messages from her that asked why he was 'not horny' and complaining that they 'never do anything' sexually.[35] This cherry-picking of evidence is often seen in fact-findings around sexual assault, with the implication that a woman who has asked for sex once should be considered to have asked for it – and wanted it – every time. Denise's own evidence made clear how she had actually felt: 'I thought that because [he] and I were in a relationship, even when I told him no and that I did not want him to do these things to me that it wasn't rape or abuse. I always felt physically violated, scared, and emotionally distressed after he did these things to me. I just didn't know I could do anything about it.'[36]

Denise was, the judge found, the victim of rape and domestic abuse in multiple forms. Yet she was not the perfect victim that women are expected to be: an innocent worthy of being rescued. The judge also found that she had brandished a knife at her ex-partner on one occasion, that she had pushed a television off its stand in a fit of anger, and how, after the relationship had ended, she had used her control over his contact with their daughter as a bargaining chip to try and rekindle the relationship, telling him that the two of them 'come as a package'.[37]

For those so minded, it would have been easy to draw

the conclusion that Denise was exaggerating what she had experienced, that she had behaved irrationally, and that certain things she had said undermined the case she was now making. Why would she want to resume a relationship if it had really been so bad? These are presumptions that fail to take into account the emotional complexity of abusive relationships: how they leave women like Denise shorn of confidence and self-respect, unable to conceive of life outside the relationship and with a warped perception of what normal and reasonable behaviour is.

It was fortunate that the case was being heard by Mr Justice Cobb, who has written some of the law in England and Wales about domestic abuse and recognised that there was no contradiction in Denise wishing to resume a relationship with a man who had bullied, raped and sexually assaulted her.[38] As he concluded: 'She became possessive of the father. That does not mean that she was not abused by the father, as he sought to persuade me. Indeed, [Denise's] description of the relationship is to my mind entirely recognisable as the behaviour of someone caught up in the whorl of abuse, who has lost any objective sense of what is acceptable and unacceptable in a relationship.'[39] He also pointed out that her lack of any previous relationship had given her nothing with which to compare her ex-partner's behaviour and that she had likely come to depend on him.

We were also reliant on the judge's understanding to avoid Denise's testimony being discounted because it was sometimes inconsistent and not in every respect accurate. Her ex-partner sought to argue that she was unreliable because she had confused dates, mixed up the sequence of some events, and not made the allegation of rape until months after the legal battle had begun. In our adversarial legal system, where lawyers are trained to constantly hunt for the thread that could unravel someone's entire account, these inconsistencies, delayed memories and misremembered details are eagerly seized upon.

Like so many women I have worked with, Denise's recollection of events had been impaired by the trauma associated with them.[40] So much so that she kept insisting that a series of threatening messages she had received were from her ex-partner, even though, at the time, she had reported a work colleague for sending them.[41] This was an issue on which she was found to have misled the court, and while she clearly had, I believe she had genuinely become confused and believed that the messages had come from her abuser. There was no mistaking the look of real shock in her eyes when this mistake was pointed out and irrefutable evidence produced. You could see her trying to work it out, as if given a box full of jigsaw pieces that had once been familiar to her but which no longer fitted together.

This shows the complexity that surrounds what lawyers and witnesses confidently brandish as fact: a single version of events that must be used as a stick to beat those who depart from it. In a custody dispute such as this, absolute truth becomes almost impossible to access under the weight of two competing accounts, his and hers, backed up by family members who weigh in as witnesses on both sides and lawyers who cross-examine them, seeking to open every flaw into a fissure. The search for truth is also complicated by the experience of trauma, the nature of abuse suffered and the passage of time. Denise had been sexually abused and raped, she had been made to think that she may have a serious mental disorder, and she had been threatened by a senior judge with the forced removal of her child.

Mr Justice Stephen Cobb (as he then was) was sensitive and acknowledged that she was still experiencing depression, and I had also seen how she was suffering panic attacks that left her almost unable to give evidence and often in tears while doing so. Moreover, like all rape survivors who must come to court to protect themselves and their children, Denise was being asked to recollect in detail events that she had been trying for years to forget. Was it any surprise that she could not recall the details in full or in their proper order and had, in some cases, blended incidents and confused perpetrators?

Regardless, I knew that the inconsistencies in Denise's account would be seized upon. When there is no substantial case to make, lawyers for men accused of domestic abuse will invariably resort to nit-picking small details, insinuating that a woman who is wrong about one thing must be lying about everything. In such situations, my typical response is to demonstrate how distress and trauma can impair an individual's ability to give evidence, and that untruths – which may be inadvertent – do not necessarily detract from the substance of what that person is alleging. While the judge did highlight instances where Denise had given misleading and untruthful evidence, he ultimately accepted her case that a deeply traumatised woman should not be punished for lacking perfect recall of her abuse, nor should she be treated as a liar simply because some things she said were untrue. 'I find that she was genuinely confused about the order of events, which have become muddled in her mind, possibly because of the passage of time . . . and possibly because of the intense emotional and possibly psychological turmoil associated with them,' he wrote.[42]

The balance of the judgment that followed was comprehensively in her favour. Mr Justice Cobb found that Denise's ex-partner had sexually assaulted her, writing: 'I am satisfied on the evidence which I have received that: i) On occasions the father forced himself on the mother for sexual intercourse, uncaring whether she was consenting or not . . . sexual intimacy which involved physical abuse of the mother ("rough sex") was initiated by the father and was probably not consensual.'[43] He also found that Denise's ex had manipulated her and tried to exploit her fragile mental state, and that 'by reason of the father's conduct towards her and in the relationship, she has been caused severe anxiety, depression, and trauma'.[44] He concluded by ordering a further hearing into the impact of this abuse on Denise and her daughter, to help inform a final decision about care arrangements, at which point her ex-partner decided to drop his case and stop seeking contact.

It was the outcome Denise had wanted: her child protected, not required by the court to have a relationship with the man who had raped her. But it was a result she had only been able to achieve after three and a half years of delays, legal wrangling, mistreatment by the system and constantly having to relive the trauma of her abuse under aggressive cross-examination. Watching her give evidence, crying throughout as she recalled the worst events of her life and was cross-examined by opposing counsel, every flaw and inconsistency in her evidence raked over, had been a heart-wrenching experience. In one respect, it was an awe-inspiring display of strength: a woman, a mother, putting herself through hell to protect her daughter. But this was a courage Denise should never have been required to show, a determination that should not have been necessary to have her story heard and her child safeguarded. As the judge acknowledged, she had been traumatised not just by what her ex-partner had done to her, but by the court proceedings that he had initiated.[45]

In the end, it was a pyrrhic victory: a result that had required Denise to re-traumatise herself, to live for all this time with the court action hanging over her, and to face threats of having her daughter taken away forever. By the time she was finally vindicated, Denise had spent longer fighting to keep her violent and rapist ex away from their daughter than she had been in the initial relationship with him in the first place. This legal torture had not only revived every detail of the abuse she had suffered at his hands; it had also created traumas of its own that would prove just as difficult to escape. It was an appalling price to pay.

Even the final vindication of Denise felt more like an indictment of the system than a credit to it. Sensitive treatment and a fair hearing should be extended to every woman and child by the family court, not simply those left holding the right straw when the caseload is shared among justices. Denise's case revealed how the system may fail women as well as giving a belated glimpse of how it should be serving them. Above all, it underlined how capricious and cruel that system is, forcing even those who 'win' to crawl over broken glass, leaving wounds that may never heal.

For that reason, even a successful outcome and the knowledge that Denise could finally move on with her life left me feeling hollow. Justice should not be so agonisingly difficult to achieve in a case where the balance of evidence is clear enough. It should not come down to what judicial raffle ticket you are dealt, beholden to the attitudes of the man (it usually is a man)[46] chosen to sit on the bench.

When I spoke with Denise after the judgment had been handed down, listening to her crying on the phone and to the relief suffusing her voice, she had one final question for me. 'Can he come back? Can he do this again?' I had to admit that he could. There was no order in this case preventing her ex-partner from bringing further applications about contact with their child. Nothing to stop him hiring a new lawyer and starting all over again. Denise was free for now, and her child was safe, but she would have to live for many more years with the latent fear that she may one day be forced back into a courtroom.

The almost endless nature of certain family court cases is something I have come to see as one of the worst features of the system. The combination of cynical legal tactics, systemic issues that cause delays, and the desire of certain men to exert control over their former partners, means that cases that should be dealt with in a matter of weeks or months can drag on for years. Sometimes I will ask the court to order that no further applications about child contact can be made for an agreed period of time, to give mother and child stability, but this is not always possible, or granted for as long as I would like.

It is understandable that women like Denise find all this overwhelming: how the court becomes a place they dread rather than one where they can expect to find justice. Working with her was just the beginning of my education in how the family court can be a terrifying and unsafe space for women who come there to protect themselves and their children from abusive men. As I was about to find out, family court can be a devastating experience not just for those unfamiliar with its ways, but even for someone who has been working in that system for their entire career. It was when I represented a fellow lawyer in family court that I saw just how debilitating a place it can be for those whose futures depend on coming to court to rake over the past.

3

Unsafe Spaces:
Fighting Domestic Abuse

As Michelle told me her story, I kept thinking that surely she had got to the worst part.[1] It was bad enough that she had endured cross-examination in court by the ex-partner who she claimed had abused her, representing himself in the child contact dispute over their young daughter. Worse that no special measures had been provided for her during the fact-finding hearing, and that under cross-examination by her ex-partner, she started crying.[2] By the time Michelle explained how the judge had found there was no evidence of domestic abuse, diminishing incidents including one in which her ex had squeezed her hand so hard that it fractured, I had almost ceased to be surprised – not shocked when she recounted how the judge's ruling had written off apparent child abuse as 'inappropriate parenting'.[3] She felt accused of behaving as a jilted woman, motivated more by jealousy over her abuser's new relationship than fear for herself and her child.

Like many women who have gone to family court in expectation of a fair hearing, only to be confronted with unsafe conditions and then finding themselves blamed for what happened to them, Michelle had been visibly affected by the experience. Her voice hovered between defiant anger as she recalled the ordeal in court and something little above a whisper as she admitted how it had left her struggling to sleep and losing her hair.

But Michelle was not an ordinary appellant. She was a lawyer herself, who before leaving the profession had done most of her work in family court. She had been involved in hundreds of cases like the one she now found herself in the middle of. 'Stand in your truth and tell your story' was the advice she had routinely given to clients trying to protect themselves and their children from abusive ex-partners. This was a woman who knew exactly what to expect from family court: where to sit, what to wear, who would speak first, how to address the judge, and what kind of questions would be asked. In theory, it should not have been an overwhelming experience, but it had been. Even knowing everything she knew, Michelle had been rocked by the reality of being the woman who must present their case, answer questions in front of (and sometimes posed by) their abuser, and put her safety and that of her child in the hands of a judge who might not have received training in domestic abuse. As we spoke, I looked at Michelle, taking in the narrow oval of her face and her auburn, curly hair. I wondered, if the family justice system can bring a woman like this to breaking point, then for whom can it really be considered safe?

Michelle had recounted the most traumatic events of her life, only to be accused of lying by her ex, critiqued for looking anxious, and told that an abusive partner had, in the eyes of the court, done nothing wrong. The judge in the case, Deputy District Judge Duncan Watson, had ruled that Michelle's allegations of domestic abuse were not proved: he concluded that there had been no assault when the ex-partner broke Michelle's hand, that the man had been acting in self-defence, and there was, in fact, no violence in the relationship.[4] If there had been, he pondered, why would she have felt comfortable going on holiday with him and their daughter after they had broken up?[5]

This is the kind of logic that is seen and heard too often, seeking to deduce the truth of an allegation from how a woman acted in response to it. *It can't have been true because she didn't leave, she didn't tell anyone, she kept on doing this or agreeing to that.* Women like Michelle must first go through the agony of telling the court what happened to them and being interrogated in an adversarial process. And then they must accept the judgment of someone who may critique the way they behaved in the face of domestic abuse. It is traumatising for victims to be told they should have acted differently or 'better' in the unique circumstances they lived through.

For Michelle, this was just the beginning of her ordeal. When she took advice from two different lawyers about appealing the judgment, one of them a senior KC whose time came at a significant cost, she was told that an appeal would be against her best interests and unlikely to succeed. What would happen, this eminent lawyer asked her, if it failed and she ended up back in front of the same judge for subsequent hearings? Was she willing to risk having to pay her ex's court costs in the event of a failed appeal?

Now, she had come to me with the same question: did she have a case? It was clear she had agonised over whether to do so. There had already been multiple hearings, each of them an exercise in re-traumatisation. Like many women in family court, Michelle was facing the harsh reality that justice could only be pursued at the cost of her own well-being. Pulling her one way was the need to put this abusive relationship behind her, and in the other, the thought that if she did nothing, her ex would get away with what he had done, enjoy unfettered access to their daughter, and always be able to say that the court had dismissed her allegations.

In the months that followed, I would learn that my new client had a talent for getting to the heart of the matter in few words. 'I just thought, fuck it, I'm going to do it,' she told me, summarising the decision that brought her to my office at chambers, where we sat as we might have done discussing someone else's case, except it just happened to be one of us at the centre of it.

Michelle's story was over. Now, it was my turn. Did I really know better than two other lawyers, including one of the top-ranked professionals in my field? At this point I was thirty-two and had relatively little experience of domestic abuse appeals. It was the summer of 2021, just a few months after I had brought Denise's case to the Court of Appeal along with three others. Perhaps emboldened by that experience, and not wanting to be just another lawyer who told a woman that it was not possible to have her allegations of violent abuse taken seriously, I decided we had to find a way.

I believed Michelle had a case. The judgment against her was a minefield sown with legal and procedural errors: the failure to implement or even consider special measures for a vulnerable witness, the inappropriate use of a criminal standard of evidence that does not apply in family court, and the judge's highly questionable definitions of what did and did not constitute abuse among them.

These were just some of the grounds on which to mount an appeal and I began to feel confident, despite some trepidation about being a junior barrister representing a woman who was far more experienced than me in exactly this field. I should not have worried, for Michelle was an ideal client, and I regularly leaned on her expertise as we honed and developed the appeal. But although our case was strong, neither of us was entirely prepared for what lay ahead, and how drawn out an already lengthy set of proceedings would become.

Michelle's case was not just an egregious example of how the family court often fails women in instances of domestic abuse. It also came at a time when the law around such cases was changing, with a new bill going through Parliament. The Domestic Abuse Act 2021 updated and supplanted legislation that, in some cases, dated to the 1980s. It established a statutory definition for domestic abuse encompassing emotional and economic forms, as well as for coercive and controlling behaviour.[6] It also clarified that children in domestic abusive households were victims in their own right.[7] And it established provisions to protect victims, including a presumption that they should be eligible for special measures when appearing in court, a ban on alleged or found abusers cross-examining their victims in court, and protections to prevent abusers from dragging out court proceedings in a deliberate attempt to traumatise their victims further.

Working with Claire Waxman OBE, the Victims' Commissioner for London, and Jess Phillips MP, I had been involved in putting forward proposals for the bill, discovering both the satisfaction and frustration of being involved in the legislative process. We would draft amendments, gather relevant evidence and case studies, join meetings with ministers and watch the bill being debated in Parliament. It felt like a chance to address some of the most glaring defects in the family court system, building a wider understanding of how the courtroom could be a place where abuse was perpetuated as much as it was brought to account.

But even as some problems were fixed in the new legislation, others continued to be ignored. One amendment I worked on was designed to prevent court orders being served to women's refuges, which risked disclosing the location of vulnerable victims to their abusers.[8] A second sought to ensure that a woman could not be left in the position of having to meet the costs of an abusive ex-partner's ongoing contact with their child. Both were rejected on the basis that they were outlier scenarios that should not be expected to arise. Subsequent cases would prove otherwise, helping to establish protections through case law that the legislation had not.

It was a reminder of the cumulative work needed to achieve progress. While an amendment may not be accepted in legislation, it will be debated in Parliament, helping to establish a reference point that can be referred to in subsequent legal arguments. In the opposite direction, legal cases that demonstrate a problem area can be used to advocate with politicians for a legislative response. The system is often slow and cautious, but each argument made or case won can be a building block towards a new law being passed or precedent established. Both halves are essential in the effort to make the justice system safer and more effective for women.

For Michelle, the new legislation had come too late. The original fact-finding hearing and judgment, which she now wished to appeal, had happened in November 2020, six months before the new Act became law. Yet even in that context, the procedural and legal failings of the case were clearly apparent. As I put together the skeleton argument for the appeal, it felt like the twenty pages we had to work with – the maximum length for a written argument – were nowhere near sufficient for the case we had to make.

First was the failure to ensure the courtroom was a safe place for Michelle as a vulnerable person bringing accusations of domestic abuse against a former partner. It was not just that special measures used to protect victims from traumatic situations were absent in this case; there had not even been a ground-rules hearing to deliberate them.[9] Provisions could and should have been made for Michelle to give evidence from behind a screen or via video link, and the judge should not have allowed a man accused of domestic violence to question his victim in court.[10] All the relevant guidance for such measures existed prior to the 2021 Act via a practice direction, which the judge failed to implement.[11]

This total absence of protective measures was only the beginning. Once the case began, it became clear that the judge was imposing a questionable interpretation of what could constitute domestic abuse. Important events were minimised, while significant weight was given to circumstantial factors, such as the fact that Michelle had agreed to go on holiday with her ex-partner after their break-up.[12] The judge found that her ex had shouted and sworn at his teenage son (from another relationship) while he was holding their daughter – then an infant – but waved this away as merely 'inappropriate', saying that the court should not expect parents to be perfect.[13] With regard to the incident where her ex had squeezed Michelle's hand so hard that it fractured, Judge Watson found that there was no assault and that there had been no violence in the relationship.[14] Instead, Michelle believed he had accepted her ex-partner's arguments that she had behaved angrily after seeing photos of him with a new partner, and that he had been trying to protect his face when he grabbed her hand so hard that it broke.[15]

In the course of this hearing, the family justice system had not only engaged in the kind of re-victimisation of women that is so familiar in domestic abuse cases, but the judge had erred as a matter of law. When deliberating on the altercation that broke Michelle's hand, he discussed in detail the criminal definitions surrounding assault, self-defence and reasonable force and described the incident as a 'count' of assault.[16] By doing so, he contravened precedent that states criminal law concepts have no place in family court, where the imperative is not to prove innocence or guilt but to establish facts on the balance of probabilities.[17] In the process, he had convinced himself that there was no violence in the relationship, that the shared holiday to support her daughter's contact with her father (when her hand was broken) showed Michelle was 'comfortable' in her ex's company, and that the unreasonable behaviour had been more hers than his.[18]

Putting together the written argument for the appeal was both difficult and straightforward. On the one hand, the grounds for appeal seemed so clear: here we had a judge who had given no consideration to Michelle's vulnerability as a witness, wrongly introduced criminal law concepts into a family court case and made decisions that seemed at best a surprising interpretation of the evidence presented. But the job was complicated by the need to distil our case into as succinct a form as possible and by the presence of a client who was herself an expert in work such as this. Back and forth we went, honing the argument and debating it point by point. Although I was Michelle's barrister, she was also considerably senior to me in law and I had a great deal of respect for her.

After weeks of work, the document was finally done. We knew we had a case. Now, the question was what kind of hearing it would receive.

'That's a complete lie, I never said that.'

Voices were speaking through my headphones as I saw the words appear on my phone, its screen lighting up silently for what felt like the hundredth time that afternoon. This was the summer of 2021, and pandemic restrictions still applied to court proceedings. As Michelle's appeal hearing unfolded, I was in my office at home, and she was in her living room. An almost constant stream of WhatsApp messages stood in for the comments that might normally have been whispered in my ear or passed to me in court as handwritten notes. It was hot, my throat was dry, and although my kitchen sink was tantalisingly close, I knew I could not get up to fill my glass with water.

Robust as our case was, it was a day that I had become more and more anxious about as it approached. As appeals usually are, it was an open court hearing, with the press dialled in. Given that the hearing addressed issues I regularly campaigned on, I felt nervous about how my arguments would be perceived under scrutiny; the stakes felt incredibly high.

I was keen to do well for Michelle, whose treatment seemed so unfair, symptomatic of how women across the system were routinely being harmed after they spoke out about the abuse they had suffered. And I was conscious that any slip-ups risked not only jeopardising her appeal but the wider issues to which this case related. There was and is no shortage of people who regard the work of feminists and lawyers much as they do the accusations of women who allege domestic abuse: by definition irksome, based on exaggeration and stemming from so-called 'misandry'. Any errors I made here would be eagerly scooped up as grist for this mill.

I was also nervous about an appeal that, while robust and strongly evidenced, was effectively asking one judge to agree that another had been badly at fault. In the back of my mind, I wondered what it would mean if we couldn't succeed in an appeal like this when the case seemed so clear and the errors so transparent.

My apprehension did not ease when it became clear that this would be anything but a quick proceeding. Every judge is different: some are impatient about barristers rehearsing points they have already grasped from written submissions, while others prefer to have the entire case presented to them orally. His Honour Judge Farooq Ahmed was in the second group. I would need to go through every single appeal ground in some detail, as well as answer his carefully phrased questions. Even speaking as quickly as I could, this occupied several hours. It felt like an eternity as I talked into the screen, one eye on my phone as messages came in from Michelle, pointing me to a piece of evidence or a point that should be underlined.

I only relaxed when we reached the section about the previous judge's inappropriate use of criminal law concepts. As I pointed to the relevant precedent, the judge interjected to comment that the point was sufficiently obvious that he did not need to be walked through it. In successful cases, there is often a moment when you can sense the tide has turned your way. As the judge warmed to this theme, pointing out how the criminal law was not just illegitimately employed in the prior hearing but had, on its own terms, been misinterpreted, I knew we had reached one of these junctures. Even as my throat was getting drier and drier, for the first time that day I began to feel calm. Then my phone screen lit up again, and I opened yet another message from Michelle. No words this time, just a heart emoji. We both realised at the same moment that her voice was finally going to be heard.

When the judgment came, it was scathing. Judge Ahmed found that, in the initial fact-finding, 'fundamental principles were not implemented, and principles and outdated attitudes which have no place in the Family Court, were imported'.[19] The judge had been 'wrong in failing to recognise and identify the mother as a vulnerable witness'.[20] His downplaying of the father's abusive behaviour towards one child in the other's presence was 'wholly inappropriate and not what one may expect a judge of the Family Court to condone'.[21] Ultimately, due to the failure to examine the allegations of abuse in their proper context and a string of procedural failings, 'the court fell into error such that the Order made by the judge cannot stand'.[22]

This was total vindication for Michelle: a ruling against her struck down and a point-by-point renunciation of the judicial process that had exposed her to such traumatic conditions, treating her allegations with suspicion that bordered on hostility. She had been the woman told by men that she was exaggerating, that a man she knew to have abused her had done nothing wrong, and that her fears for her child were misplaced. Then, she had been advised by a barrister that there was little point in seeking legal redress for any of this. In the face of all of this, she had followed her own advice and stood in her truth. And now she had won.

Or, to be precise, she had started to win. We had been successful in having the initial ruling struck down. But this simply returned Michelle back to where she had started – another fact-finding hearing to rule on her allegations of abuse and, ultimately, her ex-partner's contact with their child. With both professional knowledge and financial means, she had been able to fight the system this far. But she could not avoid being dragged into the situation that traps so many women who come to family court: an endless run of hearings that span across months and sometimes years, sapping dry every emotional and financial resource.

Michelle had not wanted to go to court in the first place. But she had been served with a court order by her ex-partner seeking contact and accusing her of making false allegations. In order to protect her daughter, she had felt there was no choice but to try and prove in a courtroom that the domestic abuse had been real. Although Michelle's professional knowledge meant that none of the torturous process came as a surprise to her, the emotional toll of the experience did. 'Why is he able to keep dragging me through this?' she would say to me.

In February 2022, the second fact-finding which followed our appeal concluded, upholding the vast majority of her allegations: that her ex-partner had assaulted Michelle and fractured her hand, been emotionally and verbally abusive to her and both children, engaged in 'gaslighting, control and denigration', and used threats of police and legal action to 'intimidate' her. He had also, Judge Ahmed concluded, bullied Michelle about her disability and upset their daughter by hitting the family dog in front of her (examples of animal cruelty are common in domestic abuse cases).[23]

Yet even this conclusive judgment, coming more than two years after the legal battle had begun, did not mean the end. Yet another round was to come. Soon, Michelle was put in the position of having to decide between what was in her best interests and what was right. Her ex-partner was a senior social worker. In June 2022, the regulatory body Social Work England (SWE) became aware of the judgment against him and applied to the court for a copy of it (the fact-finding hearing had been private and the judgment was not published). Initially, the judge was inclined to share it with them, but first, he invited submissions from both parents. Michelle was in two minds: she believed it was in the public interest for SWE to have the relevant information about someone who worked with vulnerable adults but was worried that he might lose his job as a result and withdraw his financial support for their daughter. She also feared potential repercussions from him. Initially, she told the judge she was neutral about the disclosure application before later telling him that she supported it. Unsurprisingly, Michelle's ex-partner objected. Judge Ahmed agreed with him, rejecting the application on the grounds that disclosure might adversely affect the daughter and that SWE could conduct its own investigation without the fact-finding judgment.

SWE did not appeal this decision, meaning that once again, the decision about whether to proceed fell to Michelle. She could have let the matter rest, reasoning that she had finally been vindicated in court and that she had already been through more traumatic court proceedings than should be expected of any abuse survivor. Doing so would have been the easiest thing for her and her daughter. But she could not live with the thought that a man she knew to be a bully, whom the court had found to be physically violent and emotionally abusive, could continue working in a responsible role with vulnerable people without facing a proper investigation. As a lawyer, she knew that the matter had wider meaning, too: an important test case in determining whether findings of domestic abuse could be concealed from professional and regulatory bodies.

We were back to 'fuck it'. She decided to appeal the decision herself, going back to court even though she did not have to. 'I feel like a turkey voting for bloody Christmas,' she said to me in characteristically blunt style.[24]

It was a decision Michelle should never have had to make, and which placed her directly back into the firing line: having to listen yet again to her ex-partner give what she described as a self-aggrandising speech about his behaviour, undermining the court's findings of abuse. During this hearing, Michelle was angrier than I had seen her at any previous point. 'I can't believe I'm here. The *third* appeal. How can this happen? All the money and time I've had to spend on protecting my daughter from this man.' Yet that anger also fuelled her resolve. She put herself through the hell of having her abusive relationship replayed one more time because she believed it might help to prevent others from going through what she had.

Once again, she was successful. The appeal judge ruled that her colleague had failed to conduct the appropriate 'balancing' exercise to weigh public interest needs against the well-being of the child.[25] He had not considered relevant case law around the disclosure of such information to regulatory bodies, and had been mistaken in determining that SWE could conduct a satisfactory investigation without his judgment.[26]

I suggested to Mrs Justice Knowles that it would be of great assistance to share practical guidance for equivalent cases. She set out her observations that it should be the responsibility of the court to consider the necessity of disclosure to regulatory bodies proactively, not leaving it to victims in Michelle's vulnerable situation.[27] This, more than anything, justified Michelle's difficult decision to mount another appeal. She had not only won her own case, but also helped to set a precedent for how others should be handled in the future. Men found by a court to be domestic abusers had lost a layer of protection shielding their professional lives – which might often bring them into contact with vulnerable people – from scrutiny. Having worked on cases involving abusers who are working in the emergency services, the medical profession and in Parliament, I knew the importance of this. An abusive man does not suddenly become a different person when leaving the house in the morning. What they habitually do to their spouse and children at home poses the same risk of harm to their patients, constituents, junior colleagues and more. Michelle's bravery had forced the court to take a step towards mitigating some of that risk.

Yet, as we spoke after the appeal judgment was handed down, I could see how conflicted she was. More than three years of family court and successive rulings in her favour had come at a huge personal cost: having to relive an abusive relationship that had been over for seven years but which was still dragging her through the courts. She had been called a liar, blamed for the physical abuse her partner had inflicted on her, and told repeatedly that she had no legal recourse. Her career had been disrupted, her mental health had suffered, and she had had to parent her daughter through years of instability and uncertainty.

Even now, she felt it was not over. 'We will never be free of this man' was one of the last things she said to me before we parted. Of course, this is already the case for so many abuse survivors, who must live with traumatic memories and cannot simply put the past behind them. But it is an indictment of our justice system that it often serves, as it did here, more to perpetuate this cycle of abuse and trauma than to mitigate it.

Michelle was an exceptional case, with significant legal experience and limited financial means to fight. But even she looked broken by the end, though she had, in fact, 'won' three appeals.* That is the reality for women in family

---

* Michelle's first appeal had been prior to the original fact-finding

court: even success exacts a high price, and every victory is, to some extent, a pyrrhic one. For years, Michelle had seen this through the eyes of her clients, but now she had experienced the grim and grinding reality for herself. There was an understandable bitterness in her voice when she told me: 'I feel sorry for you. I don't have to do this any more. You have to every day.' Almost every week, a client will say something like this to me.

Representing Michelle had left me with mixed feelings. In some ways, it was a model for the work I wanted to do, where appeals fought and won can establish case law to help others: more of those building blocks that give victims a better chance and make it harder for abusers to exploit the system. Through its timing, Michelle's case also showed the difference made by the 2021 Act, with its more comprehensive definition of domestic abuse, which formed part of our appeal, and the additional measures it implemented to protect vulnerable witnesses.

Yet I had also been shown what working within the system to change the system really entailed: the implicit demand that individuals should suffer to ensure that failings are fought and progress achieved. Perhaps I also realised, watching Michelle's journey from lawyer to appellant, that no amount of empathy could ever make me fully understand what it was like to be an abuse survivor who must answer questions about the most traumatic events of their lives, face hostile questioning, and submit to the judgment of

---

hearing, when she successfully argued for permission to bring more allegations of abuse to the court than magistrates had allowed, so she could plead a pattern of abusive behaviour.

someone who may call into question your credibility or ask why you seem anxious.

I learned so much from Michelle, about the law and about what it takes to keep going even when others keep knocking you down and littering the path with obstacles. I left her case more determined than ever but also unavoidably disheartened. Michelle reminded me that it is only through the bravery of women who bring their cases to court again and again that we can achieve change. That our system relies on vulnerable women exposing themselves to repeated trauma in order to make progress.

I was about to find out how true this really was. Not long before I started representing Michelle, I had taken on another client, whose case began before hers and would go on for a full year after it. When I first met Kate, I had no idea how long, complex or important her legal battle would be. It was a case which ended up becoming one of the most significant of my career: one that brought the shadowy world of family court into the spotlight, and took the struggle for the legal system to treat women equally into the heart of Parliament, where laws are made.

4

Abuse of Power:
Griffiths v. Griffiths

People associate the work of a barrister with talking, whether addressing the judge or questioning a witness in court. But the longer my career has gone on, the more I have learned that an equally important part of the job is how well you listen.

Clients do not necessarily share their story in one go, especially women who have endured traumatic circumstances and been subjected to years of gaslighting by an abusive partner. Often, an important detail will be dropped in almost as an aside, or something significant will be presented as if mundane. Sometimes, you realise that a woman is telling you that they were raped, coercively controlled or emotionally abused, but does not fully recognise what happened to them. They have suppressed it, minimised it, or given it a different name.

So it was with Kate. When we met for our first full discussion about her case, I knew that she had left an abusive relationship and wanted to contest an application by her ex-husband for increased contact with their child. But the true nature of his abuse would only become clear as we sat in her green-carpeted office on firm wooden chairs, the kind that dig into your back after a while. The discomfort almost felt appropriate: we were in this room to do the agonising but necessary work of raking through the past, talking about her relationship and identifying the information we would need to put forward allegations in court.

We had been going for a while when, for the first time, Kate really paused, thinking slowly about what she wanted to say, how to say it, even if she could bring herself to. She toyed with her bouncy auburn hair, and her normally warm, deep voice began to sound strained.

'Sometimes he would start having sex with me while I was asleep.'

I paused too, letting the words settle, knowing what I had to ask.

'Was it without your consent?'

Another, even longer pause before she nodded and said yes, not meeting my eye.

'Kate, you do know what you've just described?'

'Yes, but we were married.'

'I know, but what you've just described is rape.'

Now she did look at me. I was almost certain it was the first time she had spoken those words to a stranger. To know that a partner has forced sex on you is one thing. To understand and accept that you are a victim of rape, and that the perpetrator is the man you loved, chose to marry and have children with, is another. This is what the rapist's charter so often trotted out in court – she didn't complain, didn't fight, didn't go to the police – consciously disregards: the acute difficulty for any woman in acknowledging that rape isn't just something that happens to other people, but which in this instance also happened to her.

The incident of rape was one of a catalogue of events throughout Kate's five-year marriage that told a tale of relentless abuse. During the fact-finding hearing that followed, fifteen different events would be considered by the judge, including times her ex-husband had shoved her against a wall or onto the bed, hit her, put his hands around her throat, and thrown things at her – a box, a tray of food, and one time on holiday her passport, telling her that she could fuck off home.

These horrors spanned the evening when he had knelt on Kate on the sofa, putting his hands around her throat and squeezing; the moment when, while she was heavily pregnant, he had gone to hit her before instead pushing her onto the bed; the family Christmas when she had witnessed him grab one of his own female relatives by the throat and pin her to the wall. Between all these incidents, knotting them together, was a constant drum beat of controlling behaviour, degradation and an insistence for her to satisfy his sexual demands, culminating in the multiple occasions when he raped her while she was sleeping.

Kate's was the story of so many abuse victims, trapped for years in a relationship with a man whose threats turned to violence, whose aggression repeatedly manifested in assault, and whose coercive controlling behaviour culminated in rape. Yet Kate was no ordinary victim, nor was her ex-husband just another abuser. The nondescript room we were sitting in was her office at Westminster, where she worked as a UK Member of Parliament. She had become an MP in 2019 after separating from her abusive ex-husband, the MP and sometime government minister Andrew Griffiths. She had in fact been selected to replace him when his career ended in disgrace, after it was reported he had sent a large number of sexually depraved messages to two young female constituents. Griffiths did not deny sending the messages, though an investigation found he had not breached the House of Commons' Code of Conduct for Members by doing so.[1]

Leaving him had been hard, and the challenge now in front of her – to face him in court – would be just as difficult. In the event, the fact-finding hearing we were preparing for would be the first of many hearings it took for Kate to finally achieve a full separation from the man who had abused and raped her. Her case, which became a legal landmark, was also notable for showing how the family court compounds the trauma of women who have already suffered appalling abuse. Far from being protected and supported, Kate ended up having to fight the system and change the law to protect herself and her child from the man who had mercilessly abused her.

Meeting Kate reminded me that there is no such thing as a classic victim of domestic abuse. I have represented some women who were overtly traumatised and struggling to cope and others who were thriving at the top of their professional field – all of whom had been through similar experiences of domestic abuse. Domestic abuse has no barriers and respects no boundaries. It cuts across class, race, religion, immigration status, household income and any other distinction you could think of. Men's violence against women is universal: around the world, an estimated one in three women globally experience physical or sexual violence from an intimate partner or sexual violence from a non-partner, often from a young age.[2] In the UK, the police record 3,000 cases of violence against women and girls every single day.[3] In light of this, we should not expect victims and survivors to look, act or behave in any particular way. Yet even knowing this, I still sometimes have to check myself. To tell myself that a woman who is strong, independent and occupying a position of power can have endured terrible things, even if they show few outward signs of it.

Sitting in Kate's parliamentary office, I found a woman who was as clear, robust and assertive as her position would suggest. She felt like the definition of what you expect (or at least hope) an elected representative to be. Yet she was a victim too, of a husband who had abused her in ways that she was still trying to understand and who was now embarking on a legal case that would last almost half as long as their abusive relationship.

It is the nature of my job that, almost as soon as you have introduced yourself to a client, you have to ask them for details of the controlling behaviour, the physical assaults and the sexual violence they have suffered. However sensitively this is done, there is no escaping that, while practically a stranger, you are invading a person's privacy and asking them to recall the most traumatic moments of their lives – just as will happen again in court when your sympathetic ear is replaced by opposing counsel's demanding interrogation. As a barrister, it is your duty to prepare a client for what they will face in the courtroom. Never had this requirement felt more challenging than in that office, asking another woman to set aside the armour of her professional persona and reveal the abuse victim within.

Soon the hearing we had been preparing for arrived: I

got up at the crack of dawn and travelled from London to Derby on an empty train. I lugged my suitcase through the rainy, cold, dark streets of the city where I had been born – one that now felt left behind. Just a fifty-minute drive from Leek, I remembered the times I had spent in Derby as a child and teenager, visiting the park and the shops. I had never expected to come back here with a robe and wig in my bag. One of the realities of being a barrister is that you quickly learn the job is nothing like it is presented on TV or in movies. The glamour of lawyers wandering around historic court buildings in full costume bears no resemblance to being sent to dilapidated courtrooms all over the country.

The events Kate had to recall in that courtroom were shocking. It had been hard enough for her to tell me about them in a private conference, and it was ten times more excruciating doing so in court, with her ex-husband's barrister peppering her with questions. Still, she persevered, giving evidence that painted a picture of Griffiths as a serial abuser with little to no control over his violent temper or his sexual needs, and who matched physical assaults with constant verbal abuse, degrading Kate, calling her frigid, fat and lazy, and telling her she would be nothing without him.[4] Kate's descriptions of the worst episodes of their marriage were chilling. As she later recounted to the journalist Louise Tickle: 'Sometimes I'd actually wake up and he would just have started having sex with me. Sometimes I'd grit my teeth and just think "we're married". Other times I'd get upset. Sometimes he'd just carry on and tell me not to be so fucking pathetic. Other times if I was lucky he would stop. Those were the times he lost his temper and would kick me, actually kicking me out of the bed. He'd just keep on kicking and kicking and kicking until I rolled out of the bed.'[5]

The requirement for Kate to recall details of her abuse in court was painful enough. Almost as bad was that, having given her account, she would have to sit and listen to the man who had terrorised her give his.

While being in the same room as an abusive man is never enjoyable, I find the process of cross-examining perpetrators fascinating. You get to witness the arrogance of a man who is used to exercising power and control and who believes that a courtroom will be no different. Some perpetrators visibly enjoy giving evidence, the stage it affords them and the opportunity to be the centre of attention. This is where confidence can tip over into carelessness, as a man who wishes to present one face ends up revealing another. Often, you see a man who denies having been controlling, coercive and abusive demonstrate, in the course of answering those questions, that he appears to be all of those things.

In court, I often come across men who want to try and control the direction of a cross-examination, but I had never encountered one who, like Griffiths, seemed to have prepared so meticulously for it. He appeared to have memorised every single document in the bundle of evidence, gave answers that felt like they had been rehearsed, and insisted on making long, often digressive statements that felt more like speeches than responses to what had been asked. Her Honour Judge Sue Williscroft described him as a 'lengthy responder to most questions wanting to put an answer "in context"'. Whereas I had characterised him as having acted like a lawyer himself, she commented that 'it felt more like a politician responding to debate or questioning'.[6]

Awkward witnesses often seem to relish that they are making your work harder. When cross-examining, you want to get into a flow, to land your points like a darts player – one, two, three thudding into the board. The longer you are made to wait in between, the harder it is to build and sustain a rhythm. Not to mention that you can easily lose your way when someone is purposefully avoiding the point and steering the dialogue off topic. It didn't help that the court had allocated a specific amount of time for cross-examination and understandably the judge started pressing me to hurry up, although, in the end, she did latch on to his method and granted me extra time to complete the questioning.

As this uncomfortable dance continued, a strange duality emerged. On the surface, Griffiths appeared exactly as he had prepared to be: confident and calm, referring me to different pages in the bundle as if he himself was the lawyer. Yet if you listened to the content of his answers, a very different picture emerged. Here was an abuser who leaned heavily into denial and victim-blaming, diminishing violent incidents and seeking every opportunity to smear Kate. For most incidents, he had an equivocation and alternative narrative. Of the time he had pushed her onto the bed on holiday, and thrown her passport and money at her: 'such an inconsequential row'. Of the night he had hit her and knocked a picture from the wall: 'regrettable and silly'.[7] Of the family Christmas that had descended into acrimony and him assaulting a family member: 'She could get emotional. The food was burnt. I was frustrated she was upset.'[8] He had an answer for everything, which always seemed to involve some combination of his behaviour needing to be put 'in context', of Kate having exaggerated, or her having been responsible. According to him, she was 'theatrical', 'highly strung' and 'gave as good as she got'.[9] He accused her of driving drunk and having goaded him on the occasion when he pushed her onto the bed while pregnant.[10]

This contrast, of the apparently reasonable man delivering talking points from a perpetrator's playbook, seemed at one with how Griffiths had lived his life. I reminded myself that the same man accused of raping his wife, punching and kicking her, and throwing heavy objects at her was also the politician who had helped start an organisation to encourage more women into politics and campaigned to introduce the legal prohibition on upskirting. Griffiths was used to presenting a facade in public that ran directly counter to the vicious abuse he perpetrated in private. Now, with his carefully rehearsed performance, he was trying to explain away a catalogue of serious allegations as if he could debate them out of existence.

The hearing wound up, and the look Kate and I exchanged after leaving the courtroom, before either of us spoke a word, said everything. Her case hung in the balance. 'It might be OK, let's just wait and see,' I said to Kate, hoping I sounded more confident than I felt.

Weeks later, the judgment arrived in my inbox, and I scrolled straight through to the end, where the schedule of findings would be, listing the allegations and how the judge had found in almost every instance. My eye went down the pages. The incident where he had pushed her into the wall. *Proved*. When he put his hands round her neck on the sofa. *Proved*. When he pushed her onto the bed and threw the passport at her. *Proved*. When he hit her after a night out and knocked a picture off the wall. *Proved.* When he threw the tray of food at her. *Proved.* When he raped her 'on a number of occasions'. *Proved.* And so on, with Judge Williscroft finding on the balance of probabilities that almost all the allegations we had brought were true. Others included his 'coercive and controlling behaviour to ensure the Respondent submitted to his sexual demands', when he had spat in her face after throwing a box at her, and weeks after their child was born when he shouted 'shut the fuck up' at the crying infant.[11] After the sexting scandal, he had also tried to threaten her into giving him a public show of support, saying that she would be homeless, helpless and unable to support the child without him. Kate refused. He also told Kate that no one would believe her if she ever spoke out because he was an MP.[12]

The judge criticised him harshly, describing the assault on holiday as 'a frightening loss of control', highlighting the consistent pattern of Griffiths 'minimising how he has behaved' and commenting: 'It seems to me that it never crossed [his] mind that she would not do what he liked her to do.'[13] In turn, the judge noted that he had acted like a politician in responding to questions, apparently to avoid straightforward answers 'which he understood might not have reflected well on him'.[14] And she made clear her disquiet about his inability to acknowledge or apologise for any of his actions. Having left the courtroom fearing the worst, I was now reading a judgment which had come down Kate's way in almost every regard.

When I eventually spoke to Kate, the deep sigh she gave down the phone said more than anything about the sheer relief she felt. She had not only been a victim of appalling abuse but had put herself in the deeply vulnerable position of bringing allegations of rape and domestic abuse to family court, where she had faced both unforgiving interrogation and the distinct possibility that she would not be believed – just as Griffiths had often warned her during the relationship. She had done it because she wanted her truth to be heard, for her abuser to be held accountable and for their child to be protected. Now, all those things had been achieved. At great personal cost, she had been vindicated. She might have gone on to report Griffiths to the police, but having her allegations proved in family court had achieved all she had ever wanted – to safeguard her child – and going further would simply have meant more traumatic court proceedings.

Still, this was not the end. The case of Griffiths v. Griffiths was about to take an unexpected turn, one that would make it so much more than a legal accounting of what had gone on within an abusive relationship, and a proceeding to help determine that abusive parent's contact with their child. It was about to become a question of principle: what right does the public have to know about the private lives of those they elect to public office, can powerful men be allowed to use the architecture of the justice system to conceal the abuse they perpetrated behind closed doors, and should a woman whose allegations have been upheld in family court be made to accept a vow of silence as a result?

Privacy is the first principle of the family court. Those who become involved in proceedings, whether through their own choice or not, are not allowed to talk about what happened inside the courtroom. The judgments may subsequently be published online – though relatively few are – but the people featured in them remain hidden behind neutral labels and letters of the alphabet: the woman who was beaten up becomes 'the mother', the man who abused her 'the father', the child who witnessed it a mere capital letter. The process of anonymisation becomes one of dehumanisation.

While this is designed to protect vulnerable children, it can also act as a veil of secrecy for perpetrators. Violent men hide behind the anonymity of the court, while women who want to talk about what happened to them are forbidden from doing so – not allowed to discuss a judgment that showed their partner really did abuse them or to share the traumatic experience of having had their account attacked in court as lies and exaggeration.

Disclosing such information in a way that identifies individuals is considered contempt of court. While no one could object to the underlying premise to protect children from being identified, in practice this secrecy often proves to be yet another weapon in the hands of an abuser. Not only does he get to carry on with his life as if nothing had happened, but he can also monitor his victim's social media, reporting her for any post or comment that even alludes to what went on during the case. The initial reprimand for this may be minor – a requirement to delete the posts and a warning about future conduct – but the knowledge that an abuser can continue to exercise power cuts much deeper. So, too, does the realisation that silence has become the price of justice.

When I agreed to represent Kate, I didn't realise that hers might be a case with the power to change this.[15] If privacy is the rule of the family court, she was about to become the exception. Unlike most of the other women in this book, I can use her real name, Kate Kniveton (Griffiths when she was married and elected as an MP in 2019), only because of a case that she agreed to fight and that we won.

The privacy dilemma arose just weeks after the fact-finding judgment which found Griffiths had raped and abused Kate was handed down. We were notified that two journalists – Louise Tickle of Tortoise and Brian Farmer of PA Media (formerly the Press Association) – had applied for the right to report on it.[16] They had read the judgment and were now pushing for it to be published without the names of Kate and Andrew Griffiths redacted (their child's name, as well as some specific details of the case, would remain so). In effect, they wanted to put in the public domain that Andrew Griffiths, a former MP, had been raping and abusing his wife while sitting on the front bench of the House of Commons.

They planned to take this fight to court on the grounds of public interest. Griffiths had been an elected representative for almost the entirety of the relationship and a government minister for some of it. It was highly questionable that the violent and abusive conduct of a man who represented the public in both the executive and legislature deserved to remain a private matter. Moreover, the power Griffiths occupied through his elected office was something he had often wielded over Kate. 'Nobody's going to believe you, Kate. I'm the Member of Parliament,' she recalled him saying to her.[17]

Tickle and Farmer's legal case appeared sound, but it all depended on Kate. Having already been through the ordeal of the fact-finding hearing, and with other proceedings pending regarding the divorce settlement and child contact arrangements, did she really want to put herself through yet another legal process where the details of her abusive marriage would be raked over? Her anonymity was guaranteed unless she decided to waive it.

Just as she had when choosing to put forward allegations of domestic abuse and rape in the first place, Kate faced the choice between pursuing justice and protecting her own privacy and welfare. Initially, the decision had been clear cut: she wished to limit Griffiths' contact with their child, and the best chance of achieving this was to have the most serious allegations against him proven in court. Now, the benefit of exposing herself was more nebulous, measured in public interest rather than the safety of her and her child.

Yet Kate was not easily deterred. Having initially felt 'devastated' at the thought that her being a rape victim would become public knowledge, she soon realised that the application was a cause she wanted to support – one that would ensure maximum accountability for her abuser and, more importantly, plant a stake in the ground for transparency where secrecy had so long held sway. Soon, she was in no doubt that she wanted to go ahead, and the case was heard in the family division of the High Court in July 2021, nine months after the fact-finding hearing.

I represented Kate again in her supporting role for the application. It was a strange case: the application for publication rested on what felt like extremely solid ground, given the obvious public interest dimension, yet it felt faintly heretical asking a family court judge to agree to full disclosure of information that is almost always kept private.

The case was led by Louise Tickle's barrister. She argued

that there was public interest in knowing about the abusive behaviour of an elected official, particularly one who had invoked that office while coercively controlling his victim.[18] She also suggested that publication of the judgment would correct the impression Griffiths had given in media interviews dating to the 2018 scandal over sexting, where he suggested it was a one-off event influenced by abuse he had experienced as a child.[19] And she contended that there was public benefit in bringing attention to a textbook case of coercive control, at a time when it had only recently been criminalised and was not well understood outside professional circles. Brian Farmer, representing himself, complemented these points with a direct appeal: anonymity was something extended to victims of rape in criminal cases.[20] How could the family court justify the extension of the same privilege to a perpetrator, especially one who had been holding public office?

In support, I argued that the attempts to block full publication of the judgment represented another way in which Griffiths was seeking to exercise control over Kate, just as the judge had found he did throughout their relationship.[21] In turn, his attempt to have the judgment further redacted would infringe on her rights to freedom of expression under Article 10 of the European Convention on Human Rights.[22] I also pointed out that there was little the court could do in practice to prevent Kate from putting her story in the public record. As a sitting MP, she had the ability to speak about what had happened to her under parliamentary privilege, without fear of legal repercussions.[23] Just a mile and a half down the road from where our case was being heard in the Royal Courts of Justice, she could walk into the Commons chamber and name Griffiths as her rapist. Did the court really wish to put a de facto gag order on this woman?

For their part, the lawyers representing Griffiths focused their case on the rights of the child. The anonymity of children is rightly the cornerstone of privacy in the family court, and they sought to rely on this, also arguing that publication would have a 'catastrophic' effect on Griffiths' relationship with his child.[24] Griffiths sought to have any details that could identify the child redacted – which by definition included both his and Kate's names.[25] In effect, he sought to use the child's right to privacy as a shield for himself.

This is a not uncommon litigation tactic used by men who do not wish their behaviour in a relationship to become public knowledge. Griffiths may have been hoping to achieve the same, but Mrs Justice Lieven was not convinced. In her conclusions, she supported the public-interest argument for transparency about the private behaviour of a lawmaker responsible for areas that included women's rights. She seemed to agree that a victim had the right to tell her story.[26] She also said that publication would allow the public record that was currently influenced by the interviews he had given in 2018 to be corrected.[27] Regarding the rights of the child, she was reassured that 'X' was only three years old at the time of this hearing and would not be exposed to the immediate fallout and media scrutiny.[28] Furthermore, the information already in the public domain about Griffiths meant that the child was never going to be protected from their father's history forever: it would have needed to be explained in due course anyway. Both Kate, as mother, and the child's guardian – their independent representative

– were supporting publication. Having considered the various competing rights, the judge decided to do the same.

Her judgment was handed down at the end of July 2021, but it was not until the following January that it was finally published, after Griffiths took a technical and ultimately unsuccessful appeal to the Court of Appeal.[29]

When his appeal failed, there was nothing more he could do to prevent the truth of what he had done becoming public knowledge. For Kate, it made all the anguish she had gone through worthwhile. As she later reflected: 'It's like a feeling of freedom. I'm no longer silenced, I can speak out. It's thrown a light on his lies and how he was trying to spin it. But ultimately it gives me an even stronger platform now to bring my personal experience to what I want to do to help other victims.'[30]

Yet even with this burden lifted, the legal process was not over for Kate. A subsequent court order made by Judge Williscroft required her to share the costs of Griffiths having his regular contact with their child at a supervised contact centre.[31] She was, in effect, being asked to pay for her rapist to have contact with her child. We appealed this and won, with Mrs Justice Emma Arbuthnot's ruling establishing a presumption against victims being required to meet any of their abuser's costs of child contact. Then there was the divorce settlement, a deliberately protracted process that involved offers being made from his side, revised, responses ignored, and an agreement being withheld until the day of the planned hearing. It meant months more of stress and uncertainty for Kate, as her abuser used one of the last levers at his disposal to exercise control over her. Not to mention that she had to pay £11,000 to the man who had raped her in order to free herself of him for good.

Over three years since I first represented Kate at the fact-finding, there were still proceedings outstanding relating to contact arrangements. Like every other abuse victim, she found that the legal system required her to fight and fight again, spending money, time and above all emotional energy to ensure that her story was upheld, her rights protected, and her child safeguarded. The final hearing date did not arrive until 17 January 2024, back in Derby Family Court, where the case had started. We were before Mrs Justice Lieven and seeking an order to prohibit Griffiths from having any direct contact with the child, given the risks he posed, or to be able to make any court applications regarding contact for a period of five years. The child's guardian was supporting our case, and testified that Griffiths should only be permitted 'letterbox' contact – written messages managed by an intermediary.

As had been true throughout this long-running saga, Kate was seeking both to protect her own child and to use her influence to help other women who would one day be walking in her shoes. As she asked me in frustration one day: 'How can it be right that a rapist father has the right to be involved in their child's life?'

This question had long been left unresolved. In June 2020, the Ministry of Justice's Harm Report had recommended 'that the presumption of parental involvement be reviewed urgently' across all family court cases.[32] Almost five years later, it remained untouched. Once again it had fallen to a courageous individual like Kate to assume responsibility for pushing through the vital changes that the system should long ago have done for itself.

*

It felt grimly appropriate that the morning of the final hearing was accompanied by a bitter winter chill. Having fought for so long, Kate could finally glimpse what a future without having to relive her abusive marriage would be like. But first she would have to walk this final mile through the cold, replaying the same incidents, answering the same questions, holding the same hopes and fears about what the court would decide.

When she and her solicitor picked me up from Derby train station to drive to court, it seemed like Kate was wearing the weight of every single hearing that had come before this one. She had been crying and was hurriedly reapplying mascara as her solicitor drove, and I tried to keep my voice as gentle as possible while going over final details. Then we arrived at court and Kate stepped out to be met by waiting TV cameras. In that moment, I saw what a remarkable woman she was: all the fatigue and uncertainty disappeared from her face as she strode into court, hiding the abundant fear I knew she was feeling.

Final hearings are where outstanding disputes between parties must be resolved, which in this case primarily meant dealing with the question of Griffiths' contact with the child. Kate was applying not only to limit him to letterbox contact, but to prevent him from making any further applications for a period of five years – giving her security at last that she could not be brought back to court unless he secured permission from the judge.

We had also prepared an application to challenge the presumption that parental involvement is desirable regardless of circumstances – seeking to advance the exact point highlighted by the MoJ Harm Report in 2020, and in effect to argue that a rapist father should not continue to enjoy parental involvement in a child's life as a default. This was an application Kate brought against her own government. However, she had to withdraw it after being denied an order protecting her from being liable for legal costs if this had failed – something the then Justice Secretary, Alex Chalk MP, refused to grant. Seemingly the government, having failed to address the recommendations of its own report, now wished to prohibit a backbench MP from doing their work for them.

In court, much of the hearing felt like an action replay of prior proceedings. Griffiths still seemed to be struggling to accept the totality of what had transpired. As the judge commented, he seemed to think it was Kate who needed to be changed, adjusted or corrected through therapy and that '[his] main concern remains himself and what is best for him, rather than what is best for [the child]'.[33] He also took a shot at me, saying that I had been running a campaign against him in the media (the judge noted this, but concluded that I was 'merely representing [my] client's interests').[34]

Then I sat and listened as Kate spoke haltingly under the judge's questioning. From behind the protective screen I could not see her face, but I could hear her taking big gulps of air and sobbing.[35] Although the screen was there to safeguard Kate's privacy, I felt like I had hardly ever seen a client be more exposed in the courtroom. This was not the self-assured politician who had strode into the courtroom, but the traumatised victim, ground down by a justice system after years of having to relive her trauma.

Kate faced challenging questions. The judge asked if

she was trying to 'airbrush' Griffiths from their child's life through an application to change the child's surname, which she referred to as a 'somewhat arid debate'.[36] As someone who changed my surname to cut ties with my abusive father and match my maternal family's, I understood better than anyone else in that courtroom how important names are. It was one of the best decisions I have ever made.

But Mrs Justice Lieven was clear in her view that 'it is important that [the child] has a relationship with the father and knows him'.[37] In other cases, I have sometimes argued that forcing a child into a relationship with a rapist parent is tantamount to state-sanctioned abuse, watching those present almost gasp in horror that I could make such a brazen assertion. Yet I know from experience how damaging it is for a child to have a relationship with an abusive parent. It never leaves you. Having no parent is better than enduring an abusive parent.

Despite the adversarial proceedings, the judge concluded by ruling in the child's favour, although she limited Griffiths from making further applications for a period of only three years, not five as both we and the child's guardian had asked for. After a legal battle that had been going on for most of her child's life, Kate could finally breathe. She was now almost guaranteed, if for a shorter period than we had wanted, that her abusive ex-husband could not drag her back to court for yet more proceedings. She could raise her child free from the fear of the man who had raped and pitilessly abused her.

It was a testament to the extraordinary resilience she had shown, not only in fighting for her truth and the safety of her child, but in putting herself in the public eye to do so.

Yet Kate was also an outlier. The fact that her abuser had been an MP, and that she subsequently became one herself, gave a public dimension to the case that overturned the family court's fundamental presumption in favour of privacy. She won the right to tell her own story, as a plank of her campaigning work, allowing her to be a beacon for others who had been through what she had.

The effect was to land a blow for transparency in a hitherto secretive world. While Kate's case was in many ways exceptional, it also demonstrated the limits of privacy in such proceedings and established how this can be a tool abusers seek to exploit as a form of coercive control. This all came at a time when the pressure was growing for greater public scrutiny of family court. In 2023, a pilot programme began in three UK courts that allows journalists to report on cases if they ensure the anonymity of the parties involved, unless the judge specifically prohibits it (versus a status quo where reporting is only permitted when the judge grants an application).[38] The transparency programme has since been rolled out to other family courts.[39]

After suffering almost a decade of abuse, rebuilding her life and enduring a legal battle that stretched over several years, Kate had achieved so much more than personal vindication. Her bravery had helped to change the law around contact costs while altering the debate on the broader question of privacy and to whom it should apply. A woman who had been called fat, stupid and useless by her abuser had brought him to account. And she had changed the law in a way that would soon benefit other women.

In 2024, I represented Sandra, in a case where two journalists, Hannah Summers and Suzanne Martin, had applied to report on her story and name her former partner, Kristoffer Paul Arthur White. He had been granted unsupervised contact with their child, although he had previously been convicted of raping a young woman who he dragged off the street and a family court judge later found that he had also raped Sandra on three occasions.[40] Remarkably, Cafcass (the Children and Family Court Advisory and Support Service – the independent body that represents children in family court cases) had first recommended that the father be granted unsupervised access to the child, and then supported his case for privacy, against Summers' and Martin's argument that there was public interest in naming a serial rapist who posed a danger to other women. His Honour Judge Kambiz Moradifar, citing the Griffiths case, granted the journalists' application.[41] At a subsequent hearing, he ordered that there should be no contact between White and the child and stripped him of his parental responsibility.[42] Another dangerous man had been shown that he could not use his child's right to privacy to hide from what he had done. After White was named, Sandra was able to speak out anonymously about what it had been like to watch the family court order that the man who had raped her and another woman should have unfettered contact with her child. 'It was like being told that, despite the court's findings, Cafcass doesn't believe you,' she said. 'A judge has said it happened. But it doesn't matter that he's a convicted rapist and he raped you – he can spend time with your child. It was earth-shattering.'[43]

Kate Kniveton had not just been successful against her abusive ex-husband in court time after time. In the process, she had shown that there are fewer and fewer legal shadows in which perpetrators like Andrew Griffiths can hope to hide – making the world a little safer for women like her, and a little more dangerous for abusive, controlling men like him.

Her case taught me so much about how the family court makes women suffer as they try to deal with the aftermath of an abusive relationship. It showed how women can be brought back to court time after time, made to recount excruciating details about how they were raped and assaulted not just once but on numerous occasions, before being questioned with aggression and disdain about the most vulnerable moments of their lives, treated more like perpetrators than victims.

Kate's was the first high-profile case I had worked on in which rape had been a central allegation, but I would soon learn that her experience had not been an outlier. As I represented more rape survivors, in cases I took on while Kate's rumbled on in the background, I saw the bitter truth of what family court is like for women who bring allegations of rape to try and safeguard their children – and how those victims most in need of sensitivity and support are frequently treated. By this point I was no stranger to the harsh realities of family court for women and children, but until I began to argue cases in which allegations of rape were fundamental, I did not know quite how bad it could be.

5

Double Standard:
Rape and Sexual Violence

It was a discordant setting in which to prepare one of the most upsetting cases I had encountered. My plan had been to fly home from holiday on Saturday morning, giving myself most of the weekend to get ready for the case that would begin on Monday. When our flight was delayed, it soon became clear that if I was going to get the work done, it would be at the airport or nowhere. I scrabbled for a charging port to keep my ancient laptop working, and perched on an uncomfortably tall bar stool that was the only seat I could find. As families settled down to their breakfasts, stag do goers to their pints, and my partner resigned himself to his book, I began to reacquaint myself with the story of Mary, a woman who alleged that her husband had routinely demanded sex, often strangled her during intercourse, and on one occasion raped her.[1]

Reading the witness statements showed that Mary had already been through a deeply traumatic experience, with the alleged abuses in her marriage compounding others she had suffered during childhood. Sitting in that airport bar, speed-reading hundreds of pages, I could not have foreseen how more suffering would now be heaped on a woman who had already endured so much.

When we had first met to discuss her case, it was clear that Mary – like Kate – found it difficult to put into words what had happened to her. At our conference, her already soft voice dropped to a barely perceptible whisper when I said that, as hard as it was, we needed to discuss exactly what her husband had done to her if we were going to make these allegations in court. Tears formed in her eyes, but they did not fall.

Mary gathered herself, sitting upright in the chair. Her face hardened. Her voice became louder, almost robotic as she described what had happened to her. The look on Mary's face as she recounted these events was harrowing. I felt like I was watching her step outside of her own body, as if to physically disconnect herself from the things that she said had been done to it – the things she now had to relive for the sake of the court.

I glanced at the woman in front of me and thought of how Mary appeared in her profile photo on WhatsApp: her skin glowing, curls bouncing over her shoulders, arms hung protectively around her child, whose grinning face was painted with butterflies. That was Mary, the picture-perfect, doting young mother, and this was Mary, the traumatised abuse survivor. Part of my job is to remember that those can be two halves of the same person, and to demonstrate this in court, showing that someone who alleges they have been raped does not have to look, behave or be a certain way to be believed.

Mary was caught in the bind that so many women face when coming to family court, often brought there by an ex-partner who is seeking to have the court order that they should be permitted to spend more time with their child. For these women, one part of them is desperate to bury the horrors of the past and never speak of them again, but another knows that they may only protect the most precious thing in their life precisely by excavating and reliving that past.

It can take time for someone to face up to the reality of what they must do if they want the abuse that was perpetrated against them to be heard by the court. This much was clear from Mary's written statement about her allegations. I read it with a sinking feeling, knowing it lacked the precise details about when and how the alleged rape had occurred that the court would require, and realising I would have to press Mary to provide these if she wanted to bring the allegation. To support her case, it was important to file a more complete statement. When we discussed it, Mary told me that she had given the statement to a male solicitor and had felt uncomfortable describing the details of what had happened to a man, which underlined the magnitude of making these allegations for any woman. It showed how, for Mary, this had been an agonising experience even before stepping through the door of the courtroom.

Unfortunately, it was about to get much worse. If Kate Kniveton's case had shown me how difficult it can be to give and hear evidence as a rape survivor, Mary's would shatter any remaining illusions I had about what it means to bring an allegation of rape before the family court.

The first contact I'd had with Mary was by email. Typically, clients are referred to me by solicitors, but some will approach me directly. When Mary's message dropped into my inbox after midnight, while I was preparing for another case, it immediately caught my eye. Like so many women who contact me to ask for help, she felt trapped and did not know where to turn. After she had finally walked out of a marriage she described as abusive, contact arrangements had broken down and her ex-husband had issued proceedings to restore his contact with their child. The case had become bogged down in pandemic-related delays and it was not until months had passed that the fact-finding hearing which would determine the outcome took place.

I walked from my chambers to the Central Family Court, down Chancery Lane, past neo-Gothic windows and centuries-old shops, catching the sun that was beginning to peek through the tall buildings. I knew that a far less idyllic scene awaited me: the grey slab frontage of a building I was now all too familiar with, an antiseptic conference room with bars against the window and a courtroom without any windows at all. There, Mary would have to face her worst nightmare: giving evidence about the day she said her husband had raped her and answering questions that would come straight from the textbook of lawyers representing a man accused of sexual violence. *Why didn't you tell someone? Where's your evidence? If it was so bad, why didn't you just leave?*

This is the reality facing any woman who wants to bring allegations of domestic abuse, assault or rape to family court. It is the person making the allegations who must climb uphill, trying to convince a judge on the balance of probabilities that what they are saying is true. The burden of proof rests entirely on them. They must submit themselves to deeply invasive questioning, where everything they have said and done since the day they allege they were raped could be fair game. They must climb into a glass box and be treated like a specimen. Whereas for the other side, the work is simple and the arguments rote. You refute and discredit, saying that the claims are exaggerated, the evidence lacking, and the witnesses unreliable.

I know that it is easy to represent the perpetrator in cases like this because I have done it – required, like all barristers, to take the cases that are sent to me, regardless of my views about them, via what is known as the 'cab rank rule'.[2] I have been in the situation where I know the best legal strategy for my client is to cast doubt on everything the woman is saying and discredit her as much as possible, picking holes and building straw men. And I have had male clients who pressed me to be more aggressive and go harder. As tough as it is, there is very little you can do once you are in the courtroom with a demanding client who insists that a certain question be asked in a certain way, as long as those questions are within the boundaries of the law and our professional duties. These are rarely people who want to hear legal advice, but rather wish to use their lawyer as a tool to attack their former partner. Reconciling my feminist views with a job where I was required to represent men facing allegations of violence against women and children was always close to an impossibility. I am fortunate that the nature of a barrister's career is that you tend to become known for doing certain types of work: over time, my reputation as an advocate for women has meant that almost all the cases that come my way are to represent women.

While representing those clients, I have seen the same

98

dynamics play out time after time: watching the notes being shared and the words whispered in ears, hearing opposing counsel upping the ante in response, putting on a show for a male client who wants to control the proceedings just as they did the relationship it concerns. There is a reason that slut-shaming and victim-blaming are such prevalent features of family court proceedings: many male perpetrators demand it, and the system was built by men in a way that has accommodated and rewarded it.

I had done my best to prepare Mary for this. As I do with every client in her situation, I asked if she was prepared to put forward the allegation of rape and explained what this would entail. I told her she would have to go through what the court demands of every woman in her position: not just to relive the events but to explain them, justify her actions, be presented with alternative explanations and listen to discussions of what does and doesn't constitute rape. That is the limit of what I can do as a barrister to ensure my client is ready for court: we can discuss their legal strategy, the options they have and what they should expect in general terms. But you cannot rehearse or prepare someone, telling them what they should say or how to answer a likely question.

The line between what is and is not permissible becomes starker once the hearing itself begins, and especially once a client is sworn in to begin giving evidence. For the duration of their testimony, I cannot discuss the case with them at all, and at this point I will generally stop speaking to a client to avoid the risk of a conversation straying beyond what is permitted. There are good reasons for this rule, but it is still hard when representing women like Mary to tell them that they must face their most vulnerable moment in court alone, and that even their advocate is required to keep her distance until they have completed giving evidence.

The last chance to have a conversation is immediately before the hearing begins. It was a hot day, but the room we were in was temperature-controlled and entirely free from sunlight – it could have been any time of year, anywhere in the world. As soon as we sat down to run through final preparations, I could see how difficult this day was going to be for Mary. The order of a fact-finding hearing is fixed, and as the party bringing allegations, Mary would be giving evidence first. There was no escaping that she was about to be interrogated about her claims that she had been raped, not to mention the many other times when she said she had been strangled during sex against her will. Her hand shook as she reached out to drink from a glass of water. I tried to ground her by running through the procedure of what was about to happen. She would be sitting in the witness box, and I would ask her questions first. It was an opportunity to speak freely and to tell the judge everything she wanted to say. Then the other side would ask their questions. This might be very difficult, but Mary should remember that she could take a break at any time, and that this was her story: she knew it better than anyone. I finished with words I have heard myself say in a hundred conference rooms exactly like this one. 'Just listen to the question, breathe before you answer, try to stay calm and tell the truth.'

Mary looked at me without speaking, and I could see how afraid she was, how she knew that she had finally arrived at the day she had been dreading above all. Then she did speak. 'I know what's going to happen.' She paused. 'They're going to say I'm this damaged, hysterical woman. That I've got an axe to grind and that I never got over what happened to me as a child.' Another pause. 'It was the worst thing I ever did telling him about that.' Part of our case was that Mary's husband had emotionally abused her by continually referring to the abuse she said her father had perpetrated against her during childhood.[3]

I fixed my face, trying to be reassuring, but feeling the pang of helplessness that is such a familiar part of my job. There was nothing I could now do to protect my client from the task in front of her. Mary knew what she wanted above all – to protect her daughter from the man she alleged had been abusive towards both of them. And she knew what she had to do to try and achieve that. She was about to re-traumatise herself for the sake of her child. But knowing what was coming would not make it any easier to endure.

'I just don't understand. How can he say that? How can *he* say *that*?'

Weeks after Mary's hearing, we were meeting again, this time virtually. The hearing had been hard for her, but there had been nothing unexpected. Opposing counsel had asked the same questions every perpetrator's lawyer does, the judge had been neutral in his interventions, and Mary had got through. Now the judgment had arrived and she felt blindsided. It was upsetting enough for Mary that the conclusion had largely gone against her: the judge, His Honour Judge Marc Marin, did not uphold her allegations of sexual violence against the ex-husband, although he was critical of him in many ways.

Knowing that she had been disbelieved and that she had not been able to protect her daughter as much as she hoped was one thing. But what had truly shocked Mary were some of the comments contained in the judgment. Among several examples, she had focused on one, where the judge had written: 'I found it difficult to accept that an intelligent lady could not place the alleged rape within a very short time window given that the incident was certainly etched in her memory.'[4]

Mary expected that professionals working in the family court would understand how trauma can impact memory, and how patterns of abuse in a relationship can make it difficult to be precise about timelines, or simply that human memory is fallible. She had testified that she recalled her rape as having happened at some point between October 2011 and June 2012. That was not good enough for the judge. Mary was an intelligent woman. Too intelligent not to have known the date when she was raped, so it was implied.

Mary kept coming back to this point, and she kept repeating a question I could not answer. 'How could he say that?'

This section was just one of many in the judgment that cast doubt on Mary's evidence. First, the judge questioned whether Mary could be deemed a reliable witness, based on her acknowledged experience of childhood abuse, which he wrote may have 'clouded her view' of her husband – exactly the fear Mary had expressed to me before the hearing.[5] The judgment then proceeded to critique and question her account of the rape allegation, in a way that showed exactly why so many women fear bringing claims like this to court.

No.1: *her story changed.* The judge criticised Mary for not being able to give a precise date for when she was raped.[6] He emphasised differences in her previous statement to the police and the evidence she gave in court, lingering on variations that fell some way short of contradictions. To the police, she had said her husband 'just climbed on me', and in court that he had turned around and started to remove her clothes.[7] To the police, she had said he took off her pyjama bottoms; in court, that he took off her pyjama bottoms and her underwear ('she made no mention of removal of pants to the police,' the judge noted).[8] In court, she said he had put on a condom, but this was not mentioned in the police statement (nor had she been asked about it).[9] These were among what the judge described as 'deficits in the mother's evidence'.[10] The police had taken no further action following her report, no surprise given just two in every hundred rapes recorded by the police result in someone being charged.[11]

The scrutiny placed on Mary's story was part of the high standard to which women are often held when making allegations about rape. They are expected to have perfect recall of events that may have happened years earlier (in this case, a little over a decade before the hearing). If their accounts vary between statements, emphasising different details, this may be seen as indicative of unreliability, despite guidance from the Crown Prosecution Service (CPS) which emphasises it is a rape myth to believe that 'inconsistencies in accounts provided by a victim always mean they lack credibility as a witness'.[12]*

---

* While the CPS guidance concerns criminal cases, a barrister may point the judge towards it in a family law case. As this chapter details, I have tried and failed to have an equivalent set of rape myths added to practice directions that concern family law cases.

At the same time, if a woman's account seems too perfect, it may be deemed rehearsed and calculated. The bar for a woman to be believed often seems set impossibly high: they must be detailed and consistent (but not too consistent, because that may look like a prepared story) at every stage. No matter that recalling a deeply traumatic event is difficult or that people tend to recollect the minor details of events differently at different times, when the substance of their story is not in question. Women who claim they have been raped must be perfect witnesses, or they may not be deemed as credible victims of rape at all.

No.2: *she didn't report it.* Another of the 'deficits' in Mary's story was the lack of contemporaneous evidence. The judge noted that she had not made a police report until years later or spoken to a doctor.[13] He pointed out that she had sought help from a charity supporting victims of child abuse in the same time period but that the police had not been contacted in the aftermath, indicating that she had not told them either.[14] Among its rape myths and stereotypes, the CPS dispels the assumption that 'if the victim didn't complain to the police immediately it can't have been rape'.[15]

More than ten years after the alleged event, I had seen how difficult Mary still found it to talk about and to relive the details of it. It did not seem hard to understand why she may have felt unable to report it at the time and submit herself to the invasive (in every way) process of going to the police in the immediate aftermath. It should be noted that five in every six women (and 80 per cent of men) who are raped don't report it to the police.[16] So pervasive is our rape culture that a quarter of adult women have been victims of either rape or sexual assault; the vast majority of these go unreported.[17]

There are so many reasons why a woman may not report their rapist to any kind of authority. They may be so traumatised by the experience that they do not wish to think about it, let alone discuss it in detail with a stranger. They may not recognise or accept what happened to them, especially when the rapist was already their intimate partner.*[18] And they may fear the repercussions from that man or his family, or not feel able to break away from an abusive relationship. The psychological complexity and emotional weight of being a rape victim may cause women to respond in all sorts of ways that fall short of establishing a perfect evidence trail.

No.3: *she didn't leave.* When Mary and her husband separated, she initially went to live with her mother. She then returned to the family home for a short period before finally moving out for good. 'To my mind, it made no sense for the mother to return to the home of an alleged perpetrator of such a heinous acts,' the judge concluded, even though he acknowledged that Mary's relationship with her mother was difficult.[19] Why had Mary not gone to stay with friends, to a refuge, or used legal means to gain sole occupation of the property? All these questions were asked about Mary, her actions and her decisions. Why didn't anyone stand back and ask why her husband hadn't left the family home?

It echoed an argument often heard: if the relationship was so abusive, why didn't she just leave? This is usually said breezily, as if the situation for an abuse victim is simple. It disregards the practical obstacles for a vulnerable woman

---

* Another common experience: half of rapes against women are perpetrated by their current or former partner, and five out of every six by someone known to them.

with limited options, the psychological reality of being an abuse victim who may not wish to disclose this to friends, family or strangers, and indeed, the emotional complexity of feeling dependent on a partner who may have spent years abusing and controlling them. 'She could have walked away' is one of the most prevalent and misleading domestic abuse tropes. The period of leaving an abusive relationship is one of the most dangerous times for survivors – 75 per cent of women who are killed by their abusers are murdered when they attempt to leave or after they have left an abusive relationship[20] – which can serve as a deterrent from cutting off all contact.

No.4: *she doesn't look like a victim*. The most striking part of the case came when the judge concluded that he could not uphold Mary's allegations because the things she said could not have happened to a woman like her. 'I found it difficult to accept that an intelligent lady could not place the alleged rape within a very short time window,' he wrote in one section of the judgment.[21] And in another: 'I do not accept that the mother simply allowed strangulation to continue for so many years. She is intelligent . . . She came across as someone who would not have just accepted such conduct.'[22]

When first reviewing the judgment, I had to reread these sections to make certain I had understood. I wanted to be sure that I had read a judge say – twice – that a woman had not been raped and strangled during sex in part because she seemed too intelligent to have been a victim, in the way she described. Most people working with domestic abuse victims know how much their stories and backgrounds vary. There are no criteria or preconditions for ending up in an abusive relationship. It should go without saying that any woman can become a victim of domestic abuse and sexual violence. The idea that someone can be too articulate, too robust and too clever to be considered a credible victim is both misplaced and offensive. So, too, is the implication that a woman's perceived intellect is relevant to whether they were raped or not. The CPS specifies it is a rape myth to believe that 'strong/independent/powerful/older people don't get raped', emphasising that 'there is no typical victim of rape. People of all ages, appearance, status and backgrounds can be raped.'[23]

No.5: *he didn't know what he was doing.* While the judge appeared to question Mary's story, he seemed to accept significant parts of her ex-husband's version of events. 'I am not satisfied that [the] father realised that on any occasion the mother did not want sex or that he knew she did not consent to sex,' he wrote.[24]

Much as it had with Mary's evidence, the judgment noted that the father's story had changed over time. To the police, he had previously said that they had sex on a daily basis, even when she had been ill, but in court he 'tried to back away from his previous statement . . . clearly trying to distance himself from this remark'.[25] Yet the father's evidence was not discounted in the same way as Mary's had been. Instead, his assertions about their sex life, with victim-blaming overtones, were reiterated ('The father said that their sexual relationship was natural; the mother even put on appropriate lingerie').[26] Another of the CPS's rape myths is that 'The victim provoked rape and implied consent simply by their dress / flirtatious behaviour.'[27]

It is not that the judge had formed a particularly favourable view of the father. His judgment commented that his behaviour 'was at times unacceptable', identified 'a certain arrogance and nastiness towards both the mother and the child', and stated that he 'showed a lack of sensitivity and common sense' in introducing his new partner to Mary and their child. He noted that the father had never registered Mary as joint owner of their house, failed to financially support her when she lost her job during their marriage and stopped making maintenance payments after contact with the child fell into dispute.[28]

Yet, presented with a classic case of his story versus hers, His Honour Judge Marin appeared to elevate concerns about Mary's evidence and smooth over some of the flaws in the ex-husband's. She had not reported a rape or episodes of strangulation at the time and there were some inconsistencies in her account of sexual violence over time. In any case, was it even believable that an educated woman would have allowed herself to be treated in this manner over a lengthy time period? She had sent friendly messages to her husband at other times, briefly moved back in with him after separating, and even confided in him about her experiences of childhood abuse during the marriage, which she argued he had then used to undermine her credibility. She had consented to sex on numerous other occasions and apparently worn lingerie.

All these factors and more were presented as reasons why Mary's account of being raped should not be believed. By contrast, even though there was evidence of her husband allegedly being controlling and sexually demanding, no connections were drawn between this pattern of behaviour and Mary's allegations. The judge simply concluded that 'she allowed the father's demands for sex. I accept that the mother may well have felt worthless and lacking in self-esteem, but this was not something that the father would have realised.'[29] Mary's evidence had 'deficits'; her ex-husband's was merely 'not without its difficulties'.[30]

So many questions were raised by the judgment against Mary – the woman apparently too intelligent not to have remembered when she was raped – that I hoped in appealing it, we could also achieve wider changes in the law. In late 2022, I successfully argued for her appeal to be heard jointly with one being made by another of my clients, who had alleged that her husband raped her after removing a condom when she had consented only to protected sex.[31] She said this rape had led to the conception of the child she was now trying to shield from the allegedly abusive father. In written submissions to Mrs Justice Emma Arbuthnot, a High Court Judge, I asked her to use the two cases to consider several wider points of law, including a definition for rape and consent in family court, how judges should approach women's sexual history in these cases, and whether they should be required to warn themselves about rape myths when hearing cases and preparing findings.

The first and most important of these was a family law definition of rape and consent. We proposed a framework that would define rape as 'an absence of willingness to engage in sex', and which said that willingness must be actively demonstrated, and could not 'be inferred from silence or passivity'. A person might cease to be willing at any point prior to or during sex, and lack of willingness might also stem from a lack of freedom and capacity to choose – including when someone is intoxicated, under threat of violence or otherwise in fear.[32]

Mrs Justice Gwynneth Knowles gave several reasons for refusing to adopt either this or any other definition of rape or consent.* She noted that Parliament had declined to include a definition in the 2021 Domestic Abuse Act (although the possibility of this was never raised while the legislation was being put through) or to give guidelines as to how judges should determine such allegations. If the legislature had been unwilling to agree on a definition, she argued, it would be inappropriate for the court to do so on its behalf. Additionally, she described the framework approach as 'too narrow a prism, through which to view and investigate the true nature of an adult relationship'.[33] It risked turning the judge's job into a 'tick box exercise rather than a holistic evaluation of the evidence'.[34]

In effect, we were told that the court would not be providing clarity on this issue because it was not its place to do so, and a definition or framework would tie the hands of judges and force them to take too procedural an approach to complex, varied cases. For similar reasons, the judge also refused to set out a list of rape myths and stereotypes.

On the court's own terms, these arguments make sense. The role of family court is not to determine whether an individual is guilty or not guilty of crimes but to make findings of fact that allow judgments to be made concerning the risk of ongoing contact between parents and children. Each case is different and must be assessed on its own merits and details. Judicial discretion is all-important as judges consider

---

* We appealed Mrs Justice Knowles' decision to the Court of Appeal who refused our appeal. See *A v. B & Anor* [2023] EWCA Civ 360 (7 March 2023).

a 'wide canvas' of evidence to make their determinations.

The problem is that you do not have to look far to find cases where this judicial discretion is synonymous with stereotyping women. What use had the wide canvas been to Mary when the judge in her case refused to connect acknowledged aspects of the husband's abusive behaviour with her allegations of sexual violence?

Then the appeal comes, and women like Mary encounter the next stage: a new judge who must consider not the merit of the allegations, but the narrower question of whether the original judge was wrong in law. At Mary's appeal, Mrs Justice Knowles did accept elements of our case, acknowledging that the first judge had failed to consider if her husband's overall behaviour, even if he believed it had not involved rape and strangulation, 'was nevertheless profoundly abusive and . . . should not be ignored'.[35] She criticised his description of Mary as an intelligent woman who should have been capable of reporting a rape and seeking help (although this was described as merely 'unhelpful').[36] She also noted he had failed to apply the guidance that a detailed schedule of findings should be attached to a judgment such as this, which might have helped him to assess patterns of behaviour in the relationship.

Yet in the same breath, she upheld his findings of no rape and no strangulation, commenting that: 'The judge had the inestimable benefit of hearing from both the parties at length and was best placed to assess the credibility of their evidence.' Whatever the shortcomings of how he had approached the case, he was 'uniquely well placed to determine the factual issues'.[37] This was a judge who failed in his duty to consider the evidence regarding how one form of abusive behaviour may connect to another. He had produced a judgment without one of its most important components. Yet he was still considered the individual best qualified to have made decisions about that case, which could no longer be questioned or overturned.

When this appeal judgment was handed down, upholding the finding that Mary had not in fact been raped, she was beside herself. Some clients get worn down by their experiences in court, but not Mary. She had only become more confident and self-assured at every stage – as if each hearing, and each judicial knockback, was serving not to sap her spirit but to temper it. The lower her faith in the court dipped, the more her sense of defiant indignation seemed to rise.

'Why do they think it's OK to dismiss my allegations because I'm intelligent?'

I had no answer. There was no answer.

'How am I going to keep my daughter safe now?'

I was grateful for a question that I could do something about. The other examples of domestic abuse by Mary's husband, separate from the rape allegation, had a direct bearing on the contact he should have with his daughter. In the end, the proceedings concluded with no direct contact between the father and the child. Mary could breathe at last. All her suffering in court had been for something. She had been denied so much, but she had achieved the one thing she had said was most important when she first wrote to ask if I would take on her case. The day the case ended, I saw the hardness that had settled over her face in recent months soften into relief. She grabbed me, hugged me, and repeated, 'Thank you.'

Mary's case had come to an end, but it left so many unanswered questions about how others like it should be handled. The Court of Appeal had concluded that no legal clarity should be given about what constitutes rape or consent under family law so that judges can be allowed to get on with the job unfettered. To the court, this makes sense (it also mirrored the argument of the alleged perpetrators, who opposed a definition), but to the women who must talk about their rape in family court, it is hard to explain. When clients ask me what they have to do to get the court to uphold an allegation of rape, I have no answer for them because there is no definition or guidance to fall back on. Nothing to say whether he has to be physically violent for it to constitute rape, if she has to have resisted, if consent can be given passively, or if it can be said to have been lacking when a victim was facing a wider pattern of coercion and compulsion. As I have had to say to numerous clients, it simply depends on the judge. You might get a judge who considers all the facts carefully, takes the opportunity to refer to the CPS guidance on rape myths and stereotypes, and makes allowances for the vulnerability of a woman recalling episodes of alleged sexual abuse and the difficulty of her recalling such a traumatic event. Or you could end up with a judgment not dissimilar from the decision made by His Honour Judge Robin Tolson KC, who, in a 2019 case, concluded that a woman had not been raped by her ex-partner because she had 'taken no physical steps' to stop him.[38] He was successfully appealed.

We have no end of examples to show how far judicial interpretations of rape and consent vary. Yet the court is entirely content for this situation to continue, to avoid the difficult work of developing a legal framework on these matters, and to hope that judicial training and good intentions will fill the gap.

My work on rape cases began to increase markedly after I represented Kate Kniveton. The nature of a barrister's career is that one successful case tends to lead to others like it, and so it proved here. It was this experience that solidified my belief that the family court fails too many women, and my determination to do what I can to change that. The shock factor of these cases, and the evident trauma of the women I was working with – often buried deep – was something from which I could not look away. The problem was too big, and the human cost too tangible, for me to be a bystander. If there was any lingering doubt that I wanted to focus my career on fighting for women, these cases removed it.

There have been sleepless nights worrying about these cases, going over questions and lines of arguments in my head, and occasionally working through holidays because cases have suddenly been listed at short notice, and I have known no one else would be able to get up to speed in time. Much as I try to avoid letting my work seep into every corner of my life, it is hard not to feel an obligation to women who have been through so much, and who fear what will happen to them and their children if they lose the case.

Having represented numerous women during fact-findings and appeals and made several failed attempts to convince senior judges that the law in this area is deficient, I find the family court's handling of sexual violence to be one of its most urgent and disturbing flaws. In my experience, women do not make allegations of sexual assault lightly: the trauma of having to recount those experiences in court is simply too great for it to be done unless they believed it was truly necessary. But those women are too frequently treated with anything but the sensitivity and the seriousness that their claims deserve. This is why I continue to campaign at every opportunity to change the law through parliamentary legislation.

Of course, every case is different, and not every allegation can be upheld in court even if it did indeed happen as the party says. But every woman who makes the agonising decision to talk about the day their partner coerced them into having sex, removed a condom without their consent, suddenly started choking them during intercourse, or used religious reasons to claim it was their duty to submit to sex, deserves a level of care and courtesy from the court. Their evidence should be heard in a safe environment that minimises the trauma of having to recall such events. Their vulnerability should be taken into account, and the complexity of being a complainant of sexual abuse should be recognised when considering their actions (such as whether they chose or not to report the incident at the time, if they subsequently chose to have consensual sex with the same partner and stayed in or later returned to the marital home). Certainly, they should not be subjected to rape myths and gendered stereotypes, nor a double standard that makes excuses for men accused of rape while demanding that their victims present flawlessly in court.

These are not complex or difficult things to demand of our family justice system, but so often, I have found them to be lacking in sexual violence cases. Too many women are harangued about their decisions, attacked for minor inconsistencies in their stories over time, and criticised for having failed to provide a perfect evidence trail. Some are even treated as having lied or falsified rape, flying in the face of evidence that shows how unusual this is. The reality is that a man is more likely to be a victim of rape than to be falsely accused of rape.[*][39]

I've also noticed a disconcerting trend that when a woman alleges domestic abuse or rape, the accused will allege they have made false accusations, and the judge will sometimes uphold this claim, which is not even correct in law. If an allegation is not proved on the balance of probabilities, that does not mean it is false – it means the evidential threshold has not been met to prove the allegation. I find it extraordinary to see family court professionals – lawyers and experts – claim to specialise in 'false allegations' of rape, domestic abuse and even child sexual abuse. Given the low numbers of falsified reports, and how difficult it is to prove such abuse in the first place, it's hard to believe they could have a flourishing practice, but they do, and so-called experts (such as psychologists) with such claims on their CV are appointed in the family courts.

Knowing all of this, I always take extra care to warn a woman bringing allegations of rape or sexual assault what she should expect in court. I have to be honest with her that the experience is likely to be a difficult one, and not just because she will have to describe and answer questions about the worst day of her life. She should also be ready

---

* There were thirty-five prosecutions for false rape allegations in 2011, meaning 0.0002 per cent of men were falsely accused. The average man aged sixteen to fifty-nine in England and Wales has a 0.3 per cent chance of being raped during the course of a given year.

for pointed questioning, for doubt to be cast on each aspect of her story, and to be criticised for actions she took or did not take while reeling from the most profound trauma imaginable. She should be prepared for the fact that, even as she bares her soul and demonstrates her vulnerability to convey the truth of what happened, a judge may well conclude that he simply prefers the story of the man she says raped her – believing him credible, her unreliable. This is the reality of how the family justice system treats women making allegations of sexual violence, as if they themselves were facing trial. It means some of the most vulnerable witnesses entering the system are shown its least sympathetic face. It is an unacceptable situation that we desperately need to fix if family court is to be seen as a safe place for women where their stories will be heard fairly and treated equally.

Representing Denise, Michelle, Kate and Mary showed me the extent of what women face when they come to family court, bringing allegations that their former partner was violent and abusive. These women must relive all the terrible things they suffered and open themselves up to invasive scrutiny, and frequently contempt.

Why do they do it? Almost always it comes down to the children: their ex-partner wants more contact with them and applies to the court to try and enforce this. As a mother in this situation, either you accept that the man who abused you (and sometimes the children) should have a greater role in the life of your child, or you decide to fight.

In family court, allegations of domestic abuse and sexual violence rarely stand alone. Most often they come as part of wider disputes involving contact and custody, sometimes spiralling into bitter wars of words and worse, as parents fight for control of their children.

I was never in any doubt what this is like in practice – the way many men will push as hard as possible to tear down their former victims in court, instructing their lawyers to pull apart their evidence and be as aggressive as the system allows. But as my career went on, I came to understand that this is not the limit of what some fathers will do to try and win in court, and gain control over their children.

Increasingly, I found myself drawn into a disturbing corner of family court, where men accused of being abusers seek to turn the tables and claim that the real abuser is in fact the mother, because she has poisoned the children against him – what is known as parental alienation. It is a murky world characterised by questionable science, dubious experts and court orders that sometimes force children to move home against their will. Learning about parental alienation and representing women who were trying to combat this allegation opened my eyes to what is truly at stake when people step through the doors of family court.

6

Pseudoscience: Parental Alienation and Unregulated Experts

I squinted into the laptop screen to catch my first sight of my newest client. A pale, cautiously smiling face peered back. We were about to begin a conversation that had been long in the making. Florence was not the first client who had approached me directly to represent her, but she was undoubtedly the only one who'd had to fight in court to earn representation in the first place. Her legal battle against a situation she felt was fundamentally unjust had now been going on for several years. What made this all the more remarkable was that she was still just fifteen years old.

Florence had been put in this unconventional, unreasonable situation because, five years earlier, her father had obtained a court order saying that she should live with him. After her parents separated when she was eight, she had been living happily with her mother and having regular contact with her father. But because there were, as there often are, difficulties with a child being passed between two parents at odds with each other, the case ended up in court.[1]

As a result, Florence was ordered to move from living with the parent she had chosen to the one she had not.

When her case crossed my desk in mid-2021, I was still unfamiliar with the approach her father had used to achieve this, though it would soon become a regular part of my work. I was about to learn about parental alienation, the allegation that one parent has turned the children against the other. Soon I would see the almost extraordinary power this can have in court: how a deceptively simple argument, dressed up as science and supported by carefully chosen experts, can be used to upend children's lives, persuading the court that they should live with the parent who was accused of being abusive in the first place.

How does this all work? It often begins when a man who has been accused of domestic abuse wants his children to live with or spend more time with him, even when they say they do not want to. In a situation like this, he must find a way to invalidate the testimonies that are piling up against him. He must give the court a story more compelling than the one that says he is an unsafe parent who harmed his partner, his children or both. Often he will turn to parental alienation, arguing that the mother has turned the children against him. That she has established a psychological hold over them and is, in effect, the real perpetrator of emotional abuse.

If he has the financial means and the right legal advice, soon it will not just be him saying it. Next, he will enlist a child psychologist or other expert who specialises in parental alienation or false accusations of domestic abuse or child sex abuse. They will meet the child and may submit evidence to the court that the mother has in some way undermined their relationship with the father. Not infrequently, the child's own representative in court – their Cafcass guardian, a social worker – will line up behind this argument. And soon, the judge will be hearing evidence from the father, a designated expert and the child's independent representative, telling them that, in fact, the mother is the unsafe parent from whom the child needs to be protected. That is how parental alienation has become a regular and influential feature of family court cases,[2] even though it is not recognised as a medical syndrome by the World Health Organization,[3] the American Psychological Association,[4] or other US judicial guidance.[5] The UK's National Institute for Health and Care Excellence (NICE) has listed parental alienation syndrome as discredited.[6]

So it is that mothers who were the victims of domestic abuse can end up accused of being perpetrators, to the point where their children are taken away from them and placed with their abusers, and their contact is limited or even cut off entirely. So it is that children end up being forced to live with one parent despite consistently saying that they want to be with the other. And so it was with Florence. For five years, she had been living with her father under court order after a judge concluded her mother had alienated her from him. For almost as long, she had been trying to reverse this.

I am used to meeting clients who face unusual or challenging circumstances. But only Florence had to conduct video meetings with me while worrying that the person she was, in effect, going to court against might be sitting in the next room. I had some misgivings of my own. I rarely have teenage clients: because children are typically represented by their Cafcass guardian, a situation like Florence's does not often arise, and there is no equivalent for barristers of the accreditation that most solicitors gain before working with minors.

But Florence was, in every sense, an exceptional case. From the age of twelve, she had been repeatedly trying to gain her own legal representation, with support from her maternal family, to make the case that she should live primarily with her mother.[7] One judge had refused this, and another actually banned her from making these applications for two years.[8] By the time we first met, Florence had not only been living with her father against her wishes for a large part of her life, but had consistently been denied independent legal representation. First, the court told her that she had no say in which parent she lived with. And then it decided that she had no right to protest against this.

That only changed when, after the two-year prohibition had passed, she applied again and was rejected once more. Only when she appealed this to the High Court did a decision finally go her way. With Florence then nearing the age of sixteen, at which point her wishes could no longer legally be ignored, her father consented, and a judge granted the appeal.[9] Having read some press articles about my cases, Florence asked her solicitor to approach me as her long-awaited legal representative.

I was late to the party in a case whose history went back seven years to when her parents had separated. Initially, Florence had lived with her mother and had regular contact with her father. In the legal proceedings that began after contact broke down, the court found the father had been abusive on several occasions – he had slapped the mother and 'held Florence down and shouted at her when she had a tantrum'.[10]

Far from the case going against him, however, it was turning his way. As his own abusive behaviour was being established by the court, in parallel, the narrative of parental alienation was being established. A child psychiatrist, Dr Mark Berelowitz, interviewed Florence and gave evidence to the effect that the problems over contact had arisen 'because of the mother's distress and unresolved angry feelings about the breakdown of the relationship [which] was being communicated to Florence'. The judge picked up this thread and concluded that the mother 'was not giving Florence permission in an emotional sense' to have a relationship with her father. She ordered the contact arrangements to be reversed, and for Florence to live with her father.[11]

It was a classic example of how parental alienation can be used to flip a family dispute on its head. The father did not have custody of Florence and was found by the court to have been abusive to both her and the mother.[12] Yet with the right expert in his corner, he had been able to persuade the same judge that the mother was the real root of the problem and to rule that Florence should instead live with him. Parental alienation was the silver bullet that allowed this man to override the objections of his child, and the reality of his former abuse, to get the court to rule in his favour.

This had been decided when Florence was ten, and the intervening years had seen the unrest surrounding her care arrangements continue. At one point, her mother made allegations that led to the police becoming involved and Florence being temporarily placed with her grandparents before the court returned her to her father's care.[13]

Now, finally, she had been granted the right to be independently represented and to put her case in front of a High

Court judge. It was a simple one: she had always wanted to live with her mother and had now reached an age where it seemed self-evident her wishes should be taken seriously. I further argued that Florence being forced to live with her father did little good for their relationship, just as it was unfair to her and her mother.[14] The best outcome for all concerned was for Florence to be given what she had spent the last five years asking for.

The case seemed straightforward enough, but I still had to contend with the novelty of representing a client who was still very visibly a child – quiet and unsurprisingly anxious after so long being pushed and pulled through legal battles, spending more time than anyone her age should in the vicinity of lawyers, psychologists and police officers. While I couldn't help but admire the determination and self-confidence Florence had shown, I was also conscious of her vulnerability. Even more than usual, I was concerned about doing everything I could to ensure her welfare.

I soon learned that behind Florence's timid exterior, a confident character lurked. She asked if she could meet the judge before the hearing, and I accompanied her and her solicitor to the High Court to see Mrs Justice Frances Judd. No discussion of the case was permitted, so the meeting took the form of gentle chit-chat. Already, I was forming the strong impression of a young woman who, having had so much decided for her in her life, was now determined to take control of the situation. She had been denied a voice for so long and was not going to miss the chance to use it now.

That was reinforced during the hearing itself, which was held remotely, with Florence sitting next to me in a large conference room in chambers. Normally, a child being represented by their guardian would not attend these proceedings, but Florence was more than present. As I cross-examined both of her parents, she was closely involved, passing me notes and asking me to mute the feed so that she could instruct me verbally. She was confident, clear and in command of detail – in so many ways, one of the most remarkable clients I have represented. I had never sat with a child through a full court proceeding before, and was struck by how attentive and involved Florence seemed throughout; when I glanced to my left, often all I could see was her neat, shoulder-length brown hair bent over her pad as she made notes. But at other times, when I took her for lunch each day during the hearing, feeling more like an auntie or godmother than a lawyer, I was reminded how young she was.

Although the history of the case had been acrimonious, the heart of it was no longer especially contentious. With Florence close to sixteen, she would soon be able to decide her own living arrangements, and the only disagreement was over how her time should be split in the interim. The guardian recommended that she alternate between parents on a weekly basis, which Florence's father supported.[15] We argued that this would not reflect her wish to live primarily with her mother, and the judge ultimately agreed, ordering an arrangement that saw her granted this right for the majority of each month.[16] Five years on from the original order that had taken her away from her mother, Florence had finally got what she had repeatedly asked for. But it had taken an unreasonable amount of struggling against the system for her to get there. Florence could never get back the years of her childhood she had lost with her mother or the time that she had dedicated to a personal legal battle that started when she was not yet a teenager.

Children always suffer when the relationship between parents becomes acrimonious, but the allegation of parental alienation can cause a very particular kind of harm. It makes the child not just subject to a tug-of-war between two parents, but the focus of the allegations that are being contested in court. They must be interviewed by psychologists and their behaviour must be scrutinised: what does this or that action mean, and what does it imply about whether one parent has been trying to influence them against the other? This harm then rebounds upon the parent, usually the mother, who is being accused of alienating their child. Often a victim of abuse, they now find themselves cast as an abuser.

Representing Florence was only my first step into the strange and disturbing world of parental alienation. Around a year later, I became involved in another case that showed me the brutal psychological toll that this allegation can have on a family, and how it can so easily cause an already fraught family situation to descend into bitter acrimony whose consequences may never be undone.

By the time I represented Claudia in the summer of 2022, she was already more than three years into a court battle with her ex-husband, who had accused her of alienation and succeeded in having the court order their children should be moved to live with him.

When she had first entered this maze of legal proceedings, which would ultimately amount to around eleven different judgments being written, Claudia had been sharing custody of her children with her ex-partner, on a 50–50 basis. This had been deemed appropriate and so ordered by a judge back in 2014. But as I read the papers concerning her case before meeting her, I could see that the allegation of parental alienation had exploded in her life like a bomb. She had been found by the court to have harmed her children through alienation,[17] her contact with them had been reduced to almost nothing, and her assets had partially been frozen.[18] Her future was to some extent in the hands of Karen Woodall, a court-appointed expert, who had been given a huge amount of power – not just testifying in court but overseeing extensive therapeutic work with the children and both parents,[19] with ample opportunity to try and 'undo' what the court had deemed as Claudia's harmful and alienating behaviour.

There was no question that Claudia had been found to have behaved in erratic, desperate and even dangerous ways. In the final hearing in 2023, the court would ultimately find that she had encouraged her children to make false allegations against their father, arranged for a man to approach her children outside their school and hand them a phone she could call them on, in defiance of a court order, and that she had told her children to hit each other in a way that would leave bruises, which had led her daughter to strike herself on the face with a shampoo bottle. The judge, Mr Justice Michael Keehan, concluded that she had 'pursued her own agenda and objectives without any regard whatsoever to the well-being and welfare best interests of the children' and that she had 'seriously abused [the children] emotionally and psychologically'. As a result, she was to have no contact and 'no future role of any description in their lives'.[20]

This unhappy saga had begun in 2018 after the shared-care arrangement for the children broke down.[21] Claudia had brought a series of allegations (unspecified by the court) against her ex-partner, which were investigated by the police but did not lead to charges. The case came to court, and child experts were instructed to work with both children and parents with a view to rectifying the conflict. Their evidence to the court was unequivocal that this was a case of parental alienation instigated by the mother, who posed a real and ongoing threat of harm to her two children. According to one of them, Karen Woodall, an unregulated expert, the younger child was 'currently alienated and split from his father', while the older daughter was 'scarred and has a permanent vulnerability to her mother's changes of mood and emotions'.[22] In this expert's view, Claudia '[held] the balance of power in respect of the children's vulnerabilities'.[23] In other words, it was a textbook case of parental alienation, a conclusion that the judge fully supported in ordering a transfer of residence to the father and an initial month-long period in which they would have no contact (bar one or two supervised phone calls) with Claudia – a typical measure in such cases, used to 'reset' patterns of attachment.[24]

The original intention was for Claudia to have occasional contact with her children after this initial freeze: one long weekend in every three. Yet, almost as soon as the original order was handed down, the problems started again. The children ran away from the father's house twice within the first week, and the police had to be called to return them.[25] On holiday the following summer, the younger child ran away again, went to the local police and made allegations against his father.[26] Then that autumn, his sister was reported missing, and the court issued a collection order, as well as acceding to her demands that she have her mobile phone returned to her and that neither of the children should be locked in their bedrooms. At the same time, both children made allegations in writing to their school that their father had been violent to them and locked them in their rooms.[27] At their father's request,[28] the court ordered that the police and local authority should be prevented from interviewing the children to discuss these allegations. The court-appointed expert had agreed. It was in the successful appeal to that specific injunction that I became involved with the case. The Court of Appeal had agreed with the Metropolitan Police Service (and the mother) that Mr Justice Keehan should not have prohibited the police from interviewing the children about their serious allegations.

On the one hand, there was a clear pattern of the children appearing to resist the order that they should live with their father and have almost no contact with their mother.[29] On the other, their father was insistent that Claudia was the instigator of all these problems, encouraging the children to make false allegations, drafting letters on their behalf and even conducting surveillance on them. This was ultimately the narrative that was accepted by the court, crystallised in the final judgment that stripped Claudia of all parental responsibility but in name.[30] The case which the father's lawyers put forward, which the expert supported, and which the court upheld, said that she was a mother who had set out to alienate her children from their father, who attempted to resist and undermine all the legal orders and therapeutic work put in place to try and stabilise the situation, and who had regularly acted in ways that had directly and indirectly harmed her children.

There was another side to this story, however. This distressing series of events unfolded in such a way that Claudia was deemed an unfit and unsafe parent who should never see her children again. She had clearly made bad decisions and terrible mistakes. Equally, it is worth understanding her situation, as a woman who faced the debilitating reality of being accused of alienating her own children. Time after time, Claudia was criticised for problematic situations and the way she was participating in the legal and therapeutic processes. While the judge acknowledged that the children would prefer to be with their mother, he characterised this as a symptom of the alienation. Their real wishes were impossible to deduce, he concluded, because their expressed ones were the result of manipulation and could not be trusted.[31] Furthermore, Claudia's attempts to raise concerns about the validity of the expert testimony (at least one of the experts was unregulated by any professional body) were not just rejected but held against her by the judge, who found she took a 'wholly unreasonable and a totally ill-judged litigation tactic' by seeking to cross-examine and call into question the expert.[32] He also used this, in part, as the basis for an order requiring her to meet her ex-partner's legal costs,[33] and as a result some of her assets were subsequently frozen.[34] Her whole world must have felt like it was collapsing.

Many family court professionals have warned about the dangers of the parental alienation thesis in family court.[35] It can reduce the complex reality of family breakdown and conflict between parents involving children into a simple narrative. One parent is to blame. And because this is a gendered allegation, usually weaponised by men accused of domestic abuse, that means the mother is to blame. It doesn't matter what she says or what the children say. Under this premise, everything can be explained away under the umbrella of alienation. It, and she, is the root of all evil.

That is the almost bewitching power of parental alienation when it takes hold in the mind of those in positions of power. It is an attractive explanation because it rationalises a messy set of circumstances into an apparent sense of order: a single stitch that can seal the entire wound. Backed up by convincing expert testimony, it is legal catnip, expediting the difficult process of deciding which parent is to be trusted when the context is murky, and allegations are being slung back and forth. As my career has gone on, I have increasingly seen parental alienation as a straw that fathers are keen to offer and which professionals are eager to clutch.

The effect on those accused of parental alienation can be chilling.[36] Claudia's actions were undoubtedly extreme and unconscionable, but it is perhaps not so hard to understand how a mother accused of alienation will fight harder for her children the more she sees them slipping away. As a woman feels the walls closing in, trapping her in a situation where she is being cut off from her children and blamed more and more for the conflict in the family, she can become desperate. As the allegations mount up and damning decisions are made, a mother may make bad decisions and do things that are neither in her nor her children's best interest.

Claudia's case did not just illustrate the traumatic effect that parental alienation allegations can have on children. It also underlined the prominent role of experts in such cases and the significant level of authority that is attached to their evidence. Once an expert has become involved in a case and won the trust of the judge, they may have considerable power to work with the children and make recommendations to the court. If they testify that parental alienation is a factor, it can be difficult, verging on impossible, to argue against this.

That is despite the fact that parental alienation does not exist in any credible medical guidance, is not a recognised syndrome, or a condition that can be formally diagnosed.[37] It owes its prominence to an American child psychologist, Richard Gardner, who coined the term 'parental alienation syndrome' in the 1980s. He was a regular expert witness in US courts who encouraged the use of 'threat therapy' – the process of removing children from the supposedly alienating parent, and cutting off their contact for an initial period.[38] In 2015, the American Bar Association issued a publication describing parental alienation as 'junk science'.[39] Tragically, one of the cases in which Gardner was an expert witness involved the forced transfer of three teenage boys to live with a father they said had physically abused them. Not long after, the eldest child took his own life, leaving notes that described his life as an 'endless torment'.[40]

Gardner died in 2003, but his legacy remains alive and well across the world. In 2022, the UN criticised a decision in the Spanish courts to award custody of a seven-year-old girl to her father, despite allegations that he had been sexually abusing her.[41] Reem Alsalem, the UN's Special Rapporteur on Violence Against Women and Girls, has written on parental alienation, recognising that pseudoscience was being utilised to dismantle domestic abuse concerns, based both on research and survivor testimony.[42] Her report notes that: '[Parental alienation] has been dismissed by medical, psychiatric and psychological associations, and in 2020, it was removed from the International Classification of Diseases by the World Health Organization.'[43] The Family Justice Council, an official advisory body to the UK Government, has also issued guidance on parental alienation, stating that instructed experts should be regulated and that 'parental alienation' is not a diagnosable condition or disorder.[44]

In other words, an idea that has grown like a weed to assume outsize importance in the family court is one that has never had a serious scientific grounding, has not been recognised in the medical community and has been denounced by professional bodies. Yet, in my time as a family law barrister, I have seen it grow rather than diminish in significance. Whether or not the term itself is used, the idea of blaming the mother for the breakdown of the father's relationship with the children and responding by giving him the lion's share of contact has become established.

Academic research underlines quite how widespread a legal tactic this has become, and the way it is weaponised against vulnerable women. In a University of Manchester study which assessed and interviewed forty-five women who had been through family court proceedings in England after alleging domestic abuse, thirty-nine had been accused of parental alienation.[45] Those mothers described how allegations of alienation 'not only shifted the focus of proceedings once raised but also diminished and often completely side-lined the investigation of [domestic abuse] and child abuse'. In a statement reminiscent of several cases I have been involved in, the authors of the study noted that 'Mothers described that the more they resisted the [parental alienation] allegations and advocated for their child, the more harshly they were treated by professionals and the more they were pathologized with [parental alienation] and threatened with transfer of residency or reduced contact.' They concluded that alienation allegations 'were used against [mothers] as a weapon to minimize, deny and rebut [domestic abuse]'.[46]

The prevalence of such allegations is in no small part down to a group of father's rights activists and experts who have made working in this field their specialism. A father who is being advised by a capable lawyer may be guided towards one of these experts and make an application to the court that they be instructed to assess the parents and the children and provide expert testimony. A mother may not realise she is, in effect, agreeing to let someone who has a track record of accusing mothers of alienation have access to their children and a significant say in their future. By the time the reality of the situation has dawned on them, it is too late.

Of the many nasty surprises in my career in family court, the role of unregulated experts has been one of the most striking. In cases where the facts are bitterly contested, these people, whose qualifications may be spurious, can assume outsize importance in court, with the influence of their words impacting decisions and disrupting lives. As a barrister, you expect to be up against opposing counsel and faced with the challenge of convincing a judge of the merits of your case. But I had never anticipated having to battle witnesses whose evidence would be treated as authoritative, even when it was clearly taking a side.

Consider the example of a parental alienation case whose final appeal was heard by the President of the Family

Division, Sir Andrew McFarlane, with the judgment handed down in February 2023.[47] It was a familiar story: a mother who was also a victim of coercive and controlling behaviour had been accused of alienating her children from their father, testimony from an unregulated expert witness who described themselves as a psychologist* had supported the allegation, and an order had been made mandating the children to be transferred to their father's residence. The mother had sought on multiple occasions to have the case reopened on grounds including the expert witness's lack of appropriate qualifications and unregulated status (meaning they were not required to adhere to any professional standards and there was no mechanism to bring a complaint against them). Her lawyers sought to introduce evidence including a letter from Professor Mike Wang, Chair of the Association of Clinical Psychologists, which said of this expert: 'she has no recognised substantive postgraduate qualifications, is unregulated, should not be calling herself a psychologist, should not be carrying out psychological assessments and making diagnoses . . . in my opinion she should not be acting as an expert in court'.[48] Yet a succession of judges, including the President, deemed that it was reasonable for the court to have relied at least in part on her evidence, and was within its rights to find her 'an impressive witness'.[49] One of these judges pointed out that the mother had not originally questioned the appointment.[50] Her lawyer's argument that the expert's credentials were not properly scrutinised until

---

* It should be noted that 'psychologist' is not a protected or defined title in law. Anyone can hold themselves as such when giving evidence in court.

the final hearing, after which the children had already been transferred into their father's care, fell on stony ground.[51]

This case reinforced that, when parental alienation has been alleged in court, timing is everything. While possession may not actually be nine-tenths of the law, momentum in these proceedings matters. Once an expert has been accepted by both sides and given evidence in court, and once initial orders about residence arrangements for children have been made, these are incredibly difficult to undo. Judges are generally unwilling to discredit an expert that one of their peers has taken seriously, and they are especially wary (with good reason) of causing further instability to children by changing their living situation yet again. Whatever the merit of these factors, they present a stark reality to women who are being accused of parental alienation. Either make your counter-arguments early or expect that they will be disregarded later.

My initial experiences with parental alienation had been both frustrating and eye-opening, but they had also been instructive. It meant that when another case involving it landed on my desk not long after the McFarlane judgment, I was ready, and determined not to let another woman become trapped in the web of this insidious, often life-changing allegation.

As the day before Gemma's hearing turned into the morning of it, I was still reading the documents. I'd already been through the witness statements from her, her ex-partner and other family members, which filled a lever arch file. There was a Cafcass report about the welfare of the children. More reports from the local authority. And then the final pack of documents, which I might easily have delayed reading until the trial got underway. This was the police disclosure, with transcripts from the interviews they had conducted with Gemma and her husband, after she had accused him of assault and domestic abuse. In almost all cases I work on, the police have been involved: their evidence is usually the slowest to obtain, and the last set of documents to arrive. I remember forcing myself to glance at it, certain that it would contain nothing except a recap of what I had already read.

After hours of sitting at my computer, I had moved to my sofa to do the rest of the reading. But the moment I turned the page and stumbled on something entirely new, I went back to my desk. With the clock past midnight and many hours of work now behind me, I wanted to be certain that I was reading the pages right. What they contained had completely stunned me. In her police interview, Gemma had alleged that her husband had raped her on two occasions. She also said that he had regularly filmed her naked before and during sex without her consent. Both claims would subsequently be upheld by the judge, Recorder John Brooke-Smith.[52] By this point, Gemma and I had been working together for nine months towards the fact-finding hearing that was set to begin in under ten hours. It had already been a long road towards combating her abusive ex-husband's allegations of parental alienation and false allegations, and in many ways the real work was just beginning. Yet this was the first time I had heard about either of these sexual abuse allegations in any detail, more serious than any of the others we had already put before the judge.

I was immediately unsure about what to do. If I had been working on the case with a solicitor I would have called them up straight away, midnight or no midnight, to find out if they knew about this and whether there was a good reason for not putting these allegations before the court. But since I was directly instructed by Gemma and we had no intermediary, I had no option but to wait until the morning to talk to her about it.

After getting to sleep late and waking early, I had to stop myself from calling her first thing. This was a conversation that needed to happen in person. By the time I walked into the conference room outside of court where she was waiting, around an hour before the hearing was due to start, I couldn't help myself and came straight out with it.

'I read the police report. The rape allegations. Why didn't you tell me?'

For several long seconds Gemma held her head in her hands. When her face emerged and her eyes met mine, I wondered if I could almost see relief in them mixed up with the shock and hurt.

'I'm just so embarrassed by it. I can't speak to the judge about that.'

With many clients I would have been truly torn about how to approach such a sensitive topic with so little time available. The hearing would begin shortly, and if the allegation was not raised before the judge right at the outset, it would be too late. Quite possibly, it already was. I was fully aware what a difficult thing I was asking Gemma to do – to revisit the worst experiences of her life in the courtroom – but I also knew that it might strengthen her case. It helped that Gemma, plainspoken and in her forties, was not someone who required hand-holding. I liked Gemma. She would routinely arrive late for our meetings before court after getting stuck in traffic on the school run, pulling scraps of paper out of a plastic bag as we talked to remind herself of the points she wanted to make. Like many women who get taken to family court by their ex-partners, she had been forced to add what she called the 'full-time job' of this court proceeding to an already full plate of looking after the children and doing her existing job.

Gemma was also my kind of client. She knew what she wanted, was blunt about how she expressed it, and not afraid of arguing with me when she disagreed. So I didn't hesitate in telling her exactly what I thought she should do, even though I emphasised that it could only be her decision.

'I'm going to give you some time to think about it,' I concluded. I stepped out of the room to give her some privacy, and when I returned it was clear what she had decided. The look on her face was almost one of exasperation, as if she couldn't believe that she now had to add yet more weight to the burden she had been carrying with her through court for the best part of three years, once all previous proceedings were counted. Yet she also knew she could not avoid this: the cat was out of the bag now, the allegation was part of the paper record before the court, and her best option was to formally introduce it into our case. With less than ten minutes to go before we would be called into the courtroom, I rushed from our conference room to the one in which the other lawyers were waiting to tell them we would be bringing additional allegations of rape and sexual abuse. This bombshell was received exactly as well as I had expected.

A few minutes later we were in court, before His Honour Judge Paul Middleton-Roy. I rose to make submissions I was slightly dreading, knowing that the last thing any judge wishes to be told at the outset of a hearing is that new information has come to light. I held my fidgeting hands behind my back as I spoke, trying to keep my voice level as if this was some minor point of procedure rather than a significant, last-minute addition to our case. I said that it was only just now that Gemma and I had been able to discuss the rape allegations and that she felt ready to bring it before the court; this was something she naturally found very difficult to talk about at all, let alone in a setting like this. I also pointed to the existing CPS guidance on how and why victims of rape and sexual assault may be slow to make allegations about what happened to them.[53] The judge carefully considered our application and granted it, delaying the hearing and giving Gemma a day to make a written statement and her husband a further day to respond. He did not need to do this, but seemed to recognise the emotional burden of Gemma bringing this allegation, showing compassion and understanding in his decision.

It was not the first time in Gemma's case that a last-minute intervention had been required. When she first approached me to represent her seven months previously, in July 2023, it did not take much reading to see that she was in a precarious situation where time was of the essence. She was divorced from her husband and their two children were living with her. At the children's request, they had no direct contact with their father (an arrangement that had been endorsed by Cafcass).[54] Seeking to challenge this, he had made applications to the court and accused Gemma of parental alienation.[55] What jumped out at me was that, at a hearing in June, the court had granted an application

from Gemma's ex-husband for a psychologist, Dr Elena
Arora, to be allowed to conduct an assessment of both
parents and children. As part of this, they would comment
on whether either parent had tried to alienate the children
from the other and what the impact of this had been.[56] All
my previous experience of parental alienation cases told me
this was a flashing red light for Gemma: if her ex-husband
succeeded in introducing expert testimony into the record
to the effect that she had alienated the children from him,
it would be almost impossible to expunge.

As soon as I read the bundle, I knew what I needed to
advise Gemma: unless she appealed against this application
and prevented this expert from becoming involved in her
case, she would likely end up with the court concluding
that she had alienated her children, and granting contact
to their father at minimum. For that appeal, we relied on
the McFarlane judgment from several months before. This
had made some important clarifications about the role of
experts in general and pertaining to parental alienation
in particular. Most tellingly, he had established that the
question of alienation was one primarily for the court and
not expert witnesses.[57] He endorsed a submission from
the Association of Clinical Psychologists which stated that
'the decision about whether or not a parent has alienated a
child is a question of fact for the Court to resolve and not a
diagnosis that can or should be offered by a psychologist'.[58]
In response to the points we raised including this one, Judge
Middleton-Roy upheld the appeal on all grounds, commenting: 'The expert was being invited expressly to provide an
opinion about parental alienation. In the judgment of this
court, that is outside the expert's remit.'[59]

That initial judgment had effectively stopped the clock on the father's attempt to paint Gemma as the perpetrator by alleging parental alienation to an expert, but it still left the substance of the case unresolved. Gemma was accusing him of abusing and controlling both her and the children; he said that she was lying and had alienated the children from him. It was not until the fact-finding hearing in February 2024, where the last-minute rape allegation had to be added to the schedule, that the truth of what had gone on in Gemma's marriage was fully established.

Cross-examining the father during that hearing was one of the most bizarre experiences of my career. As the judge later noted, he frequently grinned and laughed in response to my questions, many of them about serious allegations concerning domestic abuse and sexual violence. He was sarcastic and combative, saying that he was 'amused by the absurdity that I'm a highly lunatic man' and later challenging me directly, saying, 'I understand the campaign you're running.'[60]

In between these attempts to unsettle me, he would descend into emotional spasms where he appeared to be crying, although no tears were visible, and then he would descend into anger. At a previous hearing, in 2021, apparently similar behaviour had won over the judge, who described him as 'emotionally vulnerable, frequently becoming tearful when talking about his children'.[61] Judge Middleton-Roy was less charitable, using his judgment to describe the father's testimony as 'deeply troubling' and 'repeatedly evasive in his answers to straightforward questions'.[62]

Stranger still was that the father made a point of saying during this hearing that he no longer wanted to allege parental alienation against Gemma, even stating that he had read about how 'paedophile fathers' would try and use it to gain access to their children. This despite the fact he had previously advanced the allegation in court on multiple occasions, sent Gemma an article about parental alienation with the message 'this is you', and sent similar material to a marriage counsellor they were seeing.[63]

His erratic, theatrical performance in court could not conceal the reality of one of the most disturbing cases I have encountered. The court found as fact that the father had repeatedly been physically violent and emotionally abusive to his children. When Gemma called the police on one occasion, their ten-year-old daughter had told an officer that her father had stood by her bedroom door to stop her walking through it, grabbed her wrist hard, tried to snatch her arm, and that previously he had poured freezing-cold water over her legs. He had berated her for not wanting to go to music school and called his child 'mean and an actress'.[64] On a separate occasion, while his younger son was ill and off school, during an argument he had shoved himself between Gemma and the child, with sufficient force that the boy fell and hit his head on the tiled floor.[65]

The abuse went beyond isolated incidents and explosions of temper. One of the most shocking parts of the case was that the father had regularly worn a GoPro camera around the house so that he could film everything that went on. He had also set up iPads to film when he was not at home. He berated his children, blaming them and their mother for their 'behaviour'. Ironically, it was footage from his own cameras that helped to build the case against him. Part of this had showed him telling his daughter: 'You're putting pressure on me by not coming to your music lessons . . .

Did you like us being late yesterday? Was that fun? You're making us late every day. Your behaviour's bad.'[66] While with Gemma, his controlling behaviour extended to moving a mattress around the house and instructing her where to sleep, frequently in the smallest available room.[67] He had accused Gemma of being mentally ill, communicating this to the local authority and various therapists the couple were working with, as well as seeking to have her mental health assessed.[68] And on the occasions the police were called, he had blamed all problems on her, saying that she was manipulating the children and encouraging them not to comply with him. Footage showed him complaining to a police officer: 'This is *my* weekend caring for the children and their mother is interfering. She encourages my daughter not to do what she knows she should be doing . . . My wife wants *my* time with the children to go really badly.'[69]

As I proceeded with the cross-examination, I had to remind myself that despite his apparent volte-face, this was the man who had accused *Gemma* of being the primary perpetrator of abuse, by alienating the children from him. A man who had almost succeeded in getting the court to rule that a psychologist should make assessments about the family and whether parental alienation had taken place. It chilled me that Gemma's case seemed so obvious, yet she had come so close to being deemed more the perpetrator of abuse than its victim, and potentially losing custody of her children to this dangerous man.

When I represented Gemma, it was almost fifteen years since I had been called to the bar, and five since I had begun to focus my practice on violence against mothers and children in family courts. After so many cases, hearing and reading about the most excruciating details of physical, sexual and emotional violence, I sometimes worry that I am becoming desensitised towards the shocking nature of what happens in abusive relationships. As my career has gone on, I have generally found myself less emotionally affected by the stories I encounter, whether because I feel like I have seen and heard some version of them before, or subconsciously I am trying to create distance between myself and the deeply upsetting experiences I must write arguments and make statements about.

But even with these layers of experience and psychological armour, sometimes a case will arrive where the details are so visceral and disturbing that, after hundreds of pages of reading, you almost start to imagine yourself in that house, with him shouting, locking the children in their bedrooms, and walking around with a body camera wrapped around his forehead. When I am preparing a case like Gemma's, I feel like it takes over my entire life – I ignore texts, dishes pile up in the sink and I cloister myself in my office at home until I am sure I have been through every page of evidence and built my argument from every available detail filleted from police interview transcripts, written statements and disclosure. By the end, I feel like I know my client's life almost better than my own.

In Gemma's case, we were fortunate that both our appeal and the subsequent fact-finding were heard by Judge Middleton-Roy, who took a thorough and unsparing approach to digesting the mountain of evidence and case history before him. From all this he drew clear and punishing conclusions. First he ruled that there was 'no evidence of the mother undermining the children's relationship with their father'.

Tellingly, he continued: 'the evidence before the court leads to the clear conclusion that the father has sought consistently, systematically and falsely to manipulate the mother, the children, professionals and the Court into believing that he is the victim of domestic abuse perpetrated by the mother. His pernicious actions alone have resulted in both children rejecting him. Both children are now refusing a relationship with him for reasons that are justifiable.'[70] As he might have written: yes, there was alienation, but you alienated yourself.

I have rarely felt as relieved when reading a judgment as this one. Most importantly, it laid the groundwork to protect Gemma and her children from a man who was demonstrably abusive and an unfit parent. But it also felt like a broader win, against the growing tide of cases that suggested an abusive man could turn the tables by alleging parental alienation and using hand-picked experts to build a case against his victim, negating all his own wrongdoing and often reversing the assumption about which parent a child should live with. Judge Middleton-Roy's two judgments had reinforced the need to limit the use of expert testimony in these cases, recognising that parental alienation is not a condition that can be medically diagnosed. They had also exposed the way an abusive man may weaponise the idea of alienation, reversing the roles of victim and offender and trying to present himself as the injured party. This was the first family law case where the judge referred to DARVO (deny, attack, reverse the roles of victim and offender) in his judgment. As Middleton-Roy commented about Gemma's ex-husband: 'the father has sought, wholly incorrectly to reframe the mother as a liar who emotionally abuses the children'.[71] The end result was that the father was ordered to have no direct contact with the children, his parental responsibility was restricted and Gemma had permission to change the children's surnames to her name only.[72] She also secured a costs order against the father of over £50,000.[73]

The relief I felt at the outcome of this case was mixed with a bitterness about the mothers who have suffered so much because of the allegation of parental alienation and how it can be supported by the family court system. Gemma's experience could easily have been closer to that of Claudia – her children taken away and her behaviour to try and get them back increasingly extreme, to the point of almost losing parental responsibility altogether.

Such cases do not just have a profoundly negative impact on mothers and their children. They also reveal something about our family courts – how they can fall into the trap of believing that the woman must be at fault, too open to being manipulated by abusive men, and too vulnerable to being swayed by testimony from carefully chosen experts. The court cannot and should not outsource its work, however difficult, to experts with questionable credentials and an attraction to discredited scientific ideas. Parental alienation is not just junk science and bad law. It is a symptom of how women are too often treated in the family justice system – pathologised, blamed and stripped of their rights. It is precisely because our system behaves in this way that such a dubious and debunked idea as parental alienation has been able to take root. While it is true that one parent can negatively influence their children against the other, such cases are the exception. And they should always be matters of fact for the court to determine, not ones of spurious, quasi-medical diagnosis.

Allegations of parental alienation, and the complex court battles that follow, are often the culmination of disputes that have been growing for years, as relationships break down, contact becomes strained, and ultimately two parents are left battling in court for control of their children, each hoping the allegations they are bringing will be favoured over those that are being brought against them.

Yet such court battles are not always the gradual product of a broken relationship. Abusive men do not wait until their children have reached a particular age before revealing their true faces. Indeed, one of the most shocking discoveries of my career has been to learn quite how early in relationships the patterns of abuse become established. I have seen how coercion is viciously exercised around what should be one of the most meaningful and intimate parts of a relationship – the decision about when and how to have children. And I have represented women who have been forced to fight for control of their children from the very beginning of their lives – in some cases even before they have been born.

7

Conditional: Abortion and Reproductive Coercion

'Surely they will see that?'

Lydia's expression was one I have come to know well. I have seen it on the faces of so many women I have represented in family court, as they struggle to come to terms with what a judge has said or decided about them. These women are trying to reconcile their experience of what a man has done to them with the court's decision about the relationship that man should have with their children. Their look is one of bemusement mixed with frustration – the almost hopeless sense of anger that comes from having to work this hard to establish a truth that seems so obvious.

Lydia's truth was that the man who had applied for contact with her child was the same man who she claimed had threatened to kill her and the unborn baby during her pregnancy. On the day Lydia informed this man, a sexual partner with whom she was never in a relationship, that she was pregnant, she asked him to walk away and said that she would never ask him for anything. But he didn't. According to her account, he had initially tried to coerce her into having an abortion and then, when she refused, threatened to 'make her pay' for what she had done to him. He had not been present at the birth, nor had he shown any interest in being involved in the child's life until he filed an application to the court a few months after the baby was born. For Lydia, it seemed self-evident that he presented a clear danger to both her and her baby – that is how she felt. But now her case had gone to court and, at the time of our first conversation, she was worried that a family court judge would permit this man to have a relationship with her child – the same one he had allegedly tried to prevent from being born in the first place.

During previous proceedings, Lydia's most serious allegations against the child's biological father had not been upheld, and a decision on contact had been deferred. Understandably, Lydia was terrified that this would now also go against her, and we were meeting to discuss an application that would give her the permission to appeal.

This is where I sometimes end up hating my job, because while I empathise with everything a client is saying, I cannot always tell them what they want to hear. I wished I could reassure Lydia that of course she had the right to prevent a man who she claimed had threatened to kill her from having a relationship with their child. Of course the professionals would understand that the father's litigation was an extension of the coercive and controlling behaviour he had shown during their relationship. And of course the paramount concern was not his rights as a parent but the child's right to safety. But I could not tell her any of that. The truth was that our appeal had only a narrow path to success. We would have to convince a judge that their predecessor had erred in dismissing Lydia's allegations about the threats to kill, and that the father's alleged behaviour during their relationship and her pregnancy had a direct bearing on the safety of the child.

In doing so, we would be running into one of the family justice system's most mystifying and frustrating tendencies: the apparent belief that the past can be discounted when considering what is likely to happen in the future. When determining child contact, frequently the court shows a reluctance to consider seriously what happened in a relationship prior to that child being born. Often, such allegations will be described as 'historic' or not fully relevant to the case. With a strict focus on the welfare of the child and the risks to them, it can be hard to get the court to consider abuse that happened before or during the pregnancy.*

To women like Lydia, it seems like common sense: if a man threatens you and your unborn child while you are pregnant (as she claimed), he is unlikely to have magically become a safe parent now he is litigating for contact. Yet for the court, the situation as it appears at the time of the hearing is much more significant than what may have transpired months or years before. The question is less whether a man posed a risk to his partner while she was carrying her child, and more if he represents a threat to that child now.

---

* This is a problem that goes beyond cases involving reproductive coercion and abuse of pregnant women. The MoJ Harm Report commented (p.55): 'A common theme emerging from the mothers' submissions was that all the agencies . . . and the courts, were only concerned with incidents of domestic abuse that had occurred in recent months or weeks. "Historical" allegations were treated as less relevant and victims were sometimes discouraged or prevented from talking about the cumulative effect of abuse going back over a number of years.'

For Lydia, it meant the heart of her case – the abuse she had allegedly suffered during her pregnancy – was difficult to get off the ground from the beginning.

Getting the court to take Lydia's allegations seriously was one problem. Another would be successfully arguing that the father's behaviour represented a specific kind of domestic abuse, namely reproductive coercion – the way a man tries to force a woman to make decisions against her will about whether to proceed with a pregnancy or try to get pregnant in the first place.[1]

It was only through representing women like Lydia that I learned what a prevalent form of abuse this can be, and how it turns what should be one of the happiest and most fulfilling times in a mother's life into one of the most difficult, and sometimes dangerous. I did not have to read *The Handmaid's Tale* to understand the full extent of what men may do to weaponise a woman's fertility and pregnancy. As I started to take on more cases in this area, I saw it first hand: the men who had tried to force their partners either into having an abortion or continuing with an unwanted pregnancy; the men who said they would only agree to another baby if their wives met 'conditions' such as allowing them regular sex; and a man who bombarded his partner with aggressive phone calls and texts while she was in hospital giving birth, which resulted in him being banned from the maternity ward. All these abuses speak to the same truth. Coercive and controlling men want to wield power and will use every available means to do so. For them, a pregnancy is simply an opportunity to tighten their grip.

Reproductive coercion is mentioned in the CPS guidance on controlling and coercive behaviour, but is not cited in the practice direction on domestic abuse in child contact cases. In other words, it is not part of the established legal guidance to which judges are meant to refer themselves when hearing cases such as Lydia's. The upshot was that we faced multiple hurdles if we were going to secure Lydia the right to appeal. We would need to convince a judge to take seriously allegations the court would often regard as insufficiently relevant, and which a different judge had already found against. In turn, we would need them to recognise that the allegations amounted to a form of domestic abuse which was sparsely recognised by the legal system as it stood.

Worst of all, we would have to do this on appeal. As I often do in such situations, I wished that I was talking to Lydia before her case had been heard and findings had been made. With those now on the record, it would be even harder to make our case and to achieve what she wanted – total separation for herself and her child from the man she said had threatened to kill them both.

If I was frustrated that I hadn't had the chance to represent Lydia from the beginning, she was justifiably angry that her case had reached this point. A mature, professionally successful woman, she was indignant that this man had so sought to coerce her and was now using the courts to try and pursue the same end. And she was incredulous that the court had not agreed that his involvement in their lives would represent a threat both to her and her child. Since the first hearing she had read up on domestic abuse and coercive control and was frustrated that her original lawyer had not specified the issue of reproductive control.

Lydia had put her faith in the system and believed it would offer protection from a man she felt was dangerous.

Now, she was being confronted with the reality: the challenge of getting the system to reconsider its decision and see whether it has got it wrong. Like many women who get this unwanted education in how the family court really works, she had gone from putting trust in others to doing her own homework. She told me what had happened to her was a distinctive form of abuse – reproductive coercion. And she wondered why the court had not considered this, why her original lawyer had not argued the case in those terms, and how an appeal judge might still not acknowledge it.

It was at this point that she turned to me and said that *surely* the court could see it from her point of view. Surely a judge could understand why she was so scared about this man having contact with her child. Surely they could see through what appeared to be a cynical ploy on the part of an allegedly abusive man to exercise post-separation control.

'I hope so.'

It was the only answer I could honestly give. I wished we had been having this conversation months earlier, before the fact-finding hearing, and that we could have shaped her entire case around reproductive coercion and the real risks this man posed to both Lydia and her child. Now, the presumption was in favour of a judgment that did not deal with that idea. As with every appeal, there was the feeling that you are trying to unscramble the egg.

And, as with every client, I was trying to instil confidence without providing false hope. To be realistic about the situation we were in without sounding too pessimistic. Mostly for Lydia's benefit but partly for my own: there are enough cases where you begin confident and have your hopes reduced to dust, or you win a case that seemed a certain loser. You can never know for sure until the judgment is in your hands.

I went away and prepared the argument for Lydia's appeal, telling myself that we would succeed, believing it could be an important case that helped cement the significance of reproductive control as evidence of ongoing domestic abuse. With applications to appeal, you prepare the standard skeleton argument of around twenty pages, and the judge often makes an initial determination on the papers or at a hearing. At this stage, they can say, in effect, yes, no or maybe. I hoped that we would have an appeal granted at this stage and thought, at minimum, we would get a 'maybe': the chance to put forward our case at an oral hearing. But when the response came back, it was the one I had dreaded so much that I had practically discounted it. A flat no. No right of appeal. No further recourse. No more that we could say or do.

As she heard the news, I watched Lydia's face crease in agony, revealing lines I had never noticed before. Each one seemed to represent a different kind of pain she was now experiencing: the anger that her arguments had not been heard, the anxiety for what would now happen to her child, the helplessness at being left with no place to turn. After the shock had subsided, I knew she would be left with another feeling, too, a hurt that might linger the longest of all. With the appeal having been rejected, the original judgment was now a record that could not be contested. At the stroke of a pen, the court had effectively rendered it indelible. Now, the record would always say that Lydia had alleged things about her ex-partner that were not upheld by the court. She had to live with that, forever, and the fear that, years later, her child might see it.

That is the reality of the family justice system for some women. It might refuse to acknowledge or give proper weight to the allegations of abuse they suffered because the events were too far in the past, the evidence wasn't clear enough, or the judge simply preferred his version of events to hers. The trauma of not being believed compounds that of the original abuse.

For Lydia, what lay ahead was a pain that would twist its way through months and years of her life. For now, she was in a state of simple disbelief. 'There must be *something* we can do,' she said over and over, clinging to the words like a charm. She kept repeating the mantra, unwilling to accept that such a momentous event in her life could have come via this sharp anticlimax – no additional hearing, just a written judgment that stated her appeal was rejected with no additional recourse.

I felt desperate for her, but I also owed her the truth, even as bitter a pill as this. I let her words settle and tried to keep my voice level as I spoke.

'I'm sorry, but I'm afraid you have done everything. There's nothing more that you can do.'

Another pause.

'I know it's difficult, but you do have to accept that it's over.'

It was my job to advise her of this, a fact that had now acquired steel plating, but I almost hated myself for doing so. It was a reminder that as a barrister, you are unavoidably part of the system, however much you recognise its flaws and seek to mitigate them. You can be the client's most committed advocate, but you are also their representative and guide through this unfamiliar landscape and the one who must translate its worst truths. Even though I had done the best job I possibly could for Lydia, I felt complicit because I was the one who had to tell her she had no further right of appeal in England and Wales, no way to argue her case and no chance of changing the record.

The sense of guilt was deepened by the thought that this incredibly painful conversation might be our last. If there was no more legal work to do, we would almost certainly never meet again. I would move on to the next case, while Lydia would be burdened with the aftermath of the court's decision for the rest of her life, replaying the hearing and rereading the original judgment until its words were etched into her subconscious.

That is the reality of being a barrister, and I can always rationalise to myself that there is someone else whose need for representation is equally pressing. But I could not escape the thought that this woman had lost confidence in the family justice system and that I had been a participant. However much I fight against the worst of that system, I am also a part of it, the lawyer who must tell a frightened and angry woman that the court's word is final before swiftly ushering her out of my life forever. The knowledge that there is nothing more I can do does not staunch the guilt – at having failed to achieve the result Lydia so desperately needed and at having been an agent of the system that treated her with such careless cruelty.

Lydia's case stayed with me, partly because I had not been able to help achieve what she so desperately wanted, but also because it opened my eyes to reproductive coercion as a form of domestic abuse that deserves much greater understanding by the court system. Representing Lydia was just the beginning of learning about this insidious form of coercive control, and the lengths to which abusive men will go to exploit their victims at the most vulnerable moments of their lives.

'And then there were the conditions for having another child.'

'Conditions?'

'Things I had to agree to.'

My mind was immediately racing, but I had to stop Beth from breezing ahead with her account of her abusive marriage – one so bad that her husband was ultimately convicted of domestic violence-related offences. Beth looked like any other forty-something mum picking her children up from school, or talking to you about them while making a coffee in the office kitchen. Now she was telling me about how her husband had attached conditions to her pregnancy as if she was asking whether I wanted milk or sugar.

I had never heard of someone signing up to conditions before getting pregnant, and had no idea what a list of them would look like.[2] When Beth agreed to share what turned out to be a typed document, with both their signatures at the bottom, I couldn't believe what I was reading. There were ten separate clauses in this 'contract', beginning with statements that the husband should not be expected to give up his (mostly sporting) hobbies and that Beth would not bring up the subject of having another child. Beth would agree to shop for clothes in charity shops and 'keep the house as tidy as possible'. This was bad enough, but it was when scanning the lower half of the page that my stomach began to turn. Under the heading 'sex', this absurd document became disturbing. Its clauses read:

'I will entertain all [sex] requests – whenever and whatever – with a smile on my face and as a willing participant'.

'I will provide – and receive – oral sex on a much more regular basis than currently'.

'I will be happy "to swallow" on some occasions (as I used to before we married) and also agree to "facials" on request'.

There followed a fourth condition about Beth wearing make-up and nail polish, and a fifth stating that these terms would remain in force for eternity.

In the course of my work, I have read thousands and thousands of pages of evidence concerning domestic abuse, rape and violence against women. There is very little committed to paper on this subject that truly shocks me. But this particular document did. It was, in effect, a charter for a man to rape and sexually assault his wife whenever he chose. A disgusting power fantasy which he had typed out in 11pt Calibri and made Beth sign her name to.

I couldn't believe that such a thing existed or that she had skated over it like it didn't matter. Indeed, the court subsequently did exactly the same thing. This grubby little document spoke to several things: the normalisation of coercion, control and assault in an abusive relationship, such that it is treated as normal; the abuser's desire not just to exercise control but to use every opportunity to remind their victim that they hold that power; and the fact that pregnancy and childbirth will be used as an occasion to reinforce that twisted power dynamic. The abuser may choose to assert his authority by seeking to prevent the victim from either proceeding with or terminating a pregnancy; women are twice as likely to have their male partner refuse contraception when experiencing intimate partner violence.[3] Or he may 'agree' to her preferred course of action, but only by extracting his demands in return and reinforcing that the power to make decisions resides with him alone. What he demands is almost incidental. In all cases, it is about exploiting one of the most vulnerable moments of a woman's life to coerce and control her.[4]

A successful, middle-class woman, Beth was exactly the kind of domestic abuse victim who hides in plain sight. None of the parents talking to her at the school gate would have guessed that she was being subjected to such vile sexual coercion, or how she felt so trapped by the combination of her abusive relationship and parental responsibilities that for a long time she felt like there was no escape. Her case reinforced my experience that some of the most horrendous domestic abuse happens in wealthy, overtly stable households.

Beth's experience was appalling, but she was at least able to cut all ties with this man, successfully mounting a case to oppose his contact after he was criminally convicted of domestic violence-related offences. Even so, it took months of litigation and thousands of pounds in legal costs to achieve this. For all this time she felt as if she had traded one prison for another, and only when her abuser was finally cut off from contact did she feel able to breathe easily again. Several other women I have represented have not been so lucky. Despite acute experiences of abuse, they have not been able to prevent their ex-partners from continuing to have contact with their children and, in some cases, access to their home.

Jasmine was another woman who took me aback by producing a written agreement entitled 'Conditions for third child'. The six terms included the hiring of a nanny 'so [husband] is not a weekend childminder', 'Regular (weekly) sex', '[wife] to mellow a bit and not get angry at bedtime', and 'There to be no fourth child'.

I read it, having to remind myself that I was representing Jasmine because this man, the one who did not wish to be a 'childminder', was now litigating not just for contact but *residence* – he wanted all their children to live with him and not her. It reinforced, yet again, that men like this will change their tune and argue anything as long as it enables them to exert power over their victims. And, unfortunately, the court will sometimes enable them rather than protect the women and children. In Jasmine's case, her ex-husband argued that she had alienated the children against him, secured expert witness testimony to that effect and was successful in having the court order a transfer of residence. By contrast, the document detailing his 'conditions' for their third child was not deemed relevant by the court, even though he did not deny he had written it. I don't know what ultimately happened to Jasmine and her children. With some cases, barristers follow them until the end, in others we are not always available for the next hearing or clients decide they wish to instruct another barrister or the case concludes out of court. One of the oddities of the job is that after the court hearing has ended, your role comes to an abrupt end, sometimes for good. You are left wondering what happened to that woman, and to those children.

Reading documents that said a man should be entitled to sex whenever he liked, if his partner wished to have another baby, reminded me that this is a job that can make you feel hopelessly naive. Even knowing that many relationships are abusive does not prepare you for how calculating and ruthless the behaviour of some abusers can be. Or for the way angry, violent men can be triggered by either the prospect or reality of a child being born – whether by the presence of an infant who will draw the woman's attention away from him or by the thought that she may wish to exercise bodily autonomy and not proceed with having 'his' baby.

An abuser's anger may not even stem from feelings relating to a child at all. Pregnancy 'may have a significant impact on the power dynamics of a relationship', one study has suggested, affecting everything from financial requirements to sexual availability and the roles that both partners are expected to perform.[5] In this context, violent men may wish to 'punish' the woman who can no longer provide for all their needs in the way they are accustomed. Whatever the particular pathology, the reality is that pregnancy means the norms of any relationship shift, which makes the partner of an abusive man become newly vulnerable to his need to reassert control and mitigate threats to that power.

Cases concerning reproductive coercion were a window into a side of domestic abuse I had not seen before and an insight into how that intersects with pregnancy and childbirth. The longer my career has gone on, the more I have seen how some of the most outrageous and disturbing abusive behaviour happens in this context. One client was in labour in the hospital when her husband pelted her with abusive messages, so much so that the midwife had to take her phone away from her. When he stopped getting responses from her, he started bombarding the hospital with calls, to the point where they called the police to report him for harassment.

Perhaps the saddest dimension of that case was that my client kept insisting to the hospital staff and then the police that her husband wasn't a threat and she didn't feel in danger. The truth was that she was so afraid of him that she felt the authorities could do nothing to protect her, and her only chance was to try and placate him as far as possible. This was then used against her in family court. Far too often, that is the choice forced on women. Those most in need of protection are sometimes, in effect, forced back into the hands of their abuser.

That was the predicament facing Melody, another client who alleged that her partner had mistreated both her and their children. He was initially granted contact, and the children said he had been abusive to them during the time he spent with them. But the court took his side, accepting the argument that Melody had been coaching the children and alienating them against their father. Melody was warned that she risked losing custody if she continued to press her case against her ex-partner. So she made the decision that no woman should have to make, but which felt like the only thing she could do to protect her children. Because she couldn't bear the thought of letting this man have unsupervised contact with their children, and because the court had refused to take the risk he posed seriously, she decided to go back into the relationship. She put herself in harm's way to try and keep her children safe because no authority had been willing or able to protect her.

The abuse that is perpetrated against women during pregnancy and childbirth by their partners is one of the saddest themes I have seen through my work in family court. Yet it is not just violent men who heap misery on women at the most vulnerable point in their lives. All too frequently, so does the state, wielding antiquated laws against women who wish to exercise their reproductive rights and soon find themselves facing criminal consequences. In the 2020s, approaching sixty years after the Abortion Act, women in England are still being put on trial and sent to jail for ending their pregnancies.

Susie had been prescribed mifepristone, the abortion pill, during a telemedicine appointment. She had allegedly taken the pills after the point in her pregnancy where it is legal to do so. She suffered severe bleeding and went to hospital, where an operation was performed to stabilise her. The hospital had also called the police, who turned up at her bedside, arrested her and took her to the station, where she was held in a cell for more than thirty hours. Whatever the legality of what this woman had done, there was no justification for treating her in this way, no conceivable threat to the public that required her to be arrested and jailed, and a total deficit of empathy and ethical behaviour that allowed a vulnerable woman to be criminalised so cruelly. Nor was this an isolated example. In another case, a woman I represented was charged for abortion-related offences and had her two children removed and placed in foster care. In 2023, a mother of three children was prosecuted and given a twenty-eight-month prison sentence for having taken abortion pills after the legal cut-off point. This was reduced before the Court of Appeal to fourteen months after the judges agreed that she needed 'compassion not punishment'.[6] Like Susie, she had been sent these in the post under a scheme introduced during Covid restrictions. The law under which she was prosecuted, the Offences Against the Person Act, dates back to 1861.[7]

It is a grim irony that criminal law in this country is punitive towards pregnant women while family law still struggles to understand the coercion that they may be facing. In one part of our justice system, women are pursued for questionable prosecutions that may result in a prison sentence for having terminated their pregnancies too late. In another, their pleas to be protected from violent men fall on deaf ears, such that they may feel they have no choice except to return to an abusive relationship so they can act as a human shield for their children.

Together, these problems underline the systemic failure to understand the complex realities of pregnancy and childbirth. A woman who is either trying to become pregnant, to carry a pregnancy to full term or to terminate, is going through one of the most vulnerable episodes of their life. That vulnerability may prompt them to make seemingly strange decisions, or it may expose them to the violence of a partner who feels displaced within the relationship or simply wishes to reassert their control. Whatever the case, it is a set of problems poorly understood by the state and barely accommodated.

The double life of pregnancy is something better understood than it once was – how it may be a source of physical injury and acute psychological harm as well as a precursor to the fulfilment of family and parenthood. Yet our legal system lags behind, reluctant to acknowledge the link between pregnancy and domestic violence, too keen to dismiss as 'historic' allegations that have a direct bearing on the risk of harm, and too incurious about why a woman may choose to downplay the threat she faces from an abusive man, or even to resume her relationship with him.

The idea that anyone would set out to harm a pregnant woman is difficult enough to reconcile, let alone the truth that they would perpetrate that harm *because* the woman has chosen to become (or remain) pregnant.[8] Through representing women who have experienced exactly this, I have seen and read things I would not have believed about how violent partners will behave when they feel displaced by such a dramatic change in their relationship.

It gives me a mixture of feelings which has become familiar in my work – despair at the abuse so many women suffer, often an experience compounded in court, and determination that I will not stand by and ignore what I am seeing, or accept that it is normal. There are days, when I snatch a quick coffee with a friend from bar school who has gone on to a career in corporate or commercial law, when I crave that quieter life. They work the same punishing hours I do, but I doubt they have as many nightmares about tax entitlements or intellectual property disputes. Sometimes I wonder if, had I known what working in family court was like, and what it means to be drawn into the lives of people who have suffered so acutely and are looking to you for help, I would have chosen this path. But the longer I have walked down it, the more I have realised that there is no turning back.

Rarely has this work left me feeling more helpless than when trying to represent women who have been subjected to reproductive coercion that the court refused to take seriously.[9] Telling Lydia that she had no further right of appeal concerning the man who had allegedly threatened to kill her, watching Melody decide that she had to return to her violent partner for the sake of her children, and witnessing Jasmine lose custody of her children to a man who had resented having to be a 'childminder', were some of the worst experiences of my professional life. Having had ample opportunity to see how the family justice system fails women in any number of contexts, I believe that few are let down more drastically than women who were abused as a result of being or wanting to become pregnant. They are the women who were exploited at one of the most vulnerable times in their lives, who tried to get the court to acknowledge what had happened to them, and who, to varying degrees, struggled to safeguard their children as a result. Representing these clients was a window into the agonising choices faced by women in abusive relationships once they have become mothers. Now they must think not just of their own safety but their child's.

In some cases, having a child is the spur for a victim of domestic abuse to do one of the most difficult things they can – to break away from an abuser who has spent years grooming and coercing them into believing that they have no option but to stay. Leaving can be the hardest choice a woman in this situation ever makes. But as I would learn, for some this is just the beginning of a legal battle that can stretch across continents, as abusive men leverage international law to try and bring both their ex-partner and their children back under their control.

8

Point of No Return: Child Abduction and the Hague Convention

Everything about Lisa was slim. Skinny jeans clung to her narrow figure, framed above by a tight-fitting navy jacket. Thin strands of sandy brown hair kept falling over her forehead, before she brushed them anxiously away. Some of the women I meet appear to be making themselves as small as possible, shrinking away from the intimidating prospect of the courtroom. The first time I set eyes on Lisa, I worried that she was a woman almost fading away.

Then Lisa started talking and I wondered if my impression had been misplaced. Words poured out of her tiny figure in a rush so great that she often tripped over them, picking up the next thought from the wreckage of the last. She was frantic, an odd mixture of anxiety and defiance, hugging her body in a protective stance while holding forth with a fragile kind of confidence. As she continued, I reached my first conclusion: here was a woman who was terrified about her own and her child's future. With it came a second: she had absolutely no idea what she was up against.

Lisa had done something that, to her, appeared to be common sense. She had escaped a relationship in which she had been the victim of alleged physical, emotional and verbal abuse, taken her child from their home in Australia and returned to the UK, where she had grown up. Now they were living with a relative. In Lisa's mind, she had done what she had to do, removing her child from an abusive environment, one in which they had witnessed some of her ex-partner's abuse of her (itself an acknowledged form of child abuse). She had protected herself and her child, doing what any mother would.

But she had also, in the eyes of the law, abducted her own child. Now, under the terms of the Hague Convention that governs such cases across national borders, she was faced with the prospect of being ordered to return to Australia, from where she had just fled. Her Australian ex-partner had filed an application for a return order, and through the door of her relative's house an official letter had dropped telling Lisa that she had to attend the High Court and her child may soon be put on a flight back to Australia. Unless we could make a successful case to oppose this, she would have no choice but to return her child not just to the country from which she had fled but to the same street as her abusive ex, where he was offering to provide her with accommodation as part of the legal order that required her return.

'I'm never going back.'

Lisa's eyes were insistent, belying her frail-looking body. 'He's been abusive to me. I've got the evidence.' From a plastic shopping bag I hadn't noticed until now, she started unpacking sheaves of paper and spreading them over the table in front of us. Photos of her face and body after he had beaten her. Printouts of messages between them.

Even on first impression, this appeared shocking, but there wasn't time for a detailed discussion about what had happened to her or what it meant for the case. Our hearing was minutes away, and the only question now was whether she wanted to contest his application for a summary return order.

'What's your position on going back to Australia?'

I had to ask even though I knew the answer. She would fight it, and soon I would be standing up in the High Court to state that we opposed the application on the basis of harm and because she did not have secure immigration status there. As we parted that day, Lisa looked happy, satisfied that her voice had been heard and someone was fighting her corner. But I knew that we faced an uphill climb to succeed in the case. And it worried me even more that she did not.

By the time I met Lisa, the Hague Convention had been in operation for almost forty years. Originally designed for situations where a father without custody would remove their child and take them abroad, it had drifted some way from its original purpose.[1] Now, most of the cases heard under the Convention concern mothers like Lisa, who have taken their children out of fear for their safety in an abusive home. The upshot is that a legal protection designed to safeguard children is often being used against the mothers seeking to protect them. As Baroness Hale, former President of the Supreme Court, has written: 'there may be good reasons for the unlawful taking (or even keeping) of a child. The taking or keeping parent may be the victim of domestic violence or abuse. She may have felt that flight was the only option.'[2]

This was Lisa's predicament in a nutshell. In an abusive relationship, living in a country where she had none of her own family and friends to support her, she had truly felt that her best choice was to return home to the UK with her child. Now she was on the brink not just of being removed from this country, but forced to live in close proximity with her abusive ex-partner, and the family members who she said had enabled his coercive and controlling behaviour. Lisa did not just look vulnerable. She was in an economically precarious situation, couldn't get a job in Australia due to her immigration status, and would, in effect, be entirely reliant on her abuser to provide for her and their child.

To Lisa this seemed as nonsensical as her decision to return to the UK had been obvious. How could a court of law compel her to return to an abusive environment where she had documented evidence of physical and emotional harm? How could it give a man she accused of being coercive and controlling so much say over how and where she lived?

Like so many women, Lisa believed that the court would understand her situation, take her concerns seriously and respond accordingly. She could not conceive of how a responsible authority would act so clearly against her child's interests and welfare. But in the Hague Abduction Convention, she had encountered a very blunt, prescriptive and narrow piece of law. With its focus almost entirely on expediting the process of return, it leaves little room for the consideration of wider context and the vulnerability of domestic abuse victims. As the Convention sets out, the conditions under which return may not be ordered when a child has been wrongfully removed are 1) if the other parent or carer did not have custody in the first place (or consented to the child being moved), or 2) if the return would pose 'grave risk' of harm to the child or put them in an 'intolerable situation'.[3] In practice, the bar for the second provision is incredibly high, usually amounting to a credible threat of suicide on the part of either mother or child.

The Convention directs judges to prioritise custody rights and the return of any wrongfully removed children above all else. This means issues such as domestic abuse are usually disregarded or, if they are considered at all, treated as matters to be dealt with in the jurisdiction to which the child is returning. Judges in Hague cases are encouraged to take a narrow view and frequently do. Prior to Lisa, I had represented dozens of women who were contesting return applications made under the Hague Convention. Only a few were successful, and two of those after the father had dropped the case (they involved older children, who stated their opposition to going back). Only once had I persuaded a judge to rule that the threat of harm met the threshold of 'grave risk', after the woman in question had undergone a psychiatric assessment which judged her to be at risk of suicide.

Before our second conference, I agonised over how to convey this to Lisa. By now I'd had the chance to review the evidence: her witness statement and his, the bundle of documents she had tipped onto the table when we first met, and audio recordings that documented her ex screaming at her and the baby crying in the background. I had read Lisa's account of how her ex-partner was often drunk and on drugs and how his family had explained away all his behaviour and done nothing to support her, even when he beat her. We had advice from an Australian immigration lawyer that stated

Lisa would have to return on a temporary visa and apply for permanent status in country – in other words, her right to remain there could not be taken for granted.

I admired Lisa's determination to fight the case and believed as much as she did that a return order would leave her in reasonable fear of her safety and the child's. And I didn't want to be fatalistic about her chances: there is nothing worse than an advocate who has given up on their client before they've even started arguing the case, or who lets their preconceptions about how a judge is likely to respond sway their presentation of the case. Lisa's prospects were not good, but we still had a chance. There were robust arguments to make about the threat of harm to Lisa and her child and about her insecure immigration status. As ever, a lot would depend on the discretion of the judge assigned to hear the case.

I wanted to be optimistic, to reassure Lisa that I was with her, but also realistic. As well as being her advocate, I was obliged to give her the best possible advice and prepare her for what may transpire. I didn't want to break her spirit, but nor could I afford to build up her hopes. As we spoke, going through the provisions of the Convention and the grounds we would argue her case upon, I set out what seemed to be the cold reality. The Hague Convention was disadvantageous to someone in her situation, and while her experience of domestic abuse had clearly been profound, I had seen more severe cases where judges had still ordered the child to be returned. Lisa did not appear to be experiencing any overt mental health problems, and we had no psychiatric or psychological assessment to support an argument that her return to Australia would pose her or the child a grave risk. 'I'm going to be completely frank with you,' I concluded.

'I think it's unlikely the judge is going to say you can stay here.'

As Lisa gave me one of her intense looks, I could see that she had taken in what I'd said but did not fully believe it. Whatever the rational arguments, in her heart she clung to the truth of what she was saying and believed that a judge would see it the same way. She still struggled to accept that a court would force her into circumstances that she described as 'like a prison' – living almost next door or even in the same house as her ex, among his family and entirely separated from her own. 'They're not going to make me do that,' she said. I could see that she believed it.

I wished I could share her certainty. In one of my previous Hague Convention cases, I represented a mother whose daughter had made allegations of sexual abuse against her father. He in turn argued that the mother had coached her, and she was ordered by the judge to be returned to his custody. I knew that Lisa's evidence of domestic abuse would be very unlikely to sway the decision our way. The High Court would probably take the view that, even if the things she was alleging were true, she could be protected by the relevant authorities and courts in Australia. In other words, it didn't need to be their problem. I hoped the argument about her precarious immigration status would find more favour.

When we arrived back at the High Court for her final hearing, at which the arguments would be presented, the first thing I noticed was how Lisa looked. Hague cases are fast-tracked, and it had only been a couple of months since our first meeting. Noticeably thin then, she had somehow lost even more weight since. I was shocked by how physically fragile she now appeared. It wasn't hard to see the toll that this experience had taken on her, sitting in her relative's house, counting down the days to the hearing, knowing that she was on the brink of being sent back into a situation she had crossed the world to escape.

I was about to go into court and argue on Lisa's behalf that it would be intolerable for her and her child to be sent back to the father. Whatever my doubts about how this argument would be received by the judge, I knew just by looking at her that Lisa's fears were real. Even the prospect of this outcome was causing her physical and mental health to deteriorate. The reality of it should have been unthinkable.

It was 10 a.m. and I had finished work on my skeleton argument just seven hours earlier. I knew that everything would have to go our way, and I could not afford any missteps. But I also relish the simplicity of hearings like this. There is no witness testimony, so you present your argument to the judge in one go, they ask questions, and then it ends. There is structure, clarity and a tight focus on the legal arguments, without the Punch and Judy show of questioning and cross-examining witnesses. The only downside was that I was on my feet for almost three hours arguing Lisa's case. By contrast, counsel for the father took only a fraction of the time. It was a bad sign. When you are confident in your case, you can afford to be succinct. In our position, I had to pile up every piece of evidence to try and create a picture compelling enough to sway the judge. I had never argued in front of this judge before and was none the wiser about their views after the hearing. Asking only a few questions, they gave nothing away.

The next day, we returned to hear the judgment. I entered

the courtroom expecting it to be read, but instead a short written document was handed down. I scanned it as quickly as I could, conscious that Lisa and her family were looking at me – that they would know before I said a word what the outcome was. It was as I had feared. The judge had granted the father's application for a summary return order. Lisa and her child would have to return to where they had fled from a few months earlier.

As I confirmed it to them, we were standing outside the courtroom, in a foyer with barristers and their clients filing past, the noise of many conversations merging into a busy hum. In the seconds after her fate had been confirmed, Lisa put her back against the wall and slowly slid to the floor, her head between her knees. Her loud sobs and wheezing breaths rasped above the low murmur as she hyperventilated. I crouched down, trying to comfort her, as heads started to turn our way. Eventually, a clerk intervened and found us a private room to sit in. Someone with first aid training came to help Lisa steady her breathing. The panic started to recede, but the reality of the situation could not be escaped. This woman's worst nightmare was now happening, spelled out in a court order. The law had deemed that she must be sent back into an environment where she felt she would face serious risk of harm.

This is the reality of the Hague Convention and how it has become weaponised against mothers like Lisa. A woman can demonstrate that she was abused, that her child witnessed it, and she is scared that there is nothing to protect her from that abuser if they are compelled to return. She can show that, after being returned, she will be economically reliant on that man. All that may still be disregarded simply because a legal framework that was drafted over forty years ago encourages the court not to view the whole picture but to focus on one specific part of it. Unless there is overwhelming evidence that return places mother or child at grave risk of harm or puts the child in an 'intolerable situation', they will be sent back.[4]

When it comes to the threat of further violence, the Convention comes close to suggesting that courts should cover their eyes and say what they cannot see, they will not consider. The sole nod to safeguarding comes in the form of 'undertakings' made by the father as to how they will engage with and support the abducting parent after they return. In Lisa's case, her ex had committed to providing her with accommodation and supporting her financially for an initial period. He also promised to drop the criminal charges he had levelled against her in Australia and to give up his application for sole custody. These undertakings form part of the return order and are negotiated by lawyers on both sides. Yet despite this appearance of formality, they are effectively paper promises, which would require more time and money to enforce in an Australian court.[5] The same system that doesn't listen to women who say they are at risk of violence is happy to put faith in the men who have abused them and assume that they will keep their word. In cases like Lisa's, an abusive man is considered the 'wronged' party in the eyes of the law, while his victim is deemed to be the perpetrator who abducted the child.

As I explained to Lisa once she had recovered from the panic attack, we had a narrow window to make a final appeal if she wanted – within twenty-one days of this judgment. I thought there were good grounds to appeal. Most importantly, her immigration status on return remained unclear, which could have left her unable to care for her child after being sent back to Australia. But she was adamant, just as she had been in the opposite direction at our first meeting, that she did not want to.

It was one of the saddest parts of an already distressing case. Her spirit, so clear when we first met, had been broken to the point where she no longer wanted to resist. Lisa had been abused and traumatised by her ex-partner, but it was the court order that had finally robbed her of the will to fight. She had stubbornly believed that any fair system must take seriously her account and evidence of abuse, only to see it put its weight behind the case of the man who she claimed had beaten and belittled her.

There could have been no more conclusive evidence of the injustice of the Hague Convention than the sight of Lisa, crumpled on the floor outside the courtroom, utterly broken by the experience of trying to protect herself and her child. By contrast, her ex had only had to submit paperwork and instruct a lawyer to achieve what he wanted. He had not even had to pay for a lawyer, because the applicant parent in child abduction cases receives legal aid. Now, he would have an overwhelming amount of control over both her life and that of their child. Far from being sanctioned for his abusive behaviour, he had, in effect, continued his exercise of control from thousands of miles away.

Typically, I would never hear from or about a client like Lisa after we part ways. The honest truth is that there is an element of relief in this. When you do not know what happened to someone, you can rationalise that perhaps the outcome was not as bad as feared. I care deeply about my clients and want to achieve the best I can for them. But you cannot carry every case around with you, worrying about what happened to people, wondering if somehow you could have represented them better or achieved a different outcome. Ignorance about how people's lives pan out after court is one layer of protection against this.

In Lisa's case, this was punctured several months after the final hearing when I received a message from her mother. She painted a shocking picture of what had happened when Lisa complied with the return order. The father had not upheld either of his two most important undertakings – to drop both the criminal charges against her and his custody application. After arriving back in Australia, Lisa had been arrested and now found herself in legal hell in both family and criminal courts, as well as facing continued uncertainty over her immigration status. She now feared she would lose her child for good.

Could I do anything to help? The short answer was no. All the actions Lisa faced were in a jurisdiction outside of my ability to help her secure either legal funding or support. I felt as helpless as her mother, who was also living in the UK, clearly did, but I was also glad that she had contacted me and shattered the protective veil of ignorance. I had already known just how dangerous the Hague Convention could be in effectively requiring women to return to environments that they believed to be unsafe for themselves and their children (technically the return order concerns the child only, but few mothers are going to abandon their children in such circumstances). Now I had proof that, having put women like Lisa in harm's way, it would then do nothing to protect them when the worst happened. The Convention had done its job and 'solved' the problem of a child abduction. That this had come at the cost of a woman's safety and well-being seemed not to matter. That the undertakings made in the return order had been so quickly broken would not make a difference. I felt almost as ashamed that I could do nothing to help as I was angry that Lisa had been so badly failed by an outdated Convention that had closed its ears to the threat of harm.

Sometimes, when I am talking about my work with friends outside the law, they will say that they don't understand how anyone can deal – week in, week out – with such depressing and traumatic stories. But even then, I often feel like it is hard to convey what the job is really like at its extremes: when you are the last person left fighting for a vulnerable woman whom the court is refusing to protect from her abuser. When you have to watch the fight drain out of a person because they have been through so much and know that if they stand up for themselves again, the system will probably crush them anyway. Occasionally I will try to paint this picture, but often I don't. It doesn't exactly lighten the mood over a cocktail. So I smile, say that of course it's hard but it's all part of the job. And then I go home, struggle to sleep, and think about the women and children who were not protected from dangerous men.

Lisa's case was far from an isolated example. Other women in her situation have been taken to court under the Hague Convention after escaping a situation in which they faced violence, rape, threats to life and financial control. Women have reported being coerced into moving country with their partner, so that he could use the legal system to

exercise control over them and the children.[6] And more
of the same awaits mothers like Lisa who are 'Hagued' –
forced to return to the country from which they fled. They
are acknowledged to face a whole range of risks, including
homelessness, punishment by a domestic court system that
considers her as a 'child abductor', and continued abuse
from the ex-partner they were trying to escape in the first
place.[7]

A study funded by the US Department for Justice in
2010 revealed stories of mothers who had fled to the US
with their children and had experiences that were, in many
cases, even worse than Lisa's. One woman described six
police officers waiting at her home, serving her with the
legal papers and immediately removing her two children,
dragging them away when they were clinging to her legs.[8]
Others reported that they had been ordered to return to
their country of origin even when judges acknowledged their
partner's abuse of them (one described this as 'common'),
and in one case, despite commenting that 'I find a risk
in placing this child under his father's custody'.[9] In many
of the twenty-two cases studied, all of which concerned
abused women who had left the country with their children,
domestic abuse was not mentioned in the judgment and
sometimes not even raised by the woman's lawyer.[10] Of those
who were ordered to return, four of the women and three
of the children reported that they had been further abused
by the man from whom they had originally fled.[11]

There is no shortage of evidence to show how the Hague
Convention has become open to abuse – protecting violent
men and putting their victims back into harm's way. Despite
the widespread insistence that returning children will not

face harm, the reality is that sometimes mothers or children are killed, and often cases are never monitored.[12] The need for change is obvious, and very slowly, domestic judiciaries are waking up to this reality and beginning to address the problem. In 2022, the Australian government instituted provisions allowing its courts to consider 'family and domestic violence' when deliberating over return orders.[13]

Yet despite these positive developments, there is still a feeling that Hague cases are extremely difficult to win when representing a mother who has fled an abusive partner with her child. It's why, some years after representing Lisa, I read the file on Julia's case with a sense of dread. Originally from Eastern Europe, Julia moved to another European country for work, where she had met her partner and had a child. Her daughter was now five years old and Julia had removed her to the UK, where some of her family lived, to get away from her partner's violent and abusive behaviour. It was not hard to see why she had acted. Even an initial skim of the documents suggested he was a serial abuser who had physically assaulted Julia on multiple occasions, while their child was in the room, and in some cases while other family members were watching on video calls. Since she had come to the UK with her daughter, he had bombarded her, her sister and brother-in-law with threatening messages, including after she secured a restraining order against him from a UK court.[14]

Yet even then, I wondered if we would be able to resist the return order that the father had filed under the Hague Convention, and get a judge to agree that Julia and her daughter would face an 'intolerable' situation or 'grave risk of harm' if they were sent back to the father's country. We met on the day of the hearing, and our conversation turned to the most sensitive parts of Julia's allegations of domestic abuse. I must often advise mothers that it is in their interest to share the most excruciating and embarrassing experiences of their lives in front of the judge, to ensure that the abuse they are claiming is understood. I had known this was coming and arranged for us to meet earlier than usual so that we would not have to rush.

As I talked, suddenly the grey-walled conference room seemed very crowded. On one side of Julia was her sibling, who had been allowed to attend in support of her, and on the other her translator. With the solicitor, we were five women sitting around the smallish table as I spoke. I paused for the translation, trying not to look too intently at Julia, who stared straight ahead and met nobody's eye. Her hair was scraped back and tied up in a bun, accentuating the dark pouches under her eyes that spoke of anxious, sleepless nights building up to this day of decision. She did not speak as the translation finished, but the tears that were beginning to blotch her cheeks gave me my answer. First Julia started crying, then her sibling joined in, and still the translator's flat tones conveyed my words to both of them.

Julia's case against the return order had clear merits. It included numerous, well-evidenced allegations of physical assault and threatening behaviour. On one occasion, she claimed her ex had hit her on the face with the back of his hand, with enough force that she was left bleeding (Julia had video-recorded the blood on the floor in the aftermath, and the next day her daughter had accidentally sent this to one of Julia's friends on Instagram).[15] Another time, she said he had thrown a large metal bottle at her, which ripped her top and also left her bleeding from the back.[16] Several months later, he allegedly put a knife to Julia's chest and threatened to kill her after she asked him to drink less. After she begged him to put the knife away, he hit her in the face and pushed her outside onto a balcony.[17] The same month, she claimed he beat her up, leaving her with a bleeding nose and bruised ribs. It was only after two more serious alleged assaults, including when he hit Julia in the face, locked her in the bathroom and started kicking the door – all while her sister was on a video call in the background – that Julia finally decided to leave.[18] Without making findings of fact on the specific incidents, the judge was clear that the pattern of violence had led to this point: 'I have found that [the mother] was the victim of domestic abuse comprising violent, coercive and controlling behaviour by [the father] . . . and that her removal of [the child] and flight to the United Kingdom was effected in order to escape that abuse,' he wrote.[19]

Even then, the threats continued from a distance, targeting Julia, her mother back in her home country, and her sister and brother-in-law, whom she was living with in the UK. The judge summarised the messages as containing 'abusive and graphic threats of violence, including sexual violence' aimed at Julia and her family members.[20]

It could not have been clearer that Julia had escaped a vicious, relentless abusive relationship when she came to the UK and brought her daughter with her. Yet still I wondered, after all my previous experience in Hague cases, if even this would be enough. I reminded myself how high the bar was set for a situation to be deemed intolerable. And I feared the worst after the evidence of the psychiatric expert witness, Dr

Cleo Van Velsen, who I felt was guarded in her testimony and did not commit to anything beyond saying that if the allegations of domestic abuse were found to be true, Julia could be considered to be suffering from an adjustment disorder, effectively a synonym for low mood or mild depression. She was not, the expert insisted, suffering from PTSD, although this could happen if she was subjected to further abuse.[21] I found this part of the expert's evidence hard to believe and lacking a trauma-focused approach.

When the judgment was handed to us in writing, I was almost stunned to see that the father's application had been dismissed. The judge, Deputy High Court Judge Paul Bowen KC, deemed that Julia's daughter was indeed at grave risk of harm and liable to be placed in an intolerable situation if required to return. He gave weight to the fact that the child had witnessed several of the assaults on her mother, a recognised form of domestic abuse, and that mother and daughter would be returning to a situation which left them effectively under the father's control, living in a flat that he owned even though he had committed to moving elsewhere. He found it very likely that the father would try and resume his relationship with Julia and that this would impact her fragile mental health, also commenting that, '[if] the relationship resumes, it will only be a matter of time before the abuse does too'.[22] He also noted that the father had been an unreliable witness, that he had shown himself willing to flaunt court orders by continuing to contact Julia and her family, and that his financial struggles and problems with alcohol were well established. No protective measures, the judge concluded, would be sufficient to insulate Julia and her daughter from the risk of harm these factors together posed.[23]

It was a judgment that left me deeply relieved for Julia – rarely had I been more worried that such an obviously vulnerable client was about to be placed in harm's way by the court. Yet almost in the same breath I wondered where this appreciation of the wider context and the insidious nature of abuse in a relationship had been when Lisa's application to stay in England was dismissed, or those of the other women I have represented in such cases. As is so often true in family court, women accused of abducting their own children are reliant on the luck of the draw. That will only change when the Convention itself is updated, so that we no longer rely on a piece of law that was drafted in 1980 when both attitudes towards domestic violence and our understanding of it were prehistoric compared to today (not to mention that marital rape was legal, and homosexuality was still criminalised in parts of the UK).

When I took my first child abduction case, I had never heard of the Hague Convention. I had no idea how it is routinely weaponised against women and used to bring them back into the orbit of their abusers. And I was not ready for the frustration of coming up against such a stubborn and prescriptive piece of law – one that makes it very difficult to argue on behalf of women who fear for their own and their children's safety. It represents another corner of the justice system that is skewed against women and in favour of the men who abuse them.

No woman should be put in a position where they are begging to be protected by a system that declares their welfare to be someone else's problem. The Hague Convention began with good intentions and still has an important role to play in protecting children. But it can only do so properly when it stops pretending that mothers do not exist and acting as if their safety does not matter. Without better safeguards for mothers, no child who is brought home under this treaty can ever truly be deemed safe.

Hague Convention cases showed me how the law can be used to extend coercive control across borders. Representing clients like Lisa, I saw how women can end up in the impossible situation of having to choose whether to return to an allegedly abusive household or become separated from their child. I learned how the law can hold up its hands and say that domestic violence is not an insurmountable problem because an international treaty takes precedence.

These were some of the most frustrating cases of my career, fuelling my belief that we can and must do better for women who are only trying to protect themselves and their children from the threat of abusive men. It would be in my work around female genital mutilation, where cases also came down to the question of whether someone should be allowed to stay in this country or sent back to another, that I saw how we do not have to accept the status quo, and that politics and the law combined can make a difference.

9

Hostile Environment:
Female Genital Mutilation

The corridor outside the courtroom was like a train station at rush hour. Families huddled together and young children roamed aimlessly through the confined space, toys left abandoned on the threadbare carpet. A pervasive odour of mould and staleness permeated the air, clinging to the scruffy furniture. Some shouted conversations could be heard from across the corridor while others were being held in huddles drowned out by the din. I could hardly hear myself as I explained to Malia, a girl of just fourteen, that the government's lawyer would be questioning her in the hearing we were about to enter – a hearing that would determine whether or not she would be sent back to a family who had threatened her with harm.

I looked into the scared eyes of a young teenager, in baggy jeans and trainers, an oversized suit jacket covering her white T-shirt. Now she faced the prospect of being deported to her home country, and being sent back to the father who had previously assaulted her, leaving scars, and who, she said, had now promised to perform genital mutilation. As I tried to keep my voice both calm and audible, I noticed out of the corner of my eye that the Home Office lawyers had sat down and were flicking through their papers quickly, as if reading them for the first time. An additional stack of documents sat next to them: all the other cases they would be arguing that day. For these overworked and underpaid lawyers, this was just another hearing, another box to be ticked and statistic to be recorded. For Malia, it was the case that would decide the course of the rest of her life.

Hers was the kind of story I had become familiar with over years of campaigning, academic research and legal work around female genital mutilation. Prevalent in more than thirty countries spanning Africa, Asia and the Middle East,[1] FGM involves the cutting, incising, removal, piercing or otherwise harmful alteration of the clitoris and/or labia – done variously because it is traditional, deemed aesthetic, hygienic, or to be attractive to men.[2] An estimated three million women and girls are subjected to FGM every year. Not only is this a violation of their human rights, but a practice that causes direct physical harm, including bleeding, chronic pain, complications in childbirth or infertility.[3] At Taylor House in London, where first-tier asylum tribunal cases are heard, the question was whether the risk of this fate was sufficient to grant Malia asylum. Her application had already been refused once by the Home Office, and we were about to enter the tribunal to mount an appeal.

In FGM cases I have worked on, the question is usually whether girls will be allowed to leave the UK: either a mother is trying to stop a father from taking their daughter back to a country where FGM is performed, or the local authority is intervening on the child's behalf for the same reason. It is an established pattern that families wishing to perform FGM on their daughters may do so under the pretence of taking them on holiday to a country where it is prevalent – during what is grimly known as the summer 'cutting season'.[4] FGM protection orders, which became part of the law in 2015,[5] were established to give the courts the power to prevent girls being taken out of the country in these circumstances. I had worked with a team of lawyers on a survivor-led campaign to introduce the orders, so I could hardly believe that Malia was in a situation where everything seemed to be happening in reverse. Rather than intervening to protect a vulnerable child from the risk of FGM, the government had gone to court to try and ensure she was sent back to a country where she faced the threat of life-altering mutilation. At exactly the point where the focus should have been on safeguarding, it was doing everything it could to try and send this teenager directly into harm's way.

Malia's case had arisen when she and her eleven-year-old sister Zola had come to the UK for the summer to stay with a female relative. After they told her what their father had said he was going to do to them, she acted immediately, lodging an asylum claim. Zola's application was accepted, but Malia's was not. The Home Office argued that, at fourteen, she was probably too old for FGM to be performed and that her age also made her better able to protect herself from harm.*[6] Although I understood the reasons for this heartless stance all too well, it was still hard to fathom how we could be in a situation where a girl with the visible scars

---

* The age when FGM is performed varies by country. For some communities, FGM is performed from birth until fourteen, and in other communities, the age can range from fifteen to forty-nine.

of abuse on her body did not require protection from her abusive parent, or how a fourteen-year-old could somehow be deemed safe in circumstances where an eleven-year-old was not. This was the hostile environment in action: the government preparing to separate two young sisters, send a child back to an abusive home, and chalk it up as a win.

It had led us to this crowded corridor, where I tried to look reassuring as I answered Malia's questions about what kind of things she would be asked in the courtroom. Unsurprisingly, she seemed completely overwhelmed by the experience, telling me, in case there was any doubt, that she had never been in a courtroom before. Her quiet voice, which I had to lean forward to hear above the background noise, underlined what a travesty it was that this girl was about to be put through an unforgiving cross-examination by the lawyers who sat nearby, barely taking any notice of her, doing their last-minute homework and paying no heed to the young girl whose story was contained in those papers. They had the full power of the state on their side and were using it against this frightened girl, who had been in the UK for only a few months, and was now encountering a system in which almost no one looked like her and few could share or understand her experiences. I already knew how the court, where most of the people asking questions, making speeches and handing down decisions are white, could make people of colour feel unseen and unheard. But I had never felt it so viscerally as I did when watching Malia preparing to walk into that courtroom, an intimidating place in an unfamiliar country. I wanted to protect her, but knew there was nothing I could do to make this any less of a terrifying experience.

Then, one clear, loud voice rose above all the others. Our case had been called, and I smiled at Malia and her older relative, even as I felt a knot of apprehension twisting in my stomach. We walked together to face her fate, weaving through the maze of other families who still awaited theirs.

The issue of FGM, how it should be combated by the law, and the importance of representing girls at risk of being cut has been one of the running themes of my career. In 2017, I completed my PhD thesis on the impact of the UK's criminalisation of FGM, and in 2022 I published an academic text on the subject. In between, and since, I have represented in court girls who face being deported back to a country where it is likely they will be subjected to FGM, and mothers who are trying to protect their daughters from that fate – often one they themselves experienced as a child. And while I was still working on my PhD, I played a role in helping to argue for legislation that introduced FGM protection orders, a legal mechanism to help the court recognise when a girl is at risk of FGM and to prevent her from leaving the country.

But my very first encounter with FGM in court was some time before I became involved in researching and campaigning on the issue. Back in 2013, still a baby barrister, I barely knew what I was doing, but soon found I was in good company. It quickly became clear that the well-meaning judge, who kept referring to what he called 'FMG', had never even heard of the subject in question. The case, from which he quickly withdrew himself to hand over to another judge, concerned a girl who was at risk of being taken to her wider family in Somalia during the school holidays, where her two older sisters had already been cut.

My interest was sparked by that case, but it was not until I took a year out from the bar to do my PhD that I began to focus properly on FGM. I had begun researching a thesis on deliberative democracy, the question of how to get people more closely involved in government decisions. But I quickly ran into the sands of dry political theory which was much less interesting than I had hoped.

In the way that happens when you are meant to be focusing on one important thing, I found myself dedicating more and more time to something else: the work I was doing with lawyers at the Bar Human Rights Committee (BHRC), an independent group of barristers who focus on promoting international human rights through the law. Political attention was starting to return to the question of FGM. Although it had been outlawed in the UK in 1985,[7] and an estimated 137,000 women and girls in the country were living with the consequences of it,[8] not a single prosecution had at that stage taken place. It was clear that across education, healthcare and the law, there were shortcomings in awareness around FGM and a lack of measures in place to safeguard those at risk of it. Campaigners, including the brilliant feminist Leyla Hussein OBE, an FGM survivor who had been cut aged seven, were raising the profile of the issue, and the political wheels were slowly starting to turn.

I'd already had a taste of combining the law with political activism in my work with an earlier, successful campaign to criminalise forced marriage. I knew that my ambition for a legal career to make a difference in the lives of women and girls could not be confined to a courtroom and that

I had to be willing to take the fight to other fronts. As I supported the BHRC in compiling its written evidence to a parliamentary inquiry on the issue, my PhD began to feel even more remote. Political theory felt less urgent than an issue affecting the lives of vulnerable people, where my work could help to bring about change. Before long, I had abandoned deliberative democracy. I decided to change direction and write my doctorate on the criminalisation of FGM in Britain and how the law had affected the lives of survivors.

My research showed me what a complex and multifaceted issue FGM and the law surrounding it is. I spoke to politicians, social workers and police officers who had been involved in the legislation, as well as to over eighty survivors and at-risk young girls and women. My trips to the House of Lords to interview politicians were eye-opening. The legendary Baroness Trumpington, internet famous for flicking a V-sign from the red benches at a male peer who called her old, had been the junior health minister responsible for the 1985 bill. She took me for tea and recalled how people protesting the legislation had told her, 'If you try to stop us, we'll just do it at home on the kitchen table.'[9]

It was not hard to see why the criminalisation of FGM had been so ineffective. After the legislation was introduced, little to no attention was given to the requirements of trying to abolish FGM in practice – such as the training and safeguards needed in schools, social services and healthcare. A practice thought unacceptable had simply been criminalised, with the statute put on the shelf and left there largely untouched for thirty years, barring some updates to the Act that had been made in 2003 and again in 2015.

No attempt had been made to listen to objections from FGM-performing communities, to raise awareness among the same people that the practice was now illegal, or to introduce practical provisions to enforce a ban. FGM had been outlawed in name only.

More insight and ambiguity came from my interviews with women who had themselves undergone FGM, including several focus groups. These were eye-opening and sometimes hair-raising conversations. Even bearing in mind my PhD supervisor's advice to be open-minded, as a committed anti-FGM campaigner I was shocked to hear some women talk about how they were pleased it had been done to them, that they wanted their daughters to be cut, and that it could easily be arranged in the UK.

While my anti-FGM stance did not falter, these conversations helped me to understand that the issue was much more nuanced than I had appreciated. The sessions were warm and, at points, light-hearted. 'I'll show you if you want,' one woman said when I asked her about the physical effects of being cut, sending a ripple of laughter through the room. But there was also sharper emotion and a clear divide in opinion according to age. Older women in the groups often suggested that FGM was traditional, normal and even beautiful, and argued their daughters and granddaughters might actually suffer for not being cut – stigmatised by their communities for shunning a social and cultural norm. By contrast, younger women tended to say that the practice was unjust, degrading and cruel.

One grandmother spoke in favour, even as she described how her sister in Somalia had died as a result of being cut and in the presence of her granddaughter, who talked about how painful and violating her own experience of FGM had been. Yet the younger woman also had her doubts about whether it should be against the law. 'I wouldn't want my grandmother being criminalised for it,' she said, echoing the views of others who feared family members going to prison or having their immigration status threatened.

The more I researched FGM, the clearer it became how complicated the legacy of its criminalisation had been and how challenging it was to put in place safeguards that would not be punitive towards women and families from FGM-performing communities, predominantly immigrants.[10] The status quo was that the state, in effect, discriminated against Black girls and minority girls through neglect of their FGM risk or injuries. Yet attempting to overcome this through legislation posed another threat, whereby a 'clampdown' on the practice might lead to excessive surveillance of communities that already routinely faced over-policing and racial bias directed towards often already vulnerable and excluded families.*

As the anti-FGM campaign developed, I was part of extensive discussions with fellow lawyers, human rights experts and survivors about how to strike this balance: safeguarding vulnerable girls without creating unintended consequences that would cause harm and distress to marginalised groups. The central proposal to address this was the introduction of FGM protection orders for children considered at risk of being taken abroad to be cut. When

---

* In its submission to the Home Affairs Committee, the BHRC argued that by not doing more to protect at-risk girls from FGM, the UK was in breach of obligations under international law.

granted, an FGMPO allows the court to issue a travel ban and confiscate a child's passport, as well as potentially requiring a medical examination. The measure is designed to be proactive and to safeguard a child who has been judged at risk of FGM, without criminalising parents or threatening them with care proceedings that could see the child removed from their care. Although the family court had some equivalent powers before their introduction, the protection orders were designed to formalise and simplify the process, as well as to raise awareness among front-line service workers of the prevalence of FGM and the tools at their disposal to safeguard at-risk girls.

Working with the BHRC, I supported the campaign to introduce protection orders into the new legislation. Led by survivors, we developed our case, drafted wording for the bill, and helped MPs and peers with their speeches on the issue. This was a point in my career where I knew more about what I wanted to do than how to achieve it in practice. I had done my first two years or so at the bar and did not yet feel ready for that career; then I turned back to academia, where I felt too far removed from the real world. Now, as I worked on a piece of legislation that could help to keep hundreds of young girls from serious harm, I knew I had arrived at the right place – where research, law and campaigning meet. I spent many hours working in the office of Seema Malhotra, the Labour MP and then shadow minister for preventing violence against women and girls, who submitted amendments to the bill. I thought I knew from the bar what a hectic workplace was like, but it wasn't until my experience in Parliament, watching Seema work the phones to take input from various stakeholders, typing up her draft as she stood over my shoulder and watching as she literally ran to the relevant office to submit the amendment before the deadline, that I really learned the meaning of last-minute. I enjoyed the technical rigour of the drafting, as well as the advocacy involved, as we built a coalition of political support and promoted the voices of survivors in the media. It was a collaborative process that opened my eyes to the political dimension of our legal system, and from which I made lifelong friends.

The new legislation concerning FGM passed in 2015 as part of the Serious Crime Act. As well as introducing protection orders, it imposed a duty of care on parents to protect their children from FGM regardless of what country it was performed in and on front-line professionals working with children to report cases of FGM when they encountered them. The intention was not just to empower the courts, but to overcome the apparent hesitation that existed among teachers, social workers and even medical professionals to speak up when they encountered FGM, whether because they weren't sure if their suspicions were well grounded or they feared causing offence.

We did not achieve everything we set out to with the legislation. Mandatory training for those professionals was rejected, and there were limits to the powers of protection orders, especially for those without secure immigration status. The law alone was never going to be enough to protect children from FGM: that required the kind of education, advocacy and ongoing safeguarding effort that was taken forward by Barnardo's who at that time ran the National FGM Centre. But the legislation, while not in itself sufficient, was nevertheless a landmark. It formalised and strengthened measures to protect young girls from a shocking form of harm that will affect their whole lives: in the first five years after the bill was passed, 584 protection orders were issued; in contrast, there had only been a handful of prosecutions for FGM. In the process, it showed what can be achieved when there is a concerted effort to prioritise the lives, well-being and human rights of women and girls. I was now seeing in practice what I already believed to be true: that the law really can make a difference. But, as I would discover when I returned to the bar and began to work on FGM cases under the new legislation, the statute is just the beginning. The real struggle comes in the courtroom, when law and politics collide.

The hug seemed to go on forever. As soon as we had left the courtroom Daria threw her arms around me.[11] She was shaking and sobbing, and I held on to her, worrying that if I let go, she would collapse from the grief and stress that were so clearly consuming her. We had just left a hearing where she had been informed that the court could not stop the Home Secretary from deporting her family. She, her eleven-year-old daughter, Ada, and her other children now had to leave the country.[12] As a survivor of FGM who had seen two of her sisters die in her home country of Sudan as a result of being cut, Daria was facing the prospect of having to return there with her own daughter, despite having made it clear that it was a near certainty that the girl would then be subjected to the same abuse.[13] This was no baseless claim: while the immediate order was for Daria, Ada and her siblings to return to Bahrain, where they had initially fled eight years earlier before coming to the UK, the likelihood was that they would then have to return to family in Sudan, where the prevalence of FGM is above 85 per cent.[14] Ada was squarely in the age bracket where she was most at risk of being cut.

This was early 2019, three and a half years after the legislation that introduced FGM protection orders and a case that would test their legal limits. To the fair-minded, Daria and Ada's case seemed unarguable. Ada had lived in the UK since the age of three and spoke only English. A family court judge had already granted a protection order because of the risk of FGM. Yet, in the crosshairs of the oppressive immigration climate, all this context was disregarded. As the judge indicated his ruling at the end of the hearing we had just left, I had looked over to the Home Office team and saw them patting each other on the back. For them, deporting a family simply meant a job well done, even if it meant risking that a girl would suffer FGM. This was the system in action: cruelty by design, prosecuted with enthusiasm.

Daria first came to the UK in 2012. After her long-running asylum claim was finally rejected in 2018, she was informed that she would be deported. Refugee support workers and the National FGM Centre became involved when Ada told her teacher what was happening. The teacher reported the case to Suffolk children's services, who lodged an application for an FGM protection order. This was duly granted, and there the case could have rested, with a vulnerable child having been safeguarded. Not as far as the Home Office was concerned. From its standpoint, the family court and a local authority had no right to intervene in a way that contradicted its asylum decisions.[15] After years of austerity, it was willing to commit taxpayer money to go to court and ensure that a vulnerable mother and her children were deported after all.

Because it was an issue of precedent – if the FGM protection order could override the deportation order – the case was heard at the most senior level by the President of the Family Division, Sir Andrew McFarlane. The legal question was whether family court had the jurisdiction to tie the hands of the Home Secretary when it came to matters of immigration and asylum. It was an important case and there were lawyers everywhere you looked: barristers for the local authority made the case for the protection order it had secured; with my senior, Karon Monaghan KC, I was representing Daria; while Ada was separately represented, and two government lawyers put forward the Home Office case.

Sir Andrew McFarlane was sympathetic and praised the intervention of the local authority as 'commendable and appropriate',[16] but he concluded in his judgment that the point of law was clear. While the family court had acted properly, it had no jurisdiction to grant orders that overruled a secretary of state on these matters. All it could do was make its own findings around safeguarding and risk of harm and invite the Home Office and its tribunals to consider them. Nor, as we had argued, was the deportation order in breach of Daria and Ada's rights under Article 3 of the European Convention on Human Rights, which states that no one shall be subjected to torture, inhuman or degrading treatment or punishment.[17]

There was no question that Daria was one of the most vulnerable clients I had ever represented. She spoke no

English, was in clear distress throughout the proceeding, and a later psychological evaluation showed that she was suffering from an acute case of post-traumatic stress disorder. Despite the obvious difficulty she showed in giving evidence, she was required to take the stand and answer questions at a final hearing. While doing so, she sobbed throughout and, at one point, suffered what appeared to be symptoms akin to a panic attack. I was on edge for every moment of her short testimony, desperately uncomfortable that she was being forced to do this and incredulous at how the Home Office had treated this woman – who had seen two of her own sisters die as a result of being cut, and was now terrified that she would have to watch her own daughter suffer the same fate. At the subsequent family court hearing, Mr Justice Roderick Newton concluded: 'It is difficult to think of a clearer or more serious case where the risk to [Ada] of FGM is so high.'[18] It could not have been more obvious that this was someone who warranted protection by the state, yet it was still trying to ensure she was put on a plane and sent to a country where her daughter would not be safe. And in the face of this, the family court had no power to protect Ada.

I was not instructed to work on Daria's immigration appeal, so sadly I lost touch with her case and never found out what happened to her. But her case has remained with me, both as a symbol of the relentless cruelty of the UK government's approach to immigration and asylum, and as a reminder of what it really takes to protect women and girls from harm through the law. Seeing the very measure I had worked to introduce prove insufficient in a case of evident risk emphasised that these are truly intersectional issues: the girls most at risk of FGM also face uncertainty and discrimination concerning race, immigration status, housing, financial security and a host of other issues. In the UK, we had a series of Conservative governments talk with a straight face about protecting girls from FGM while gleefully enacting a punitive immigration and asylum system that deports those same girls to countries where their risk of being cut is severe. The work to safeguard those girls goes so much further than any law around FGM can on its own. It is only when the toxic environment itself is dismantled that meaningful progress can be made towards undoing the status quo – one in which the state shamefully abandons exactly those children who are most in need of its support and protection.

At Taylor House, the courtroom itself felt like an oasis of calm after the chaos outside, with so many people waiting to have their cases heard. The sudden quiet was a relief but also seemed to emphasise the vulnerability of Malia, my fourteen-year-old client, who would shortly take the stand in this white-walled room and be required to answer whatever questions the Home Office lawyers saw fit to throw at her.

Sometimes, sitting in the courtroom, watching opposing lawyers bombard vulnerable clients with accusations and assumptions, I have to remember where I am and stop myself from standing up to intervene too often. This was an acute example, as the government lawyers questioned Malia, accusing this young teenage girl of having a 'vested interest' in exaggerating the risks she faced. They asked if she could not protect herself from the risk of being cut and whether she just wanted to stay in the UK to have a better life. It was a reminder that no allowances are made for the age and vulnerability of girls and young women in legal situations that are already distressing. As the questions continued, Malia's answers became shorter and shorter. She looked down, unwilling to make eye contact. I was sure that she was trying to make herself disappear from a situation that felt intolerable. Not enough allowance was made for the fact that this was a girl who faced the horrifying prospect of her own genital mutilation, not to mention a separation from her sister that could go on for years. I wondered if these people had daughters of their own and what they would say or do if those girls were sitting in Malia's place right now.

Clearly, no such thought had occurred. These lawyers had their case to make, and they pressed on with no heed to humanity or circumstance. I was grateful that the judge – young, female, northern and recently appointed – counterbalanced this by showing empathy and compassion that was otherwise lacking in the courtroom. She had spoken gently to Malia, making eye contact as she explained how the proceeding would work and what would be required of her.

I then put forward our case that the West African country to which the Home Office wanted to deport Malia had a high prevalence of FGM, despite the practice having been outlawed there. Because it appeared there had never been a single prosecution for FGM in that jurisdiction, I argued that there was every reason to believe that the authorities would not intervene to protect this girl from a father who had already physically harmed her. I also made the point that was most glaring to me: there were almost no reasonable grounds under which asylum could be refused to a fourteen-year-old girl facing exactly the same circumstances as her eleven-year-old sister, whom even this government had seen fit to safeguard. I outlined what this would mean in practice: not just one child sent into harm's way but two sisters who depended on one another separated – Zola enrolled in school in the UK and unlikely to be able to see Malia again before she turned eighteen.

I sat down with the usual relief at having made the arguments I spent hours rehearsing in my head without stumbling. But I also felt disbelief that we were really here in a courtroom, with lawyers for the government trying to argue that a fourteen-year-old needed to be separated from her sister and sent back to a family who had promised to abuse her. Even knowing how the hostile environment works and having fought against it before across numerous court proceedings, I was shocked at the Home Office's approach to this case – choosing to divide a family simply to pursue its blanket policy of granting asylum to as few people as possible.

The judge summed up by saying that it was a complicated case and she would be sending on her judgment. It was an emotional moment when it arrived four weeks later, granting the appeal: happiness that Malia had been spared from the fate that deportation would have delivered her to, but also anger that we had had to fight so hard for a girl whose need for safeguarding should not have been in question, and whose case should never have gone this far. A girl in her situation should never be made to advocate for her own needs in the face of hostile questioning or be reliant on effective legal representation and an understanding judge to secure the fundamental human right of being free from torture and harm.

It summed up much of my work with FGM, which has shown me both the best and worst sides of our justice system. While there are many good intentions to protect vulnerable girls from this harm, too often those are chewed up by a political and legal machine that is so myopic in its aims that it will gladly deport at-risk girls, ignoring and trying to diminish the risk of FGM simply to tick a box and hit a target.

Researching this subject and representing clients in cases concerning it has brought me into contact with some of the bravest women I know, who have fearlessly shared their own painful histories of being cut so that others might not have to go through the same suffering they did. It has pitted me against colleagues in the law whose callous approach to sensitive cases I can scarcely believe, even as professionals who will say they are simply delivering on the brief that has been given to them.

Through my work on FGM, I learned how much can be achieved at the point where law meets politics and activism – new laws can be passed, novel legal remedies can be found for old problems, and awareness can be developed where it matters most. But I was also shown how fragile those achievements can be, and how easily undermined are the protections of the law. In the process, I internalised something that would serve me well in other aspects of my work: in the face of a system as relentless as the hostile environment, only an ongoing campaign that is every bit as determined can hope to succeed. The work to abolish FGM does not end with the statute book but must continue into every area of law, politics, healthcare and education that pushes young women and girls into harm's way. Until every vulnerable girl is protected, none will be truly safe.

My work on FGM has been a consistent feature of my career that has also summed up many of its best and worst parts. Just as I have found when working on sexual violence cases and representing mothers accused of parental alienation or child abduction, FGM has shown me that trying to bring about change in court is so often a case of one step forward, one step back. For every case you win and change to the law you effect, there is a decision that goes against a vulnerable victim, or an appeal that falls short of succeeding. The relief and satisfaction of cases won is never quite sufficient to drown out the concern about the women and girls you did not win for – who were sent back to a place where they face the risk of harm, forced into a questionable child-sharing arrangement, or told by the court that the terrible things that happened to them were not believable.

Occasionally, however, I have found myself taking cases that seem to rise above this tit-for-tat exchange of one won and another lost – where every bit of progress seems to be stalled by an example of the system's worst tendencies reasserting themselves. As my career has gone on, and I have seen the seeds planted by earlier cases influence those I am now arguing, I have done work that makes me feel I am achieving something more than making an occasional dent in the tide. It was when representing Chloe, in a case that spanned many of the issues I have worked and campaigned on – from how the court treats vulnerable witnesses and allegations of rape to the law around domestic abuse, coercive control and parental alienation – that I began to see that perhaps change really is possible.

10

Reversal:
Turning the Tide

After almost six hours of travel, time spent preparing for the case that would begin the next day, all I wanted to do was sleep. At the less-than-luxury hotel which I had booked, I arrived at the front desk to find a note redirecting me to the bar. The moment I walked in, I saw him: I could hardly have missed him, a burly figure holding a half-drunk pint of lager and an open packet of crisps in front of him, part of a sparse crowd watching football on the TV. I looked at him and for a few seconds our gazes locked.

I already knew this man disliked me: he was the ex-partner of Chloe, the woman I had come to Carlisle to represent in a fact-finding hearing. We had already won an appeal to enable this hearing to happen in the first place: now the man sitting ten feet away from me would have to spend the next few days answering allegations that he had raped Chloe, been controlling and emotionally abusive towards her, and physically abusive towards his son. His glare confirmed just how deep that dislike went, which was confirmed by his posts about me on social media, calling me a misandrist and a toxic feminist. Somehow, we had ended up staying in the same hotel – the four-day duration of the hearing that was set to begin the next morning suddenly started to feel like weeks.

This was May 2023, almost a year since I had taken on Chloe's case, and around four years since the legal battle between the two over child arrangements had begun. When she approached me directly for representation, I thought her case sounded like so many others I had done before. Her relationship had broken down, contact arrangements with their son had become fractious and disputed, and soon her ex-partner filed an application for contact that had now dragged on for several years. Although the pair had been fighting in court all this time, in essence the dispute was simple: she had made serious allegations of domestic abuse, rape, and inappropriate parenting, saying that the father's contact posed a danger both to her and the child. He retorted that Chloe had been alienating the child from him, had tried to obstruct contact, and that when it came to the allegations against him, she was exaggerating what had happened and was playing the victim to try and get her way.[1]

Another familiar part of Chloe's story was that the father's allegation of parental alienation seemed to be working. When she instructed me in 2022, she wanted to contest a series of court orders that permitted the father to have contact with their child. She felt especially aggrieved that her most serious allegations had not been properly considered during the legal proceedings so far. Although she had put statements on the record alleging that she was raped, emotionally abused and subjected to coercive control, she regularly received the response that the father's contact should continue regardless. The child's Cafcass officer had noted in several reports that 'the issue of controlling behaviour was noted . . . and not seen as a barrier to contact' and that the allegations 'should not have an impact on the arrangements for [the child] spending time with his father'.[2] In passing, the same individual blamed Chloe for having dragged out the court proceedings.

Chloe felt that the court and Cafcass had not properly heard her allegations against the father, let alone assessed their impact on her son's welfare and her own well-being, and I agreed. It seemed like a classic case where the court's pro-contact approach, and its willingness to give credence to the suggestion of parental alienation, were lining up against a mother who only wished to protect herself and her child from a man she said had done appalling things to them both. It was an all too familiar story.

As soon as I met Chloe, I had liked her and known she would be a good client to work with. When we spoke, her round, expressive face would narrate every flicker of emotion as at times she almost laughed at the absurd lengths it had taken to have her case heard, and at others was driven close to tears of frustration, flicking back strands of chestnut hair as she peppered me with details. With a mathematics background and a high-powered job, Chloe took a forensic approach to gathering and conveying information, and was aghast at how the system appeared to be taking her ex more seriously than it did her. As she said to me when our conversation turned to parental alienation: 'Where's the evidence? Where. Is. The. Evidence?'

Chloe had mountains of her own evidence, but before we could put it to the court, first we would need to win the right to appeal. At the time we first met, in spring 2022, the most recent court proceeding (in December 2021) had ordered contact with the father after denying Chloe's application for a fact-finding hearing to deal with her allegations. Fortunately for Chloe, there were numerous procedural irregularities and shortcomings in this process that gave her scope to appeal.

It was while putting together the argument for this appeal that I began to feel that Chloe's case was more than just another contact dispute between parents. In preparing a written submission like this, your job as a barrister is to make the judge's life as easy as possible: summarising the arguments and pointing them towards the relevant law, practice directions and notable cases they should consider when determining the case. As I did so, I found myself relying not on distant legal history but cases I had myself argued during the preceding years, and legislation I had contributed to.

One clear issue with the previous hearing was that Chloe had not been granted any special measures when giving evidence. I pointed the judge to the relevant sections of the Domestic Abuse Act 2021, which oblige the court to take into account the vulnerability of a witness and how this may impact their ability to give their best evidence.[3] This was the same Act where I had supported legislators including Jess Phillips MP in making amendments on the specific issue of vulnerable witnesses and special arrangements. In Chloe's case, she had contacted the court before the hearing to request that she be given a separate waiting area from her ex, and a screen that prevented her having to see him while she gave evidence. Despite this, and possibly because the date for the hearing had been moved, none of this was in place when Chloe arrived at court.[4] Compounding the issue was that no ground-rules hearing had taken place – the piece of procedure that exists to make sure issues such as protective measures for a vulnerable witness are taken into account.[5]

Mrs Justice Morgan granted our appeal on this point, and then moved on to the second ground: the fact that the judge had not heard Chloe's allegations of domestic abuse and coercive and controlling behaviour or considered their relevance to her son's welfare. In effect, the previous judge had decided that a fact-finding hearing was not necessary because the child's Cafcass guardian (their designated representative in court) had advised that the allegations were historic and '[did] not prevent safe arrangements' for contact between father and child.[6] In other words: what was the relevance of alleged rape and domestic abuse when the issue at hand was contact with the child?

In my argument on this point, I had been able to cite one of my previous cases (*Re H-N & Others*), the joint appeal I had brought before the Court of Appeal in 2021, representing Denise – the woman who had been threatened by a judge with having her child taken into care and adopted.[7] This was the case which had helped to establish that the court should be taking the issue of coercive and controlling behaviour more seriously, and that the whole point of a fact-finding is to establish whether a pattern of this behaviour exists, '*because of* the impact that such a finding may have on the assessment of any risk involved in continuing contact [with children]' (my emphasis).[8] In effect, that earlier judgment had said that the court should be doing exactly what the judge in Chloe's case had failed to do – determining whether a pattern of abusive behaviour exists, and considering in light of that whether the perpetrator of that abuse should continue to have contact with their children.

In her appeal judgment, Mrs Justice Sarah Morgan expressed surprise that no reference had been made to any of this by her predecessor, given the acknowledged importance of *Re H-N* in establishing guidance for how cases such as this should be heard, and the fact it had been recently published at the time of Chloe's hearing. She described it as a 'surprising omission' and went on to criticise the earlier judge, His Honour Judge Christopher Dodd, for having relied excessively on the Cafcass recommendation, and not having set out his own reasons for why Chloe's allegations were not fully considered.[9]

The upshot was that Chloe's appeal was upheld on both grounds. She had won the right to put her allegations before the court, and fight for the safety of her child in the way she saw fit. She was thrilled at the outcome, and I felt elated too. Reading the judgment, and the way it relied on and quoted generously from *Re H-N*, I reminded myself how I had pushed for that case to be heard – how it had come about when I was reading through the papers for Denise's case, wondering how we could secure her permission to appeal. I thought about how it had succeeded in getting the Court of Appeal to issue advice about domestic abuse cases for the first time in twenty years. Now the judgment was being used as the legal basis to allow a woman to stand up for her child's safety and her own. It was exactly what I had set out to achieve back in 2019 when I told myself that I could no longer sit back and accept the family justice system treating domestic abuse victims so dismissively. It felt like, for once, I had achieved something more than to argue the case in front of my nose, and then the next one. It felt like change.

Chloe's successful appeal had felt quietly momentous, but the real work still lay ahead of us. All we had won at this point was the right for her allegations to be heard and considered. Now she would have to go through the excruciating experience of so many women in family court, recounting the invasive details of how she was denigrated, emotionally abused, coercively controlled and ultimately raped by the father of her child – the man who was sitting in the hotel bar when I arrived the night before the hearing.

The story of how Chloe and her ex had ended up in this legal battle was extensively documented in a mountain of evidence. 'The Court bundle now stands at 6,808 pages. I have read them all,' His Honour Judge Clive Baker commented wearily at the outset of his fact-finding judgment.[10] These told of a relationship that had been through various different stages – most of them casual, with the couple never living together – but which had seemingly been defined throughout by the man's domineering, coercive and frequently violent behaviour.

Chloe alleged that his attempts to control her had begun from the moment she became pregnant, at which point she said he had tried to persuade her to have an abortion, and that he had said something about wrapping her up in carpet and throwing her in the river (he claimed this had been a joke).[11] She described an undercurrent of coercion, denigration and jokes at her expense, from making her hide when his friends visited to calling her by abusive names, posting unflattering photos of her to her social media accounts, and changing her order when they ate at restaurants.[12] In one of the many text messages between the two that were introduced as evidence, she had written to him: '[You're] so bad for me. You nit pick and have a go constantly. I'm never good enough or doing it right and to be honest I can do without it. I've never ever been in the company of anyone so critical of me . . . You batter all of [the] self worth I have out of me.'[13]

Chloe's evidence also included details of how this man had behaved in a cruel and abusive way towards their son. She alleged that he would bite the boy's fingers 'until he cried', stand on his fingers and laugh when he fell over, and that he had regularly pulled hairs from his arms and legs.[14] All of this had been on record at the time of the December 2021 hearing, yet somehow Cafcass and the court had been satisfied that this was a father who should be granted unsupervised contact with his son.

When I cross-examined the father on these points, he behaved in a manner now familiar to me when I am questioning men accused of being abusive and controlling. Just as had been the case with Andrew Griffiths when I represented Kate Kniveton against him, I was dealing with a man accused of cruel violence who seemingly had an innocent explanation for everything. He hadn't been biting his son's fingers, he said, but would put them in his mouth and 'nibble' in 'a playful way'.[15] He hadn't stood on the child's hand to hurt him, but had been playing a game 'where he would put his foot over his [child's] hand'.[16] And the time when he had been hugging his son goodbye before pushing him to the floor, resulting in a cut to his hand? That too was 'part of a game and the consequences exaggerated by [Chloe]'.[17]

He used the same narrative when trying to explain away Chloe's allegation that he had put his hands on her breastbone and moved them gradually towards her neck, 'to see how high he could get until [she] could tolerate it no further'. This too had been 'a game' and the judge noted that 'he denied receiving any pleasure from causing her to panic'.[18] Chloe's version of the same incident was that 'I have a phobia about things on my neck, I do not like it being touched. [He] thought it funny to place his hands on my neck whilst I was lying in bed until I was terrified.'[19]

When the father could not put his own spin on an allegation, he simply accused Chloe of making it up or being confused. As the judge summarised his argument at the appeal hearing: 'he submits that she has done her best to present herself as vulnerable . . . to sway the view and engage the sympathy of the court. He says that she has trawled the internet so as to see what she needs to say to achieve the desired effect.'[20] Later on, the father made it clear that he believed I was part of this conspiracy against him. While the fact-finding hearing largely took place over four days in May 2023, it also included a further day in court in July, after further evidence had been gathered. In between, the father took to social media to leave comments about the case under some of my social media posts. One of the most telling read as follows: 'False accusations in a family court against men require no proof. Toxic feminists like Dr Proudman or organisations like Women's Aid push the persecution of men and encourage women to lie and make false accusations just to get their way.'[21] I was shocked that someone would think it wise to direct these kinds of messages at one of the barristers involved in their case while it was ongoing, but not surprised to learn that Chloe's ex spoke like a men's rights activist.

The most serious of what he deemed the false accusations was Chloe's allegation that he had raped her in 2017, forcing sex on her when she had just come out of the shower and was undressed, and while their son was sitting downstairs. This was contentious not just because of the serious nature of what Chloe was alleging, but because she had introduced the allegation relatively late in this long-running case. She had first spoken about it in an interview with the child's guardian in April 2021, and gave a full statement in October that year, shortly before the hearing at which contact would be decided. Following that hearing, she had contacted the police to report the rape.[22]

Unsurprisingly, the father had responded with a series of equivocations: he told the police that they had often had sex after Chloe came out of the shower, that they had been having sex fairly frequently during this period (Chloe said this had stopped several years before) and that because the sex was regular it was 'not a standout incident'. Moreover, he asserted, 'no-one could force [Chloe] to do anything that she did not want to do' – a classic non-denial denial. She had never told him to stop (she said she did), and he considered her account of what had happened to be 'a mix of other events'. Not to mention, according to him, she 'considers everything abuse'.[23]

This was a classic 'he said, she said' – a woman who alleged with considerable detail that her former partner had raped her, telling her 'you love this', stopping her when she tried to grab her towel, and later apparently texting her to say 'you loved it. This is what you want to happen.'[24] And a man who said they had been having sex like this all the time, that he couldn't remember, she hadn't said no and anyway, he couldn't force her to do anything even if he wanted to.

I had seen this pattern in so many previous cases involving rape, and had read with despair too many judgments that sided with the easy narrative of denial: *she didn't stop me, I didn't realise, why is she only mentioning this now?* So it was with some surprise and a huge amount of relief that I read how Judge Baker had handled Chloe's rape allegation in his judgment. His assessment was a model of carefully weighing the evidence and putting all available information into the fullest possible context.

He began by considering why it had taken Chloe so long to make the allegation when she'd had 'ample and repeated opportunities' before April 2021. He noted that she had made clear in one of her statements that she felt her 'concerns . . . were being ignored' and that 'a very serious and new allegation could be an attempt to exert control on a situation that was not progressing as [Chloe] intended'.[25] Had Chloe been opportunistic in making this allegation and was she trying to get revenge?

The judge considered this, but reminded himself that almost every other allegation she had made 'has at its core a basis of truth', and that her ex had rarely been moved to deny her claims outright. Indeed, he commented that both Chloe and her ex had been largely truthful in their evidence and that 'most factual disputes related to interpretation rather than outright denial'.[26] He used this lens – of common facts and differing perspectives on them – to try and determine what had in fact happened. In their regular text exchanges, the father had often pressed Chloe for sex and she had mostly rebuffed him, though she had also sent some sexual messages to him and at times consented to sex. Because of this, the judge concluded, 'he considered [Chloe's] expressions about their relationship to be negotiable'.[27]

Based on this context, the judge attempted to reconstruct what had happened on the day Chloe alleged she had been raped. He found that, on the balance of probabilities, the father had gone upstairs planning to have sex with Chloe and expecting that she would consent, because she had before. He took the fact she was naked as 'an indication of her willingness' and carried on in spite of her 'muted' protests, which had not been more vocal because she was in shock and her son was sitting downstairs. The father had carried on, convincing himself that this was another of those occasions when Chloe had said she did not want sex before later agreeing to it. Nevertheless, Chloe 'made it clear that she did not want sex' and 'at no point did [she] consent to sex'. Accordingly, the judge found that the rape had taken place.[28]

In previous cases, I had often seen judges consider rape as if one or two of the many factors involved in such an allegation could be decisive: recall how Mary was criticised because the details of her account had varied over time, or a judge deemed it unrealistic that this 'intelligent' woman did not know precisely when she was raped. Too frequently I had seen judges struggle to grasp context, fail to take into account the pressures on women when making an allegation of this nature, and give more credence to the reasons why a rape allegation might not be true than those which suggest it may be.

By contrast, Judge Baker went to great lengths to weigh all the evidence in front of him. He showed empathy in considering why Chloe had not made the rape allegation earlier, while also considering why this might have undermined it. He was also scrupulously fair in considering the father's evidence, and ultimately presented a version of events that sought to rationalise how both of them had recalled the incident as they had. Crucially, from all this context he had pulled out clear conclusions: whatever the father may have believed or wished to believe, Chloe had not consented to sex and she had made her lack of consent clear. He had continued having sex with her anyway, and that meant he had raped her. I read this section of the judgment both relieved for Chloe, and angry on behalf of all the women I had represented who had not had the benefit of such a careful, empathetic approach to their allegations of rape. The care and precision shown by this judge should be the norm.

The finding of rape was one of several in the judgment, including that the father had done things to his son – such as pulling out hairs from his arms and legs – that 'were simply inappropriate with respect to any child and can objectively be considered abusive, albeit at the lower end of the spectrum'.[29] The judge also concluded that the father 'would engage in behaviour that would cause [the child] physical pain' because he believed it would help 'inculcate resilience and fortitude'.[30] And he found that the father had pursued sex with Chloe in a way that was 'exploitative of [her] vulnerabilities', as well as using his social media

– including posts about her, and photos taken of her without her permission – to the degree that he 'further compounded and built upon the trauma that [she] has suffered'.[31] He threw out the existing court order which granted the father contact and said that the child arrangements should be considered separately at a final hearing.

For that final hearing, the question was what approach Chloe wanted to take. The easiest thing was to make her application – what you are asking the court to order – as limited and focused as possible. After the findings against the father, an order banning him from all contact with his son was realistic. But Chloe wanted to go further: in her steady, unerring, logical way, she told me that it wouldn't be enough simply to stop her ex-partner from seeing her son. She, and he, would only feel safe knowing that the father was out of their lives for good. Not to mention, as she told the court, the stress of having to deal with her ex in some form actively limited her ability to be a good parent.[32] So we worked together on a series of applications not just to prohibit the father's contact, but to remove his name from the child's surname and to terminate his parental responsibility – the legal basis of parenthood and its associated rights.

This was not some spiteful attempt at punishment, or at exacting revenge on a man with whom her relationship had entirely broken down – indeed, at the fact-finding, the judge had specifically noted that he did not believe Chloe was motivated by revenge.[33] What Chloe really wanted was to be free from a man whose abusive and controlling behaviour – which had now been found as fact by the court – had left her devastated and damaged. As she said in her police interview, which was introduced as evidence during the fact-finding: 'He's broken me. I'm quite a smart person. Good job, nice friends. Always looked after myself. He's kinda broken that confidence or that assurance that I'm okay. I've bottled this away for years.'[34]

Chloe was in no doubt that her and her son's lives would be safer and happier if they no longer had to deal with this man, but would the court agree? While many of the father's abusive actions and behaviours had now been found as fact, an order to deny him contact and strip him of parental responsibility would go much further. It would say that there were no circumstances under which contact with his son could be considered safe or beneficial. I thought Chloe had nothing to lose by making this application, but I had no idea whether or not she would succeed. Representing Kate Kniveton, I had already seen how difficult it was to have a court order that a child's name be changed to include the maternal family name. Terminating parental responsibility (PR) was a step beyond that. Such applications are rarely made, and seldom successful. Removing PR is the ultimate interference with a parent's fundamental human right – to make decisions about their child. I did not know whether Chloe would succeed but I did believe it was the outcome in the best interests of the child.

Across the two days of the final hearing, in December 2023, I set out her case. The harm this man had done to Chloe and his son had been upheld by the court, and she had made clear that continued contact was both harmful for her and also restricted her ability to be a good parent. In turn, her son had said – in interviews with his legal guardian – that he did not wish to have any contact with his father.[35] Continued contact would be harmful, retaining this man's name would be a reminder of past traumas, and in these circumstances there was no good reason for the father to retain parental responsibility. It was notable that we could only apply for his parental responsibility to be revoked because he and Chloe had not been married – if they had been at any point, there would have been no circumstances under which this could have been taken away.

We had to wait more than a month, over Christmas and New Year, to learn the outcome. When the judgment arrived, I read it almost open-mouthed, so decisive were the findings and the arguments that supported them. All of our primary applications had succeeded: a no-contact order was made, the name-change application was granted, parental responsibility was revoked, an order was imposed preventing the father from bringing further proceedings about contact until the child turned sixteen and Chloe secured an award of costs to be paid by the father.

Just as striking as the judge's orders were his reasons. While he acknowledged the evidence of harm, and the risks that continued contact would pose, alone these might not have been enough to give Chloe the outcome she wanted. The judge also considered a compromise solution: was there a middle ground where mother and child could be protected, without the father being stripped of all his rights? He concluded that there was not, and for this he blamed the father for refusing to come to terms with his behaviour or accept the court's previous findings.

The father's written statement to the final hearing had shown that he was unrepentant, repeating the debunked claims that Chloe had exaggerated and fabricated her allegations and had alienated the child from him. He wrote that Chloe was someone 'who has openly lied and exaggerated their other accusations' and that 'I maintain my position that [she] made the rape accusation out of desperation to "win" and has convinced herself in the meantime that it happened.' Chloe, he insisted, 'regards it as an absolute that [the child] is "her ball" and I am not allowed to play . . . [she] has failed to consider or is ignorant of the damage she has caused to [the child's] emotional wellbeing and his relationship with his father.'[36] He rounded off his statement with blatant victim-blaming: '[Chloe's] stress at court proceedings is the result of her own actions and [she] has refused to take any accountability for that.'[37]

Despite everything that had transpired in court over the previous six months, Chloe's ex continued to make the same arguments as he had at the outset. In his statement, he had asked the court to order family therapy with 'sanctions in place should his mother continue to alienate [the child]'. The judge rejected this, arguing that when the father completely repudiated the mother and child's versions of events, and there was no common ground to build upon, it left 'no room for any form of therapeutic work known to this court'.[38]

He was equally firm in explaining why he had ordered the father to have no contact and no parental responsibility. It was evident, he wrote, that a continued relationship with the father would be deeply distressing for Chloe, and that this distress would also have an impact on her son. In terms of the child's welfare, after years of turmoil and uncertainty over how he was cared for – including various occasions on which the police had been called while he was present – he needed stability, for his mother 'to be able to provide him with the best care she can', free from 'distractions, traumatic triggers and emotionally exhausting issues'.[39] Ultimately, he concluded: 'The mother has proved herself entirely capable of meeting [the child's] needs. The father has not.'[40]

Reading this judgment was a cathartic experience for me. First and foremost I felt deep relief for Chloe, a woman I had come to admire, and who could now look forward to a future without having to deal with a man she said had left her feeling broken and helpless. When I had first taken on her case, I feared that she was another mother about to be dragged down the dangerous rabbit hole where the allegation of parental alienation would be used to chip away at her credibility, parental rights and personal safety. For years she had battled to have her voice heard and her concerns taken seriously. Now she had been vindicated entirely, with a judgment more comprehensively in her favour than I could have imagined.

This had been about Chloe, her son, and their lives, but for me this case was also personal. It felt like an echo of many others I had argued over the preceding years: the women whose rape allegations were disbelieved, the women who saw abusive husbands use parental alienation to gain more contact and control over their children, the women who were portrayed variously as having lied, exaggerated or been unreliable, the women who tried to protect their children but were let down by Cafcass and other child protection agencies. Bitter experience had made me fearful that Chloe would face the same fate. But through a combination of her own determination, her ex-partner's myopic approach to the proceedings and a judge who had exercised great care in considering the evidence, she had escaped that.

By doing so, it felt like she had torn down so many of the fake narratives that women encounter in the family justice system: that they make things up, convince themselves of things that are not true, act as controlling influences over their children and use the court to try and punish men they no longer like. Time and again I have seen those narratives advanced by men, and sometimes upheld by the court itself. Not this time. In this judgment, I saw the reflections of arguments I and others like me had spent years making. When Judge Baker wrote that 'the father's continued involvement in the child's life would be, for the foreseeable future, continued court-sanctioned abuse of the mother', I could almost have punched the air.[41] And again when he said the following with regard to removing the father's name: 'Each school report or medical document that arrives with the father's surname on is a reminder not only of what has happened to her but also the truth that she must come to terms with i.e. that her son is also [her ex-partner's] son.'[42]

This was a judge who had stepped into Chloe's shoes and imagined what it would be like if he ordered her to continue dropping off her child with the man who had raped her, sewing his name onto every piece of school clothing, and having his Christmas presents under the tree each year. He had understood the far-reaching emotional trauma that comes with being a victim, including the impact of the mother's trauma on the child, and he had chosen to protect both of them from it.

Chloe's case was also one of the first hearings that had

a transparency order in place, which meant accredited reporters could attend the proceeding and write about it. Indeed, a journalist and legal blogger sat through the fact-finding hearing and final hearing and various articles were published in the mainstream press. Since the decision, Chloe went on to make a highly unusual and important application – she asked the High Court to allow her to speak and write under a pseudonym about her case, in particular sharing the initial miscarriage of justice that she and her son suffered. Even though she said she would do so anonymously to prevent her son being identified, she needed permission from the family courts, otherwise any mention of the private proceedings in public could be deemed contempt of court, meaning she could be fined or go to prison. Her case marks many firsts. She is an extraordinary woman and a brilliant mother.

For much of my career working in family court, I would have thought a judgment like this impossible to achieve. But reading this one, it felt like every bit of work campaigning for victims to be treated better and heard sensitively, and every case trying to establish where and how the court had got it wrong when it comes to domestic abuse and rape, was worthwhile. It was only a single case, but it was one that showed the system can change and it can do better. It was one of the most significant and hopeful results of my career.

It came at a time when hope was something I badly needed. For while I had been fighting Chloe's case over the preceding eighteen months, I had also become embroiled in another long-running saga which would have significant ramifications for my career – leaving me wondering if I had a future at the bar. This was not in family court but concerning a case I had argued in it. It was not a hearing but a tribunal. And the client was not a woman trying to protect herself or her children. This time the person under the microscope was me.

11

Backlash:
Complaints, Abuse and Threats

I had known the man sitting opposite me since I was a pupil barrister. A senior barrister complete with pinstripe suit, pinkie ring and posh accent, he appeared every inch the Establishment figure. In fact he had, like me, come to the profession as an outsider from a working-class background. Now a consummate insider, he was about to share a secret the repercussions of which would take years to be fully felt.

He had been my mentor for years, so when he got in touch saying we needed to meet, it didn't occur to me that anything was wrong. I had barely placed our drinks down on the Caffè Nero table in Holborn, with my cavapoo Ted settling himself at my feet, when he dropped his bombshell.

'You are going to be in a disciplinary tribunal.'

'What?'

'Your tweets. You will go to a tribunal for that.'

'My *tweets*?'

I didn't need to ask what he was referring to. A few months earlier, in March 2022, the judgment had been handed down in a high-profile divorce case where I had represented the wife, Amanda Traharne (both her name and her ex-husband's, the former barrister and judge Christopher Limb, had been made public).[1] I thought Amanda had been treated poorly by the family justice system. Rather than agreeing an early financial settlement, she wished her case to go to a final hearing so that she could place on record her allegations against Limb of domestic abuse and coercive and controlling behaviour, which she said led her to being coerced into a post-nuptial agreement. A senior judge, Mr Justice Nicholas Mostyn, granted her permission to do this, but when the hearing arrived the case was heard by a different judge, Sir Jonathan Cohen, who criticised Amanda for 'prodigal expenditure on costs',[2] and wrote comments in his judgment about her, including that 'she was desperate for the relationship to work', 'the pressure that she was under was self-created' and that, 'whilst [her] psychological makeup and previous history of relationship breakups had deprived her of being able to make a rational and considered decision as to what was in her best interests, this was not caused by [the husband's] conduct'.[3]

By contrast, when dealing with the allegations against Limb, Cohen's judgment appeared to me to be lenient. Amanda said her ex-husband had sought to control aspects of her life, from when she ate to where she went, who she had contact with and how often she went to church. She accused him of trying to pressure her into drinking alcohol when she did not want to, driving recklessly to intimidate her, screaming threats of violence at her, and 'withdrawing affection' and 'sulking' if she refused to comply with what he wanted, including having sex with him.[4] She also detailed allegations of incidents where he had roughly twisted her arm after she ruffled his hair, and thrown books in the air during an argument, one of which had struck her with sufficient force that she had to go to hospital, where she was diagnosed with concussion.[5] He denied her allegations.[6]

Yet although the judge described Limb as 'reckless' regarding the books incident, and noted that he had repeatedly 'shown a temper which should have been controlled',[7] he rejected the suggestion that Limb's behaviour amounted to a pattern of abuse. '[He] has the louder voice and speaks at length,' the judge wrote. 'He loves conversation and vigorous debate. [She] on the other hand is quieter, she retreats from confrontation, and bottles things up.'[8] And in another section: 'The clear impression that I have is that this was a relationship that at times was tempestuous and that [he] would on occasions lose his temper . . . I do not accept that [she] was in fear of physical harm. There was no reason for her to be and she expressly told the police that she did not have such a fear.'[9] (This was the only, glancing, reference in the entire judgment to the police having been involved in certain events being considered.)

I was worried about the impact on Amanda of this judgment, and the way it treated the very serious allegations she had steeled herself to put before the court. It was with a sense of helplessness that I sat in the virtual meeting with her wider legal team to discuss the judgment. As voice after voice chimed in, warning about the severe costs of mounting an appeal, I desperately wished we were in the same room so I could give her a hug. The case was over but Amanda, like so many women who go through family court, would have to live with the judgment and what it had said about her for the rest of her life.

My role in the case was done, but I remained frustrated

by many of the comments that the judge had made about Amanda, and the subtext they seemed to carry: the idea that her relationship history and 'psychological makeup' had impaired her decision-making, or that the pressure she was feeling was 'self-created'. A woman had come to the court to have her allegations of coercive control heard and considered. The court had rejected her evidence, but it had also effectively characterised her as mentally unstable and lacking in judgement, and suggested she was wasting its time ('I very much regret that so much energy has been devoted to exploring this subject,' Cohen had written. 'It has also been entirely unnecessary.')[10]

It was with those thoughts in mind that I turned to Twitter (as it then was) and posted a summary of the Traharne v. Limb judgment. 'This judgment has echoes of the "boys' club" which still exists among men in powerful positions,' I wrote.

It was at this point, you might say, that the trouble began. As I had expected, my tweets were met with a chorus of criticism from the usual legal suspects, who regularly accuse me of misrepresenting the law, failing to understand my subject (including my own cases and in areas where I have helped to make the law), bringing the profession into disrepute and undermining victims' confidence in the family court. Often, these hand-wringing messages come with the sentiment that it is surely time that I was held to account by my regulatory body, the Bar Standards Board (BSB). In this instance, I knew that a formal complaint was coming because Christopher Limb's solicitor, Charlotte Leyshon, had tweeted that she was going to make one, and she encouraged others to jump on the bandwagon with her

('@twitter, do your work,' she wrote). But there had been complaints before, all of them unsuccessful.

Several months had passed since then, and I had heard nothing. I had assumed that a complaint would be made and dismissed in the usual way – thanking the individual for their concern and informing them that it would be kept on my file for future records. There was no reason to think I had gone beyond what I was entitled to say. This was not the first time a barrister had commented publicly on a judgment in this way, and I believed I was protected by changes that had been made to the BSB code of conduct, permitting barristers to express 'personal opinion' about their cases, lifting a historic prohibition.[11] After the initial backlash I had even shown my Twitter thread to a senior barrister, who laughed off the idea that my comments were actionable.

And now I was sitting in a café with one of the people I trusted most in the law looking right at me, telling me that this was serious and I had to prepare myself. Then he told me how he'd come across this information. Earlier that week, he had attended a dinner at one of the Inns of Court where I had been 'the talk of the table'. The discussion between the assembled judges, barristers and solicitors had, apparently, mostly concerned me, my tweets and whether I would be taken to tribunal. Some were desperate for me to be made an example of, while a few had supported me. But the consensus, my mentor said, had been clear. The BSB had been looking for a test case to establish what barristers could and couldn't say on social media about judges and their judgments (the BSB deny this). I was going to be their guinea pig.

If I hadn't been so shocked, I might have laughed. One of the things that had most enraged critics was my remark about the existence of a 'boys' club'. And now I was being told that a table of mostly senior men in the law had recently gathered in one of the Inns of Court to debate what should be done about me over a five-course meal and vintage wine.

Implicit in this was that one of those men was not just an interested observer but had power within the BSB to potentially decide my fate (the BSB deny this). My informant had left the dinner in no doubt about the outcome of that decision. 'They are going to make an example of you. You will get that letter through the post soon.'

I struggled to take in the full gravity of what he was telling me. Five minutes ago, I had thought we were meeting for a friendly catch-up and gossip. Suddenly, it seemed as if my career was hanging in the balance. Once the matter went to tribunal, anything could happen, up to and including a large fine or having my licence to practise suspended.

Campaigning the way I do, I know that I will attract disagreement, criticism and even abuse. For some of my peers, activism has no place in the law. They believe that a barrister should quietly represent their clients and nothing more, or that to criticise the court risks doing more harm than good (on which point we could not differ more, but it is at least a disagreement in good faith). Others appear to resent that I am a young woman with a busy legal practice and a media profile – despite the bar's stuffy dress code and arcane language, it is no more insulated from back-biting, bitchiness and professional jealousy than any other walk of life.

All this I had taken for granted and accepted. But I was

not ready for what was now coming. I hadn't considered seriously that people with an axe to grind might be able to get their agenda adopted by the regulator of my profession, a body with the power to do much more than send admonishing messages on social media.

'But they can't.'

I heard myself speaking the words, as if briefly separated from my own body. The complaint being made was one thing. The knowledge that it was being taken seriously, when it came from a source with such obvious motivations, had stunned me. I repeated the words, looking up at the face of my mentor, seeing an expression I knew so well – the mask of concern, sympathy and reassurance that a lawyer learns to wear when breaking difficult news to their client. Now I could hear my past voice too, from dozens of conversations outside courtrooms and in sterile conference rooms. *I'm afraid it's gone against us. The appeal has been denied. He is going to get contact.*

A wave of mild nausea hit me as I realised what conversation we were really having. He was on my side of the table, and I was in the client's seat, taking in the news that didn't make sense and struggling to grasp the workings of a system that seems pitted against you. So often, I had been in his chair, observing the shock and anger but not feeling it. Now I was the one who had to hear that news and to experience the sensation of stepping suddenly into thin air. It was just the beginning of learning what it is really like to be on the receiving end.

In the months and years that followed, as my tribunal grew from the figment of a bad dream into a grinding reality, with lawyers being instructed, evidence assembled and arguments prepared, my mind kept going back to one client. I thought of Michelle, the family lawyer whom I had represented through multiple appeals as she fought to have her ex-partner's abuse of her recognised by the court. At the time, she had told me that the experience of representing clients involved in protracted, traumatic legal battles was no preparation for being the subject of one. Even watching and counselling people through such a process does not allow you to understand what it is really like.

Now I knew the truth of what she had said. I discovered what it is like to carry a burden that you cannot set down, to be trapped in a cycle of thoughts that you cannot escape, however often you travel around it. I learned what it means to tell yourself late at night that you are being dramatic and exaggerating the risks and to wake up the next morning fearing that maybe it really is as bad as you think. Most of all, I found out the agony of being kept in limbo. The complaint against me was made in April 2022. In August, I received a summary of the allegations being considered and that autumn I submitted my responses. In February 2023, I was sent the decision of a regulatory panel, which referred the matter to a full disciplinary tribunal. The final hearing of that tribunal would not take place until December 2024. My life felt on hold. Now I knew why so many clients had told me that the real agony was having to wait months and years for hearings to be scheduled, evidence to be compiled and decisions to be made. How you are the system's prisoner until it finally gets around to dealing with you.

It didn't matter that many friends and colleagues tried to reassure me, telling me that it was a first offence, I would have due process and the outcome would not be too severe. I had never imagined that the complaint against me would get this far. Once bitten, I was not going to be twice complacent. And I could not get the words from that initial conversation in the coffee shop out of my head. *They are going to make an example of you.* I knew it wasn't just about the tweets I had sent or the question of where barristers should draw the line on social media. The Establishment had picked its battle and decided to send a message. There was no guarantee at all that the sanction would be proportionate.

Reading the allegations against me was enough to realise that this was a matter where proportion had well and truly been lost. One of the two claims being referred to the full tribunal was that I had 'failed to act with honesty and/or integrity, and/or failed to maintain [my] independence, and/or behaved in a way which is likely to diminish the trust and confidence which the public places in [me] or in the profession'.

Two of the tweets I had posted were cited as supporting evidence. In the first, I had written that the judgment in Traharne v. Limb 'screams of excusing the alleged perpetrator and blaming the victim. Oh, he liked vigorous debate and she was quiet – what does she expect? As if his temper and throwing things at her is permissible.' The allegation against me read: 'The tweet . . . was inaccurate in that it referred to the Respondent husband "throwing things <u>at</u>" the Applicant wife, which did not reflect the evidence or findings.'

Here is what Sir Cohen had written on this matter in his judgment: 'In March 2013 in the course of another argument, W [Amanda] threw a cup onto the floor in exasperation, whereupon H [Limb] took hold of some books and threw them in the air. One of them hit W on the head leaving an abrasion and bruise and at hospital she was also diagnosed with concussion. W agrees that the books were not thrown at her but once again, I find that H was reckless . . . he showed a temper which should have been controlled.'[12] In other words, during a fit of temper and an angry row Limb had thrown objects that had struck Amanda with sufficient force that she had required hospital treatment. Yet the important issue was that I had used the word 'at'. (Earlier in the thread, I had directly quoted the section from the judgment on this incident, which should have negated any misunderstanding.)

In a similar vein, the second tweet deemed to have been in potential breach of the code of conduct had included the words 'it was found that H [Husband] is violent and has a temper where he drinks & resorts to aggression'. The BSB charged that this 'was inaccurate in that the Judge did not find that the Respondent husband was violent or that he resorts to aggression'.

Here are some of the findings Cohen had made concerning H's (Limb's) behaviour: 'W was in bed under the bedclothes and H was sitting on the bed undressing when in frustration (as he says) he brought his hand down on the bed from on high, holding the shoe or shoes which he had just taken off. In doing so he hit W's leg which was under the covers. It was a forceful blow . . . I do not think that H intended to hit her, but he was plainly reckless in what he did.'[13]

'In March 2017 W says that she ruffled H's hair as she was walking past him, and that he then grabbed her arm and twisted it . . . I accept that it happened, but I do not find that it was the cause of any deliberate or reckless injury.'[14]

'On 25 March 2018 there was a further argument which resulted in H grabbing the duvet from the bed and marching off downstairs to sleep on the sofa leaving W naked on the bed.'[15]

'The clear impression that I have is that this was a relationship that at times was tempestuous and that H would on occasions lose his temper . . . I do accept that the arguments and H's temper during them caused her distress.'[16]

So the judge found that Limb had (perhaps inadvertently) struck Amanda with a 'forceful' blow, that he had grabbed and twisted her arm and had thrown objects which in striking her had caused her to become concussed. He said that she had been caused distress by a temper Limb struggled to control. And by describing these behaviours as 'violent' and characterising his actions as 'aggression', I had potentially committed misconduct sufficient to undermine my own integrity and that of the profession as a whole. I knew which of these claims I believed to be exaggerated.

It was not just the accuracy or otherwise of what I had written that the BSB wished to bring me to account for. It was also the tone and presumed intention of my tweets. Its second allegation stated: 'The tweets . . . viewed individually or cumulatively were seriously offensive, gender-based, derogatory, designed to demean and/or insult.' On this basis, it provisionally determined that I was in breach of its code of conduct, concerning the core duty to act with honesty and integrity, to remain independent and not to undermine public trust in the profession. The original charge cited the following excerpts from my thread:

'*I will never accept the minimisation of domestic abuse.*'

'*Demeaning the significance of domestic abuse has the [effect] of silencing victims and rendering perpetrators invisible.*'

'*This judgment has echoes of the "boys' club" which still exists among men in powerful positions.*'

'*Isn't this the trivialisation of domestic abuse & gendered language [?]*' (In reference to the judge's comment 'that this was a relationship that at times was tempestuous and that H would on occasions lose his temper'.)[17]

'*This couldn't be a clearer example of the pathologisation of a victim and the blaming of a victim.*' (In reference to the judge's comment about Amanda that 'her need to maintain the relationship eclipsed her cognitive understanding'.)[18]

'*The Judge is undermining not only W's mental health & wellbeing as a woman, but he is also throwing a Miss Havisham spin on W, as a failed unstable wife.*'

'*The Judge turns a blind eye to H's previous partner stating that H is controlling.*' (In reference to the judge's comment that Limb's ex-partner said he tried to control her, but because he seemingly did not succeed in doing so, her statement should not be considered important.)[19]

'*A misogynistic tale as old as time, the woman is failing to get what she wants so she makes dramatic allegations.*' (In reference to the judge's comment that Amanda 'has set her sights far too high [financially]'.)[20]

The language I employed in my thread may sound provocative but it was an honest personal view, as a feminist and barrister. I use social media not as a forum to debate with fellow lawyers but as a tool to raise awareness of issues about the law and family court with a wider audience. My critics argue this is simply attention-seeking, just as they seem to believe I live some glamorous life, where the reality is much more about long train journeys to stay in budget hotels and eat takeaway food out of cardboard containers, while representing clients in courts up and down the country. Whatever people choose to believe, the real reason I use social media is that I have found it is a tool for change, supporting my work in court, in Parliament and with the media. These are mutually reinforcing spheres of influence, and I have made the most progress when putting effort into all of them.

In my thread about Traharne v. Limb, the argument may have been sharply expressed. But everything in it was an honest articulation of my disagreement with the judgment – views I felt entitled to express under the protection of Article 10 of the European Convention on Human Rights, which guarantees the right to freedom of expression,[21] and the BSB's own code of conduct, which allows barristers to express personal opinions about their cases.

I believed the judgment *had* trivialised allegations of domestic abuse by favouring innocent explanations for each of the assaults Amanda had alleged and attributing the problems in the marriage to a clash of personalities. I believed it *was* fair to describe as victim-blaming how the judge had commented on Amanda's mental health, including that her 'psychological makeup and previous history of relationship breakups had deprived her of being able to make a rational and considered decision as to what was in her best interests'.[22] It *is* a misogynistic tale as old as time that women will exaggerate in order to get what they want, and the judge had given no reason for dismissing many of Amanda's allegations except to say he did not find them credible. And I *was* concerned by how the judge had declined to put Limb's alleged behaviour in a wider context, effectively dismissing the evidence of his former partner, whose allegations of controlling behaviour he dealt with in a few sentences.

These were not stand-alone criticisms intended to excoriate a single judge but examples of themes that I see too often in my work in family court, which I have written and campaigned on consistently for years. Case law is full of documented examples of how family court judges have excused the behaviour of perpetrators and used gendered language to suggest women are to blame for their predicament. In this context, my comments were not, as the BSB alleged, 'designed to demean and/or insult the judge' but to raise awareness of issues that my experience tells me are prevalent barriers to justice. I wanted to show through a real example how outdated attitudes can and do have a direct bearing on legal outcomes.

My dispute with the BSB and those who had complained about me was not just about the specifics of language. It went right to the heart of the case against me – that my comments were at risk of undermining core duty 5 (CD5) of its code of conduct, which states: 'You must not behave in any way which is likely to diminish the trust and confidence which the public places in you or the profession.'[23] I found the idea that my public criticism of a judgment could cross this threshold troubling. The essence of this allegation seemed to be that trust and confidence can only be maintained if we pretend that judges are always right, and that only fellow judges (in the course of appeals hearings) are equipped to scrutinise and critique their work. A judiciary that is open and responsive to criticism, accepting of scrutiny beyond its own garden walls, is surely one strengthened by the process and not undermined.

To put in context the allegation that I had breached CD5 of the code, I looked at other recent cases where barristers had been investigated on this basis for their use of social media. One such complaint was upheld against Anthony Bennett for messages sent to another barrister, who only later learned that the anonymous Twitter account that had been trolling him was being run by Bennett, a member of his own chambers. The tweets had accused the other barrister (who is Jewish) of being a 'lying propagandist', of believing someone 'is the wrong type of Jew', saying he had 'gone full fash propaganda' and that he was 'an absolute danger and a hater of leftist Jews'.[24]

A second example was the complaint upheld against Martin Diggins, who, in 2017, responded to an open letter published by a University of Cambridge student calling on its English faculty to decolonise the curriculum. Diggins had used a Twitter account in his own name to respond to her letter as follows: 'Read it. Now; refuse to perform cunnilingus on shrill negroids who will destroy an academic reputation it has taken aeons to build.'[25] For their respective breaches of the BSB's code, Bennett was fined £500 and Diggins £1,000.

Now, my posts critiquing and challenging a judgment were being held to the same standard as a profoundly racist message about a young Black student and a bullying campaign against a Jewish barrister for his work campaigning against antisemitism. Not only that, but as the BSB's Summary of Allegations made clear, my actions deserved to be considered at the highest level of seriousness, graded red and treated as possible professional misconduct. The sanctions facing me included a potential £50,000 fine, a twelve-month suspension of my licence of practice and an order to pay the BSB's legal costs.

As well as taking what felt like a disproportionate approach, the BSB also seemed to struggle with the issues in its own case. As part of one allegation, it accused me of 'gender critical' views in respect of my comments on the case, which implied that I hold the view that sex is assigned at birth and cannot be changed (in a case concerning two cisgendered people). I think they were trying to say that my comment about the 'boys' club' had been gender-based and offensive. When I complained, the wording was removed from the list of allegations, but I received no apology for what was a serious misrepresentation of my views.

As well as looking at cases which the BSB had pursued, my legal team and I examined those which they had not seen fit to take forward. We found multiple instances of male barristers posting derogatory comments about judges and judicial decisions on social media where no action had been taken. A cluster of these concerned His Honour Judge Robert Linford, who in July 2023 had suggested that bail should be denied to defendants who waited until the day of their trial to plead guilty, with the result that courts were often going unused despite a backlog of cases to be heard.[26]

'Hey Siri, please show me an example of unlawful conduct and abuse of power by a holder of judicial office,' wrote one barrister on X in response to this.[27] 'This is a) awful in itself; and b) unfathomably stupid,' commented another barrister.[28] 'It should be remarkable that a member of the Judiciary thinks that they can get away with issuing such a policy,' argued a third.[29] At a preliminary hearing, we argued that as a woman and a feminist, I had been held to a higher standard than numerous male colleagues, who had been allowed to call a judge stupid and said he had acted unlawfully and should be sacked, whereas my messages criticising a domestic abuse judgment had been deemed 'offensive, derogatory language'.*[30]

I didn't need to wonder if I was the only female barrister being pursued by the regulator with what felt like especial vigour in this period. A few months before my preliminary hearing, the BSB had its case dismissed against Ramya Nagesh, a commercial barrister who had been charged after falling asleep during a hearing she was attending virtually. She provided medical evidence showing she had been experiencing fatigue, sleep disorder and Covid at the time, and was cleared: her lawyers said one of the tribunal members had described the BSB's conduct of the case as 'very troubling'.[31]

If I felt there was an eagerness to bring the full weight of the profession's power down on me, I was only beginning to understand the maze I had entered. Not until I tried to make complaints of my own about the bullying and abusive messages I regularly receive from fellow barristers did I really appreciate the extent of what I was up against.

*

- *When you're screaming into the wind on a stormy night, how long does it take for people in white coats to come and escort you back to your padded room?*

---

* This was taken sufficiently seriously by the tribunal that it ordered the BSB to bring witnesses and explain why it had treated me differently.

- *What is Proudman on? If you want to be a shock jock, apply to a radio station. If you want to be a barrister, stop being a cunt.*
- *Proudman is a self-publicist who cynically uses women's suffering to promote herself.*
- *It's time she was taken down, I'm afraid.*
- *It takes a particularly monstrous ego to think that 'Do you know who I *am*?' makes you anything other than an insufferable wanker. Repellent person.*
- *I drawn [sic] to the conclusion Proudman is truly ignorant, blinded by ideology or cynically spinning this story for her own brand.*
- *Do you think that the dreadful Dr P is genuinely ignorant/confused or do you think that instead she posts this sort of tripe (knowing it to be legally unsound) in order to boost her following amongst the deplorable who lap up this sort of content? I fear it may be the latter.*

This is just a small selection of posts that have been published about me on social media. All of them were written by fellow barristers, some of them part-time judges and several of them KCs, the most eminent and high-ranking figures in the profession. Some of these senior lawyers have posted such comments anonymously (though their identities are well known within the profession) and others under their own names. A number of them have made it the habit of several years to publish derogatory comments about me – critiquing my appearance, my posts, my media appearances and my cases in a way that feels obsessional. Perhaps the most high-profile legal account on social media, The Secret Barrister, published a since-deleted post in response to one of mine that decried 'childish attempts at attention-seeking' and 'the damage that is being done to public legal understanding by self-promoting narcissists spouting errant nonsense about the law'. My original post had asked 'where's the justice?' in reference to Gary Glitter having been released after serving only half of his jail sentence for sexually abusing three schoolchildren, during which time he breached licence conditions by seeking to access the dark web, which had led to him being returned to custody. Clearly, my point was that his release in the first place had been unwarranted and unsafe. It should not have surprised me that this innocuous post led to such a strange response. By this point, I was used to how barristers talked to and about me on social media. Between them, they have seen fit to call me vicious names, to imply that I am mentally ill, to call my motives into question and to say that I am pro-rape. And these are the people who complain that I am bringing the profession into disrepute.

Having been through this cycle on seemingly multiple occasions, I now recognise every line of the chorus that is chanted against me. They start by questioning my knowledge: I am not a criminal lawyer and should not be commenting, as I sometimes do, outside my practice area. They would certainly never dream of doing so (these are mostly men with a posting history that runs into tens of thousands of comments, opining daily on a suspiciously broad range of issues). Then they deny my experiences: they have been working in court for decades and have never heard of a judge using rape myths or giving an easy ride to perpetrators. These things just don't happen. (No matter that they do, and that published judgments in my own cases attest to it.) Next, they query my motives: I can't be doing this work because I actually care about the women I represent and the issues I advocate for. It must all be a bid for media attention, for personal gain, for notoriety. At this point, having warmed to their tune, they start to mix in insults: *vile, narcissist, egotist, shrill, self-publicist, certifiable idiot.*

Soon, they are commenting on my appearance, making playground insults about my name (La Proudman, Proud-person, St Charlotte, Charlatan) and suggesting I am a phoney because I changed it in my early twenties, adopting the surname of my maternal family. And from there it is but a short trip to the inevitable destination: a full-throated blast of misogyny, reprising the greatest hits from the good old days. 'Maybe her husband ought to take away her mobile phone & send her back to the kitchen to get his dinner,' read one message in a Twitter thread discussing me. (In case my colleagues at the bar feel unduly victimised, I should make clear that one was from a solicitor.)

The abuse I can take, although it is, of course, totally unacceptable and entirely mind-boggling that senior members of the profession feel empowered to behave in this way. There is not a prominent woman in any field who isn't subjected to this treatment in some form by inadequate men who cannot accept that we exist in their professional spheres, let alone that we do so while wearing make-up, talking about our achievements and questioning their assumptions. The messages I receive in this category are hardly worth thinking twice about. The ones I do find myself rereading, getting angry about and having to restrain myself from responding to are comments that cloak their meaning in faux reasonableness – a word to the wise, a concern for the profession, the desire to 'correct the record'. These people say they do not want to attack me (and, of course, they distance themselves entirely from people who do in response to what they have written). But they wonder out loud if I am really helping the causes I profess to believe in, what my clients think about me and whether solicitors should instruct me. What do other members of my chambers make of these antics? Has anyone (i.e. an older man) spoken to me? And when is the regulator going to do something? These are the barbs that I find truly insidious: they intend not just to hurt me but to stop me; to leverage every bit of Establishment power to make me be quiet and play nicely.

I know that is the intent because when I made a subject access request to the BSB to disclose the complaints made about me, they had to send me the dozens of (anonymised) complaints that had been submitted to them by fellow barristers, none of which had met the threshold for action to be taken. One in particular summed up the inexplicable anger that I seem to provoke in some of my peers. This barrister complained that in 2021 I had written an article for the *Guardian* commenting on Kate Kniveton's case, which stated it was 'sickening and perverse' that she was being required to pay for the man who had raped her to have supervised contact with their child (splitting the costs with him 50–50). That was a matter we appealed to the High Court and won, helping to establish a 'strong presumption' against victims being expected to meet their perpetrator's costs in such circumstances. I had fought for my client, helped them to overturn an obvious injustice and contributed to case law that stands to help other women escape this kind of financial penalty. And another barrister tried to intervene and have our regulatory body declare that, in the course of this, I had committed misconduct and should be sanctioned.

It says it all that the same people who make a hobby of arguing that I don't know the law and can't do my job also kick and scream while I am winning an important case and helping to set a precedent that protects rape victims. The reality is hard to escape: there are people working at the bar who simply do not want it to change, who do not wish its flaws to be highlighted and who are willing to fight against anyone who attempts to do so.

I am certain that some of my colleagues do all this – questioning my professional abilities, my motives and my sanity – with the indulgence of the same regulator they often try to weaponise against me. When I compiled a bundle of the abusive messages I had received from over fifty other barristers, and asked the BSB to consider how they could be permissible within the code of conduct, I received, after nine months, only bland stonewalling in reply. Some of the tweets had been 'unpleasant and inflammatory', it told me, and 'would have been unpleasant and difficult for you to read'. But they had not breached the code of conduct ('I would like to emphasise that we are committed to addressing bullying, discrimination and harassment at the Bar,' their letter continued, pointlessly). At this time, I remained under investigation for my tweets about the Traharne v. Limb case, which the BSB had deemed 'seriously offensive, gender-based, derogatory, designed to demean and/or insult' – though I had used language that would not have been out of place in an appeal court. By contrast, other barristers had directed tweets at me calling me cunt, dick,

wanker, vile narcissist and friend of the rapist but had 'not
. . . breached the BSB Handbook on these occasions'. Their
Article 10 rights entitled them to scream abuse at me, while
mine apparently did not enable me to make public criticisms
of a judgment. I only wished that I could be surprised.

What other lawyers say about me and try to do to me is
bad enough. But what starts with them doesn't end there.
When senior members of my profession make abusive
comments against me, it encourages others to follow. Every
time a fellow lawyer wrings their hands about me in public
or sends a barely disguised subtweet, it threatens to open
a sewer of the worst misogynists, men's rights activists and
violence fantasists the internet has to offer. These people
hardly need an excuse, and the derogatory comments from
barristers – court experts – give them all the permission they
need to get involved. Some of the comments in response
to what lawyers have written about me on Twitter include:

- *Good thread btw. I'm debating doing some research to
  find out who this annoying cow of a solicitor actually
  is lol.*
- *Hey everybody, come look. I've found something thicker
  than this year's Boxing Day turd.*
- *Are you fucking stupid . . . you thick cunt.*
- *She seems in need of psychotherapy but in the meantime
  her personal issues are not doing her profession any
  favours.*
- *Is it a disciplinary offence to be crap and a bit loony?*

Such comments can spill over from the online sphere and

into my working life. I learned as much during Chloe's case, when her ex-partner went on Facebook during the lull in the fact-finding to post abusive messages both about and directed at me. Not long afterwards, the rapist Andrew Griffiths would make similar claims at his final hearing, suggesting I was running a campaign against him.[32] Gemma's ex-partner claimed he, too, was aware of my 'campaign'.

None of these men benefited from making me the focus of their ire in court, but I had been shaken by how the abuse I had become accustomed to receiving online was now infiltrating the courtroom. All the more because this came not long after the social media hatred targeting me had taken a disturbing turn.

By late 2022, over seven years since I criticised a solicitor for sending me a sexist message on LinkedIn and entered the public eye, I thought I had seen all the internet had to throw at me. There had been periods when I cut myself off from social media and others when I had used it intensively. On balance, I felt it was worth putting up with the abuse in return for being able to get my message out beyond the legal profession.

Then, a new account popped up. Called Rx Redpill, it billed itself as a 'men's right [*sic*] educator and activist group'. The red pill is a standard reference point in men's rights activism, deriving from the film *The Matrix*, promising to liberate the recipient and help them see the 'truth' that men are being oppressed by a liberal, feminist and female-dominated world. Rx Redpill's YouTube videos reflect this, with titles such as 'Is Feminism a Hate Group?', 'Feminism Is the Gender KKK', 'Should Men Avoid Marriage Altogether?' and 'Are Asian Men at a Disadvantage in Dating?'

Out of this ideology has grown the incel (involuntary celibate) online movement of men who define themselves by their sexual unworthiness. In place of the red pill, incels talk of the black pill – a nihilistic belief that relationships with women are impossible for them, used to promote the idea of violence against women as the necessary response. Men with professed incel ideology have committed mass murders in the UK, USA and Canada, and it is increasingly recognised as a form of terrorism – in the UK, incels made up 1 per cent of referrals to the anti-extremism Prevent programme in 2021/22.[33]

I knew this kind of misogyny existed – something more orchestrated, deep-rooted and sinister than the vast majority of abuse that is directed at me. But until I clicked on an Rx Redpill video with my name in the title, I couldn't have known how it would feel to be targeted by it. On the screen, a man appeared, dressed in a white lab coat and dark hoodie. Against the dark background, the vertical lines of green code from *The Matrix* were scrolling. The man's face was concealed behind a plastic Guy Fawkes /*V for Vendetta* mask – white with cartoonish dark eyebrows, a curling moustache and a goatee. With no preamble, a mechanically distorted voice started speaking. 'This video is directed towards the embarrassment to the legal and academic profession, Dr Charlotte Proudman.' I hit the space bar on my laptop, pausing the video. I realised that my hand was shaking and, for over a minute, I couldn't make it stop. I looked at the mask and it stared back at me. Five seconds had been enough to confirm that this was something different – a threat from a person who had gone to great lengths to appear dangerous, and was succeeding.

It had occurred to me before that an extremist might one day try to find and harm me physically – to silence me not just through professional sanctions but through the most basic expression of a man's hatred for a woman he cannot abide. This stray, often-dismissed fear now took solid form, settling over me as a weight that I knew could never be removed. The video on my screen was not someone firing off a tweet while travelling between meetings or after a few glasses of wine at home. It wasn't the spasm of a few seconds, but the work of careful planning and evolved intent. This person had singled me out and made this elaborate video for the sole purpose of letting me know they existed, that they hated me and that I should be afraid. 'You are a toxic piece of excrement that encourages violence against men,' the voice intoned once I had finally steeled myself to continue watching. 'You openly advocate for discrimination against men and female supremacy.'

A new, even deeper sewer had been opened, and I did not have to wait long to see what would emerge. Just two days after the Rx Redpill video was posted to YouTube and shared on Twitter, a reply to one of my tweets caught my eye: 'Proudman and the like are openly using Marxist techniques to drive this division. The intent has always been to create a culture war, which ushers in the cultural revolution. Hitler used the same techniques.' Another two days on, and this account's absurd abuse had turned into threats. 'Oh we're not done yet my dear . . . We're going to see you stripped of your titles. You'll be lucky to get a job in mcdonalds by the time we're finished.' Six days after that, the threat was manifested. The same account tweeted a photo at me of a man crouched in bushes, dressed in military camouflage, a helmet pulled down over his eyes, camo paint smeared over his face and a gun pointing straight out of the screen – straight at me. Forty minutes later, a message followed: 'For years, anyone who stands up for Male Victims has been stalked, harassed, doxed, our children's lives have been threatened. Those days are over . . . what you project, you receive. The difference? I'll enjoy it, and you'll panic as I inhale your last breath.'

This message was from David Mottershead, a man in his early forties from west Wales who claimed to be an ex-soldier. In 2023, he was prosecuted for harassment invoking fear of violence in relation to his social media posts targeting me. I gave evidence in court, but he was acquitted on the main charge, though convicted for possession of an illegal knife and issued with a five-year restraining order preventing him from contacting me. This was a man who had sent me a picture of himself pointing a gun and who had promised not only to kill but torture me, writing in another post: 'I'll find out your blood group so I can keep you alive long enough that you'll understand.' The judge, His Honour Judge Rhys Rowlands, merely described his actions as 'extraordinarily unwise' and commented that Mottershead 'has got issues'.[34]

Mottershead's trial and my involvement in it were an unwanted opportunity to see what it is really like to be in court as a woman trying to keep yourself safe from a dangerous man. First, I was denied the special measures I had requested, including a screen so that the defendant could not see me giving evidence, nor would I have to look at him. I had asked for these not only because of the prior death threat, but because Mottershead had then posted a subsequent video after he was charged, in which he had described me as 'one of the most notorious feminists in the UK, one of the most violent, bigoted individuals in the UK', and said that 'we are going to court, and we're going to shut this motherff . . . down'.[35]

Secondly, I had to watch as defence counsel tried to use my social media posts to smear me, including one where I had commented that an image of that year's royal coronation was 'a beautiful photograph of white male privilege and entitlement'. It was laughable to try and make this relevant to the case.

And thirdly, from the defendant and his lawyer came the minimisation – the suggestion that the posts had not been so bad, that my distress had been unnecessary and that Mottershead was not a misogynist with violent fantasies but simply a concerned men's rights activist who had never intended me to read his messages.

His Honour Judge Rowlands then directed the jury to consider that, for Mottershead to be found guilty, they must be sure that he had wanted me to see his messages, that they had led me to be in fear of violence and that this was a fear he would or should have been aware of. The verdict was not guilty. Now we had added death threats to the list of things that men were apparently free to target me with on social media. Mottershead's messages had scared me, as he obviously intended. Like so many of the experiences recounted in this book, receiving a targeted death threat like this is something you cannot fully understand unless it happens to you. It is not easy to dismiss something as the work of a Walter Mitty crank when the gun is, quite literally, pointing in your direction.

His campaign against me had also demonstrated the

dynamics of abuse on social media. Like a single cancer cell that duplicates, evolves and grows into a life-threatening tumour, online harassment has a metastatic quality. It changes its form, moves to new places and gathers pace and momentum as it spreads. Someone may begin by writing in honest disagreement about an argument I have made. The next person, egged on by their example, won't make it about my ideas or my work but about me – my supposed ignorance, false motives and lack of professionalism. The one after that abandons all pretence at argument and descends into pure insults. And the one that comes after them won't consider me as a person at all, merely a symbol of an idea they loathe, so much so that they feel empowered to say that they will torture and kill me and that they intend to enjoy it. The abuse slides downhill from the moral high ground to the depths of bigotry and violent hatred.

It wasn't just barristers and men's rights activists taking aim at me. On 15 April 2022, a Mr Philip Grimwade accused me of 'spouting drivel'. On 3 June 2022, he wrote 'Proudman is a vile narcissist . . .' in reply to a tweet by a male criminal defence barrister, about me. On 20 November 2023, Inspector Phil Grimwade was dismissed from his employment by Nottinghamshire Police and banned from policing for life for carrying out a 'deliberate and targeted' hate campaign on social media against women MPs, lawyers and police officers, which spanned six years. He was found to have engaged in misogynistic, abusive, unprofessional and gross misconduct at a police standards hearing.[36]

The worst and most disturbing harassment I have experienced coincided with the period when I was under prolonged investigation by the BSB for social media messages of my own. I was being targeted with vile abuse while I prepared my defence against the case that my criticism of a judgment had itself been offensive and insulting. When I wasn't wondering if my legal career was going to be taken away from me, I was asking myself if it was worth it. Should I keep working in the way I did, being vocal on issues which made me a target? My critics like to claim that the publicity is the point of what I do, rather than a means to the end I really seek – to make the family court a better and safer place for women and children. They argue, in effect, that I enjoy being sworn at, called mendacious and self-seeking, accused of believing things I do not and occasionally targeted by extreme misogynists who appear to wish me serious harm.

There were days when I wondered if it wouldn't be better to mind my own business and build my practice, taking the system's reward for not speaking out against its serious flaws. I considered, as I had earlier in my career, withdrawing from social media altogether. To have a nicer, quieter, safer life when I wouldn't have to read disgusting things said about me or wonder if the purposeful-looking man on the street is walking past me or towards me. For months I see-sawed between the easier life and the one I knew could make a difference.

The turning point came when I least expected it, during a conference with the KC who agreed to represent me in my disciplinary case with the BSB. I had quickly come to rely on her calm, focused and careful advice, and at one point, I couldn't stop myself from blurting out what was really on my mind.

'What do I do when this all comes out?'

She looked at me, pen raised over the page on which she had been taking notes, and gave a characteristically neat and clipped smile.

'You just carry on being you.'

It was all I needed to hear. Another of those galvanising moments in my career that has restored my energy and refreshed my desire to do what I know is right. I would not be quiet, backing down in the face of abuse. I would not give the people who harassed me the ultimate pleasure of knowing they had won.

Soon, I had written an article for *Counsel*, the bar's trade journal, detailing my experiences of harassment and showing how sadly typical this is at the bar.[37] According to the biennial survey of the profession in England and Wales, 43 per cent of women barristers have been bullied, harassed or discriminated against online. In person, women were three times as likely as men to be subjected to these forms of abuse. A majority of women of colour working as barristers (58 per cent) had experienced this, compared to 15 per cent of their white male colleagues.[38]

If my resolve needed any final strengthening, it came in the aftermath of that article, in which I wrote that it had been nine months since I'd sent the BSB a dossier of the abuse directed at me by fellow barristers on social media, and I still had not received a meaningful response. The real story soon found its way to my inbox, in the form of an email that Mr Mark Neale, Director General of the BSB, had sent to members of his team following my article. It was, he wrote, 'important that we do now communicate with Dr Proudman in response to the evidence which she submitted'. Just over a week later, I received the BSB's official response, telling me that messages from fellow barristers calling me every name under the sun had not breached the code of conduct. Nine months of inaction had seemingly yielded to an investigation conducted in the course of eight days.

Mr Neale concluded his message by telling his team to request space in the next edition of *Counsel* to regain the agenda. 'We can't just let Dr Proudman have the last word,' he signed off. This from the boss of the organisation that was supposed to be the dispassionate regulator of my profession, conducting a neutral disciplinary process concerning me. I had long feared that this was personal, and now I knew for certain. I was equally sure that I was not going to accept my fate without a fight.

12

Decision:
Three Days in Court

'You're going to drop this now, aren't you?'

My legal team could hardly keep the smiles off their faces as they came back to the conference room where I had been sitting alone. Apparently, these were the first words my senior counsel, Mark McDonald, had said to his opposite number on the BSB side. I knew his tone would have been jovial, but the message would have been equally clear. This was a different kind of law from the one I was used to, and he was a different kind of lawyer. He had wasted no time in letting the other side know that they would not be getting an easy ride.

It was the morning of the final hearing in the BSB's case against me, the first of three days that had come after several years with the threat and reality of these charges hanging over me. In a room at Gray's Inn, the kind of anonymous, fluorescent-lit space in which I had spent so many days of my working life, three tribunal members would sit in judgment on my career.

When I'd met up with my lawyers earlier that morning, in a Caffè Nero just up the road from the branch where I had first learned about the charges against me, the anxiety in my stomach was offset by the thought that the waiting was finally over. I was lucky that I even had a legal team behind me. Less than a week before, Mark's co-counsel, Monica Feria-Tinta, had not been due to occupy the seat she was about to fill. Then, as I left a meeting on the Strand the previous Thursday, in darkness and with the rain hammering down, my phone screen had lit up. It was my lead barrister, who I had been working with on the case for months: he was incredibly sorry, but his ongoing trial had overrun and would not be finished in time for Tuesday morning. Just five days before the most important hearing of my career, half of my legal representation had vanished into thin air.

These situations are not uncommon, and one option is to apply for an adjournment – to have the hearing delayed on account of unforeseen circumstances. But as I looked out onto the grim winter scene, huddling under my umbrella, I knew that I could not bear to wait a day longer. It was now thirty months since the BSB had first presented its allegations against me: two-and-a-half years to think about the consequences for my career, reputation and finances if I lost this case. Almost a thousand mornings for me to wake up wondering what the day of my tribunal would finally bring. Anything was better than more waiting. If it really came to it, I would represent myself.

Without waiting to find somewhere warm or dry, I called my solicitor, Manveet Chhina, and Mark. And then I remembered Monica. An internationally respected lawyer in fields including free speech, environmental litigation, human rights and arbitration involving sovereign nations, she is also experienced in tribunal and regulatory cases. We had emailed and spoken a little about some aspects of my case, but it was months since we had discussed the looming tribunal. As I dug her number out of my inbox, I knew it was a long shot that she could help me. There was as much chance she was in the middle of a complex international case in The Hague as she was sitting in her chambers office in London.

When she answered, I knew that there was little else to do but beg and hope. 'Monica, I am calling you in a state of crisis and despair. Please, please will you represent me.' Although I had to strain over the noise of the traffic and the falling rain to hear it, her voice was reassuring. She would try and move some things around and call me back. When she did, it was with the news I had been desperate to hear. She could represent me, working alongside Mark. Within an hour, I had both lost and found a legal team.

Now we had several long days and nights to finish preparing my case together. I had already committed countless hours to this, working with my lawyers to draft skeleton arguments and witness statements. My own statement and exhibits stretched to over 100 pages, and when I received the BSB's response I was astonished to find that it was more than seven times as long.

For months, I stole hours at the beginning and end of each day and at weekends to do this work while I maintained a full caseload. Even as someone accustomed to long periods sat in front of a screen, digesting and drafting texts, this process started to feel like a form of torture. One series of papers would simply spawn another; one set of responses would receive answers that posed even more questions and required extra evidence to be chased down.

As I sat, read and typed, the stress of the process knotted itself through my body: first my shoulder started to ache, then my neck and finally my back. With each keystroke the vice that was gripping me seemed to close a little tighter. So bad had the pain become that I took a steroid injection in my shoulder the week before the tribunal, worried that it was about to become immobilised.

I spent all this time stuck in what felt like a closed loop, doomed either to be working on my case or thinking about it. When I could no longer bear to sit with the consequences of having the charges against me upheld, I would immerse myself in a corner of evidence, a page of my witness statement or a detail of case law as a distraction. And when I had stared at the screen for so long that the words were no longer making sense, I would close the laptop and be banished back to my thoughts. I was as terrified about the outcome of the case as I was desperate for this purgatory to be over.

As we traded paper back and forth, I kept coming across new things to dumbfound me. One came when, in early 2024, I was told that the BSB had appointed Philip Havers KC as the judge to oversee my case. An anonymous informant suggested I check his entry in *Who's Who*, which showed that he was a member of the elitist, all-male (as it then was) Garrick Club. Flicking the pages of the book, I turned to the entry of Sir Jonathan Cohen, the judge whose words I had got into all this trouble for tweeting about. It confirmed, as I already knew, that he too was a member. The absurdity of the situation spoke for itself: one judge and member of an exclusive men's-only club was about to rule on whether I had written things that were derogatory and offensive about another judge who was a member of the same exclusive men's-only club. And one of the things he would be deliberating was my comment that Cohen's judgment 'had echoes of the "boys' club" which still exists among men in powerful positions'. Even though there was no suggestion the pair had discussed the case, I submitted an application to Philip Havers KC that he must recuse himself from the case because of the potential conflict of interest, which he then did.

The following month, Sir Jonathan Cohen was listed as the judge in an appeal hearing where I was representing the rape victim. I requested that he be recused on the basis of his Garrick membership, both because my client felt he might be biased against her on account of his being part of a male-only club and because one of the participants in the case had also been a frequent visitor to the Garrick. Another judge granted my application. It felt like a tacit admission that perhaps there was a boys' club after all, and that it might represent a problem for the judiciary.[1]

Around the same time, I was involved in the successful campaign to have the Garrick open its doors to female members after over 190 years.

By the time my final hearing arrived in December 2024, I had been wallowing in the case for so long that I no longer knew what I thought was going to happen. Whereas my senior counsel, Mark McDonald, was fresh to the case and infectiously confident. He proved to be exactly the advocate I needed. He was what might be called a characteristic criminal barrister: more minded to pick up the phone for a reassuring chat than to sit down and draft a position statement. As he said, there were thousands of pages of evidence and argument in this case and he had certainly not read them all. He also had trouble remembering the name of his co-counsel, given they had only just met, and kept asking me to remind him as we made our final preparations that morning. When we at last sat down in the tribunal room, I glanced over at his notepad, expecting to see the bullet points of his opening statement. The only thing he had written down was Monica's name.

Mark may not have been in command of every detail – he was almost cartoonishly deflated when I pointed out that he could not stand to deliver his opener, because in a tribunal everyone sits – but he was ebullient, assured and had grasped perhaps the most important element of the whole case: its overblown and disproportionate nature. It was bordering on the absurd that our professional regulator, which every barrister helps to fund through annual fees, had committed so much time, energy and money to prosecuting me for a series of tweets that had avoided exactly the kind of personal attacks and unparliamentary language that other barristers regularly used against me without sanction. The costs involved had been made very apparent to me just days before this hearing, when the BSB sent me a schedule detailing the £38,000 it had spent on barristers' fees in my case – using the eve of the tribunal to hammer home what I would be liable for if I lost. It felt, yet again, like bullying.

That morning, with costs, charges and career consequences on my mind, I was a mess of anxiety and nerves. Mark, by contrast, seemed to regard the whole thing as faintly humorous. He was in tune with the almost surreal atmosphere that morning, which became apparent as I walked into Gray's Inn with him, my legal team and partner. Each step along the cobbles felt like more of an effort than the last. I wanted to turn back, to run and hide from this thing that had been bearing down on me. The grey sky and icy wind seemed to be telling me that nothing good could happen that day. And then I heard it: a rhythm that I soon recognised as words. 'Witch hunt, witch hunt, witch hunt.' As we rounded the corner, I saw that we were not the first people on my team to have arrived. Around a dozen people were gathered with a megaphone and placards. 'Double Standards Board,' one read. 'Blatantly Sexist Board,' said another, in colours mimicking the BSB's own logo. Out of the corner of my eye I saw little groups of barristers, wigged and gowned, stopping to view the unusual scene, one or two to take photographs. I wondered how many protests there had been in the six and more centuries where lawyers had gathered and worked here.

I looked at the faces and saw Florence, whom I had represented as a fifteen-year-old, with her mother, both holding placards. There were people who had been my clients, and who had come from as far as Edinburgh to show their support. Mostly women but also some men whose relatives I had helped. There were even faces there I didn't recognise at all. On the day the future of my career would be decided, I now had some of the people who had been part of it standing alongside me.

When we moved inside and settled into our first-floor conference room, the chanting from outside could still be heard as we ran through final preparations. Then the clerk came in to ask how many people we needed seats for in the tribunal room. As we ran through the list, Mark interjected:

'Don't forget the placards.' Momentarily taken aback, the clerk recovered to offer a smile. 'We haven't got enough room for the placards. But if we did, they could come in too.'

The protestors may have lightened the mood, but there was no escaping the heavy reality of the tribunal. Ever since I had first read the allegations against me, I had been thinking about this day and playing through different scenarios in my head. Like every case I am part of, I had mentally prepared statements, questions and answers, trying to anticipate the moves of opposing counsel and the interventions of judges. Usually this is a process of days or weeks, and I am in the box seat, asking and answering the questions. This time I had been chewing over the case for several years, but I had almost no agency over what was going to happen. I was at the centre of the hearing yet relegated to being a spectator. I had almost no idea what Mark was going to say or how the judges were going to respond to the arguments before them. On the most important day of my life, I felt powerless.

We filed into the tribunal room quietly, the jokes forgotten and the protestors now silent. Behind us were windows looking out across the quadrangle, the last autumn leaves strewn over lawns that I always imagined to be pristine. Then the blinds were drawn and only a sliver of daylight was left. The judges took their seats and there was no longer any avoiding what was to come.

'Accept or deny?'

The English language has a wonderful diversity of expressions for the simple act of saying yes or no. In a criminal court, a defendant pleads guilty or not guilty. In the House of Lords, peers declare themselves content or not content with the motion before them. And in a professional tribunal, as a respondent you either accept or deny the charges in front of you. Five were being read to me, and five times the question was put. Five times I heard myself saying the word 'denied'.

I had wanted to maintain my composure, but even at this early stage it cracked. After so much immersion in the details of the case, there was something almost shocking about hearing the charges presented bare – those thousands of pages stripped down to their essence. Even though I knew each charge off by heart, the words thudding down one after the other – *misleading, misconduct, derogatory, seriously offensive* – made me feel like I was hearing them for the first time. Even before the clerk had completed reading the second of the five charges, I had started crying. I was grateful that the tribunal chairman, His Honour Judge Nicholas Ainley, picked up on my distress and stepped in to speed up the reading of the remaining charges, so that only the salient points were read out and I could respond.

Then came Mark's opening statement, in which he set out some of my career history, putting my tweets about Traharne v. Limb into the context of years in which I had been advocating on behalf of women in both the family court and the wider legal system. It made me smile when he recalled how I had campaigned to have women represented on the walls of the Great Hall of Lincoln's Inn – one of my early efforts at feminist advocacy at the bar – and the 'great disturbance' this had caused. It was a reminder of how far I had come in my work, but also of the common threads that connected it. So too was the fact that some of my former clients had come to support me and were sitting almost next to me in the row of chairs that passed as a public gallery. They were close enough that one was able to hand me a tissue when I started to cry as the charges were read.

Despite the detailed arguments that had gone back and forth as the BSB and I exchanged witness statements, my defence was premised on a simple case: in making my comments, I had been exercising my right to freedom of expression protected under Article 10 of the Human Rights Act and the European Convention on Human Rights. It was Monica who had emphasised to me that this was first and foremost an Article 10 case, and who made those arguments to the tribunal. I had been exercising my rights to freedom of speech as a feminist, expressing views which are protected by UK law. Moreover, despite the BSB's case that I had misled the public about what was in the judgement, as she pointed out, most of my tweets had been not statements of fact but of opinion.

To have the charges upheld, the BSB would need to prove that I had exceeded what is permissible under Article 10 and 'lost' its protection. It was a simple question that should not have taken several years and thousands of pages of argument to resolve. I was quietly reassured that in his demeanour and early interventions, Judge Ainley seemed to concur that the case was a fundamentally straightforward one, in which the primary task was to establish where the line should be drawn between protected speech and professional misconduct.

Equally reassuring was my sense that the BSB was not in full command of its case or the evidence it had sought to marshal in its favour. In bringing the charges against me, it had considered my Article 10 rights and deemed that I had exceeded them with my comments. One of the authorities it had relied on was the case of Morice v. France, concerning a lawyer who had previously been convicted of defamation in French courts after his criticisms of a judge were published in a newspaper. But when his case came to the European Court of Human rights, it ruled that this process had violated his Article 10 rights and awarded him damages.[2] The BSB pointed to a section of the judgment that stated a lawyer's freedom of expression must be circumscribed by 'the usual restrictions on the conduct of members of the Bar . . . [whose] rules contribute to the protection of the judiciary from gratuitous and unfounded attacks'.[3] In addition, the case had stated that 'lawyers cannot . . . make remarks that are so serious that they overstep the permissible expression of comments without a sound factual basis, nor can they proffer insults.'[4]

Yet a close reading of Morice v. France showed that it added more to my case than it did to theirs. The ECtHR judges had stated that 'it is only in exceptional cases that restriction . . . of defence counsel's freedom of expression can be accepted as necessary in a democratic society'. They had emphasised that 'a high level of protection of freedom of expression . . . will normally be accorded where the remarks concern a matter of public interest . . . in particular, for remarks on the functioning of the judiciary'. And they had underlined that 'save in the case of gravely damaging attacks that are essentially unfounded – bearing in mind that judges form part of a fundamental institution of the State, they may as such be . . . subject to wider limits of acceptable criticism than ordinary citizens'.[5]

In other words, this case had established that there were

quite wide parameters for a lawyer to make public criticisms of a judge, especially when doing so on a matter of public interest. To demonstrate that I had overstepped the bounds and lost my right to freedom of speech, the BSB would have to show that I had made 'gravely damaging' and 'essentially unfounded' attacks in the course of my tweets.

It was not the first time that the BSB appeared to have misconstrued case law or evidence in its eagerness to push forward with the charges. First it had got into a muddle over gendered language and gender critical views, accusing me of the second when it meant the first. Things got stranger still at a preliminary hearing, where my team argued that it was discriminatory that I should be charged for my tweets when male barristers who had posted abusive messages about me using terms such as 'cunt' and 'wanker' had not been. If cunt was such an offensive word, the BSB's lawyer retorted, how come she had found several uses of it on my Twitter feed? This was true, though the difference between a man hurling the term as an insult and a feminist using it in an empowering way ('We're all cunts and bloody proud,' I had written) should not have been hard to discern, especially given this lawyer was a woman and feminist. Mark McDonald made exactly this point to her prior to the tribunal, in his own inimitable way. 'I used to wear a T-shirt that said, "Paki and proud". Would you wear that?'

It was on the second day of the hearing that I felt the BSB had really started to clutch at straws. It introduced a number of cases to illustrate where lawyers and other regulated professionals had exceeded their right to freedom of speech and been sanctioned. One of these was the case of Martin Diggins, the barrister who had been fined £1,000 for a disgusting tweet targeting a young Black woman, which had made reference to 'shrill negroids'.[6] Another was the case of a doctor whose registration had been suspended by the General Medical Council for publishing videos that promoted bizarre conspiracy theories about the Covid pandemic.[7] A third was the case of a barrister, Forz Khan, who had his practising certificate suspended after spreading rumours that another barrister had stalked and raped a woman and threatened to kill her to cover it up (the length of his suspension was reduced on appeal).[8] While all three cases had contained discussions of Article 10 protections and their limits, it seemed bizarre to have my relatively tame criticisms of a judge's ruling on domestic abuse put on a par with such extreme and disturbing examples. As it had with Morice v. France, the BSB appeared to be saying my case was similar where it suited their argument and different when it did not.

Way back when I was first notified about the charges being considered against me, I had reviewed the Diggins case as an example of a barrister who had been found guilty of the same conduct breach as was being alleged against me (to 'diminish the trust and confidence which the public places in you or the profession'). To me, the comparison made obvious the disproportionate nature of the charges being brought against me. I could hardly believe that I was now sitting in a tribunal hearing, listening to the BSB argue that my case and his were in some way equivalent.

I was not alone in this view. Judge Ainley interjected at one point to comment, regarding the Khan case, that 'the background facts were wildly different from what we're dealing with here. And it might be said wildly different in their seriousness.' One of his two 'wingers' on the three-person panel, the barrister Naomi Ryan, pointed out another inconvenient truth for the BSB. Diggins had been reprimanded and fined £1,000, a relatively low-level sanction, despite the shocking nature of his comments. Did that help to explain, she asked, where the threshold should be drawn between protected speech and misconduct? In other words, to prove its case did the BSB not have to show that my tweets had been at least as bad as those which had used racist language to bully a young woman of colour?

After all this time and effort to prepare its case, the BSB had made its best arguments and at least two of the three decision-makers appeared unconvinced. There had even been audible laughter when its lawyers, Aileen McColgan KC and Leo Davidson, argued that I had misled people when I wrote that Limb had thrown the books 'at' Amanda, when the judgment had merely said that he threw books in the air and they had struck her. In that fleeting moment, a little pressure seemed to drain out of the room. Without uttering a word, someone had pointed their finger and called out that the regulator had no clothes. People were finally seeing that the BSB had waged a multi-year campaign against me in no small part because of my use of a two-letter preposition. Laughter increasingly felt like the apt response.

When I went home that night, I felt confident enough to begin drafting a statement in the event of the BSB's case being thrown out. Even then, I checked myself and tried to keep preparing for any outcome. On the basis of the evidence presented, the case seemed clear, and the judges had been tipping their hands through their interventions and questions. Yet I reminded myself that one of the most dangerous games a barrister can play is to second-guess the judge. I have seen enough examples of where the judge will appear to be going against the lawyer whose case they are ultimately going to side with – whether to test their own assumptions or make a show of neutrality. This ordeal was grinding to a conclusion, but victory was not yet in the bag.

Fortunately, I did not have to wait long on the third day before Judge Ainley delivered his summation. A few minutes into this, he began reading out the tweets that were at the heart of the case: a single social media thread which had led to a case that encompassed hundreds of hours, thousands of pages of documentation and tens of thousands of pounds in legal costs. Hearing these fateful words being narrated in the judge's steady, slightly clipped tones was an oddly reassuring experience. Had it really all been about this? About me writing that I could never accept the minimisation of domestic violence, that there was a boys' club among men in powerful positions, that my client had been pathologised as mentally ill and victim-blamed, and that the judge had turned a blind eye to important evidence about Limb's character and behaviour as an intimate partner? Were these sentiments so serious that they risked undermining the very profession whose seemingly solid walls surrounded us as we sat in Gray's Inn? Had it been worth all that time and money to make their point?

And after all this, had they even made out their case? Judge Ainley calmly declared that they had not. 'The tweets, insofar as factually inaccurate at all, are so only to a minor degree,' he concluded. 'But certainly in our judgment, not to the extent necessary to found a charge of lack of integrity.' Had I gone beyond what freedom of speech permitted me to say as a legal professional? 'We do not consider that she has lost her Article 10 protection by reason of anything that she wrote.' Had I undermined the profession or the public's trust in it? Here the judge unleashed his howitzer, a line picked up in almost every media report of the case. 'These tweets would not have been pleasant for any judge to read . . . these remarks may even be thought to be hurtful. But they are not gravely damaging to the judiciary. We take the view that the judiciary of England and Wales is far more robust than that.'

And with those seventeen concluding words he dismissed a case which had occupied almost three years of my life. As suddenly as this nightmare had begun during that cosy chat gone wrong in Caffè Nero, now it dissipated. I knew I was experiencing something I had often seen my clients go through in court, where months and years of anxious waiting have finally given way to vindication, but they are not yet ready to believe it. They appear dazed, ask you to repeat the conclusion back to them and struggle to take it in. It is a state of disassociation where the body has not yet caught up with what the brain knows to be true – one form of comprehension not keeping pace with the other, much as we see the lightning of a storm before we hear its thunder.

There were hugs, some more tears, and I went outside to give a statement to the media, hardly conscious of what I was saying. Nothing really settled in my mind until I woke up the next morning with the familiar pocket of tension in my stomach. And then I remembered that it was over. I had spent my last late night worrying about this case and the last early morning slogging through paperwork on it. I no longer had to worry about the impact on my career.

I had won. It was only as this thought took solid form in me, spreading warmth where for endless months there had been fear, that I realised the pain in my shoulder had gone.

In the days and weeks that followed the dismissal of the charges against me, I felt relief in many forms. Relief that spoke through a body no longer contorted and twisted with tension, meaning that I could, quite literally, move freely again. Relief that the threat to my career was gone: there would be no fine, no suspension, no lasting mark on my reputation. But most significantly, the relief was that I was now free to fight on.

The BSB had made this whole issue about me and my alleged misconduct, and for several years I was forced to focus inward, justifying and defending myself against charges which the tribunal eventually deemed to be unfounded. But my real battle, as it always had been, was about the legal profession and the family justice system, and how women and children are treated within them. I had taken to social media in the first place following the Traharne v. Limb case not in a fit of pique but because I thought it illustrated an important point. I knew from experience how many women have experienced something like Amanda Traharne did – not only having their allegations dismissed but also their character brought into question. As the cases in this book have shown, it is sadly too common for women not only to be disbelieved by the justice system but in the process discredited, left feeling desperate and broken by the things that have been said about them.

From early on in my career, I have known that to change this we must expose it. Of course, there are many cases where the system functions well, treats victims appropriately and delivers justice fairly. But there are still too many instances when that is not true. The lesson of my career has been that we must highlight those problems, we must bring them to public and political attention and we must endeavour to fix them. Without relentless focus, flaws are simply left untreated. When the Harm Report commissioned by the Ministry of Justice was published in 2020, it revealed serious issues in how the family court handled domestic abuse cases and a widespread loss of confidence among victims. In 2024, when Cafcass published a new policy on domestic abuse, its chief executive was moved to apologise, saying: 'I am sorry that some four years on from the Harm Panel report, there are still children and adults in family court proceedings who do not receive the protection they deserve and require.'[9] This was putting it mildly, but made an important point: in a secretive and insular system, the alarm must be sounded loudly and regularly for change to happen. Progress can never be taken for granted.

If the BSB had succeeded in upholding its charges against me, it would not just have been hugely damaging to my career and reputation. I believe it would also have sent a message that anyone wishing to challenge the legal establishment over its failings regarding women, domestic abuse and child contact would be doing so at the risk of their career. It would effectively have been saying that the hurt feelings of judges should be taken more seriously than the ruined lives of women and children who have had their allegations dismissed or been ordered to have regular contact with a man who is known to be abusive.

Once the sheer relief of being cleared had dissipated,

I was able to appreciate that my tribunal hearing had reinforced some important principles. One was that the judiciary is indeed robust enough to absorb some criticism. And the second was that legal professionals should have an expectation of significant free speech protection when speaking about issues in the public interest, such as how the courts handle cases of domestic violence.

The BSB had arranged an entire tribunal process that had ultimately upheld my right to do the kind of advocacy I do, in the way I choose to do it. It had helped to validate how I interpret my professional duty as a barrister: not just to represent clients in court to the best of my ability, but also to highlight examples of injustice that I observe within the system, striving to make the system work better for the future victims of domestic abuse, coercive control and rape, and for the children of abusive households whose whole lives can be upended at the stroke of a judge's pen.

The BSB, and the barristers who brought complaints against me to it, had wanted to stop me. It had sought to send a message. But the one that was returned said something quite different. It said that criticism is justified, as long as that criticism is grounded in fact and not gravely damaging to the judiciary. It affirmed that free speech matters, including for people who are telling harsh truths to a world that is unused to wider scrutiny. And it upheld that the walls of the system would not come crumbling down because a woman in her thirties had sent some tweets.

Undermining that system has never been my aim. I am proud to work within it, for all its flaws and my frustrations with them. It was what I wanted to do from the day I first sat in court and watched a young female barrister on her feet. I know many dislike how I go about criticising the system and trying to change it, but I hope that most of my peers would agree that the principle of fighting for the law to be better, and the freedom to try and achieve that, matters. My work is just one small part of that, in one corner of a set of institutions that hold sway over tens of thousands of lives every year, including many vulnerable women, children and victims of appalling abuse.

My battle against the BSB ended in vindication. It also helped to bring my career back to where it started – speaking up in the face of many people telling me it would be wiser to stay silent. When a solicitor sent me an unsolicited sexist message in 2015, while I was still a very junior barrister, the easy course would have been to let it pass. By making my response public, I brought a torrent of criticism on myself from the media and within the legal profession. But it also helped to earn me a platform to keep speaking on these issues, to highlight injustices and to advocate for change. My experience at the hands of the regulator led to much the same result: while it made me doubt myself when the storm was fiercest, by the end I was proud of myself for standing my ground. I was more determined than ever to use my voice to make a difference.

That determination is based on the knowledge that there is still so much work to be done – fighting for women like me to be present in the profession so we can help women whose needs are too frequently ignored and whose stories are too readily brushed aside by the family court. I do it because the people who rely on that work to live without fear often have no voice. And the people who wish to defend the status quo speak with deafening force.

I keep going because I am constantly reminded of how sexism and misogyny are everywhere in the legal profession, even when you are in situations and with people where you feel safe. When the online harassment of me was at its worst, I sought the advice of a male barrister I had known since my early days at the bar. During a friendly drink in his home when his wife was upstairs, my emotions got the better of me. I cried as I recounted some of the worst things other lawyers had written about me on social media. 'Oh sweetie,' he said, then he stood up, hugged me and put his hands on my waist until they crept down to my bottom. It was sexual assault – taking me back over a decade to the taxi where a male barrister's hand had moved from his court papers and onto my thigh. I left and never spoke to him again. I wish I had been braver in the moment. I wish I had said something, anything. I wish I had slapped him. I wish I had screamed. But like so many victims, I stayed silent.

My journey through the law and the family court has shown me both how deep-rooted sexist attitudes and actions are, and how painstaking the work to address them must be. I have learned that you can only change the system one step at a time, by exposing a flaw and fighting for a victim of it until that person, and that problem, can no longer be ignored. It is slow, agonising work, which the system fights and resists at every turn – denying that the problems exist, pleading that they are impossible to solve, playing for time or trying to discredit the person attacking it.

But I, and many others like me, do that work because at the heart of every case are people who rely on effective representation and whose futures may hinge on what the court decides. Women who are trying to escape the legacy of an abusive relationship and to protect their children from abusive and violent men. Children who wish to have a say about which parent they live and spend time with, who are at risk of being sent back to an abusive household or to a parent who intends to mutilate them in the name of tradition. Some of my clients end up staying in touch for years, sharing updates as their children grow up. A few have gone on to train as lawyers themselves.

So many cases end in outpourings of emotion because the people in them are so vulnerable – worried about what may happen and reliant on the court to ensure their safety and well-being. I have lost count of the number of hearings that have ended either with the client hugging me, out of sheer relief, or with me having to console them because they are distraught at the outcome and have no idea what they will do next. I have seen too many women leave the family court in a state of bleak despair, not yet comprehending what has happened to them or what their life will now look like. Women who know that they must share the care of their children with the man who beat or raped them. Or even, who realise that they must now go back into a household with that man as their only option to protect the children.

Like any barrister, I have had my share of wins and losses, some successes against the odds and other setbacks where I could hardly credit the outcome. But it is the losses that remain with you. Not just the existence of them but the manner – judgments that excoriated the women in them, penalised them for not having behaved differently in the aftermath of a serious sexual assault, questioned their motives for having brought forward allegations of abuse or lined up behind a damaging narrative that she was lying, exaggerating or had turned the children against their father.

For every advance we have achieved in getting the law and the family court to protect women, it seems there is another judgment around the corner that will base itself on rape myths, blame a woman for the abuse they suffered or refuse to recognise a woman as a victim of domestic abuse and coercive control because she appears composed and is professionally successful.

More broadly, there are times when it feels like progress is being made – the 2020 MoJ Harm Report, which crystallised many of the issues facing women and children in family court, the 2021 legislation that created a statutory definition for domestic abuse encompassing coercive control and the wider sense of momentum towards combating sexual violence against women in the aftermath of #MeToo. But there are also many occasions that make you feel like nothing has changed – when a court tosses special measures onto the bonfire, professionals indulge in victim-blaming or use arguments that imply misogynistic stereotypes as old as time. When a fellow member of my profession sends abusive messages to me and our regulator decides that they have a right to free speech that apparently extends to gender violence. When you read about yet another case where a barrister has had to be reprimanded for inappropriate sexual behaviour towards a younger woman. Sometimes it seems that however many battles those of us who want change are winning, we are still losing the war.

At these times, I have to remind myself that the law can and does change. We have shown that through the campaign to raise the legal age of marriage, preventing girls under eighteen from being coerced into unwanted marriages. Through the introduction of FGM protection orders that have helped to prevent hundreds of girls at risk of being cut from being taken out of the UK for that purpose and the criminalisation of virginity testing and hymenoplasty. Through the precedents that say that women should not be expected to pay for men who raped them to have contact with their children; that women living in refuges should not be at risk of having their location disclosed to the men who abused them; that judges should consider making professional bodies aware of findings of serious abuse perpetrated by one of their members; that abusive and dangerous men cannot hide behind the privacy rights of their children to escape scrutiny.

Those protections will not always be sufficient, and there are still so many more that are lacking. But you can only change the law through the law – updating statutes, introducing case law and changing the attitudes of the people who are responsible for interpreting them. A barrister can only fight the battles put in front of her, represent the clients she is given and attack one injustice at a time.

I don't know how long it will take to achieve change that feels meaningful and lasting. I don't know how realistic that goal even is. But I do know that there will continue to be women who come to family court, having already been through a worse ordeal than most of us can imagine. They will show unbelievable courage to fight their case, do what they can to protect their children and even try to help other women who will face similar circumstances. Those women deserve advocates. They deserve fairness. They, above all, deserve change. Every week of my working life, it is women like this who inspire me, each of them a reminder that it is never a good time to stop fighting for a cause you know to be right.

As the second-wave feminist activist and US lawyer Florynce Kennedy said, 'You've got to rattle your cage door. You've got to let them know that you're in there, and that you want out. Make noise. Cause trouble. You may not win right away, but you'll sure have a lot more fun.'

Acknowledgements

This book encapsulates over a decade of advocacy on behalf of women and children, a journey that has been possible only through the unwavering support of an extraordinary network of survivors and professionals. These individuals have long championed the rights of victims and fought for legal and policy reforms. My work is one small piece of a larger movement dedicated to transforming the justice system for women and children. Throughout the numerous cases I've handled, I've relied on the wisdom and guidance of others, whose insights have helped shape my approach and strengthen my arguments. Although barristers often work independently, I have been fortunate to be part of a community unified by a common goal of justice. It is through our shared efforts that progress is achieved.

Thank you to every mother who has fought to protect her child from domestic abuse within family court proceedings and undergone the pain of re-traumatisation.

Thank you to the judges, legal professionals, social workers, therapists and experts dedicated to safeguarding survivor parents and children from the lasting damage caused by domestic abuse.

Thank you to my agent, Adam Gauntlett, and my

publisher, Jenny Lord, for believing in me and supporting my effort to highlight the systemic problems in the family justice system through this book.

I would like to express my deepest gratitude to:

Dr Adrienne Barnett, whose lifelong devotion to reforming family law for women and children has achieved significant milestones. I am truly thankful for your intelligence, patience and kindness, which have had a profound impact on my work and life. Your contributions have set the stage for important changes that will benefit many.

Natalie Page, I am immensely thankful for your boundless energy and fearless approach to cases. Your campaigning has been invaluable, and I am proud to work with you in pursuing change.

Dr Rachael Grey and Bo Grey, whose strength and remarkable courage have continually inspired me throughout my journey. Your story serves as a powerful reminder of the importance of perseverance.

Dr Elizabeth Dalgarno, for your commitment to victims, regardless of the obstacles, I am sincerely grateful for the passion you bring to this cause. I am thankful for the knowledge and perspective you have shared.

Kate Kniveton, a survivor of domestic abuse and the family court system. Representing you in the family court and witnessing you advocating for other survivors (as an MP and now former MP) was an honour. Your bravery in reforming the presumption of parental involvement with an abusive parent is inspiring, and I am pleased to have been part of your journey.

Thank you, Apsana Begum MP, for your courage and resilience in facing personal and legal challenges. I'm grateful you entrusted me with your case, resulting in your ex-husband's removal from the Labour Party. Your belief in justice, fairness and the rights of marginalised people inspires my work every day.

Dr Leyla Hussein OBE, Hoda Ali and everyone working to end FGM in a generation are an inspiration, leading the fight with determination. Special gratitude goes to the survivors who have shared their stories with extraordinary courage, ensuring their experiences will protect and empower others.

Anthony Metzer KC, a mentor for nearly a decade, you have taught me to embrace my true self and shown me that feminism and the law can indeed coexist. I value your guidance and the example you set as both a legal professional and a champion of women. Your influence has been instrumental in shaping my approach to campaigning and legal practice. Thank you to Roderick Johnson KC and to Goldsmith Chambers.

Dr Ann Olivarius KC (Hon) OBE, a trailblazing lawyer and a true hero. You paved the way for me and countless other women in law, breaking barriers and reshaping the field. Thank you for all you've done to advance justice for women across Britain and America.

Professor Catharine MacKinnon, thank you for your contributions to feminist legal theory and for showing the ways women are subordinated under male dominance in society and law. Your work changed my career trajectory.

Dexter Dias KC, whose vocation to justice and human rights is admirable. I am thankful for your guidance, which has been invaluable in my journey as an advocate for women and children.

Thank you, Baroness Helena Kennedy LT, KC, FRSA, HonFRSE, for leading the way for female barristers and breaking barriers for future generations.

Helen Pankhurst CBE, a feminist icon and ally. I am thankful for your encouragement and the strength you have lent to this movement, and to me.

Louise Tickle, a journalist of unparalleled courage and integrity who dares to speak truth to power. I am deeply grateful for your campaigning for a transparent family justice system.

Hannah Summers, a journalist whose work is crucial in holding the justice system accountable. You have shone a light on issues that others might shy away from.

Claire Waxman OBE, relentless in your efforts to transform the family justice system. Your leadership has been a source of hope for many in the movement for reform.

Dr Jessica Taylor, whose groundbreaking work on the pathologisation of victims has influenced my understanding of trauma. Your work has reshaped how I represent clients in the family courts. Your friendship and support, along with Jaimi Shrive's, have been invaluable.

Dr Emma Katz, for educating people on coercive and controlling behaviours and how they affect children and mother–child relationships. Countless mothers know their realities are valid, and they are not alone, thanks to you and your work.

Jolyon Maugham KC, thank you for relentlessly fighting the good fight despite all obstacles – and showing that change can be achieved.

Felicity Gerry KC, thank you for your exceptional support and collaboration on our work to end FGM. Your expertise and dedication to advocating for justice in this critical area have made a significant impact.

Allison Quinlan, whose wisdom and camaraderie have been a source of strength as we've navigated the difficult terrain of the family courts – and shared a mutual love of animals.

Manveet Chhina, you are a true kindred spirit and fellow disruptor in the family courts and beyond. Your friendship has been a source of strength and comfort. I'm especially thankful to you for representing me against the Bar Standards Board (pro bono).

I am immensely grateful to Monica Feria-Tinta, Mark McDonald, Alison Padfield KC, Sophie Belgrove and Simon Clarke for the hundreds of hours of work in the case against the Bar Standards Board – exemplifying faithfulness to defending women's voices in the legal profession.

Jess Phillips MP, Rt Hon. the Baroness Harman KC, Jessica Asato MP, Ellie Reeves MP, Sarah Champion MP, Dame Vera Baird DBE KC, Stella Creasy MP, Alex Davies-Jones MP, Dr Marie Tidball MP, Tonia Antoniazzi MP, Anna McMorrin MP, Rt Hon. Louise Haigh MP and the Rt Hon. the Baroness Royall of Blaisdon, for your advocacy for victims. Your work is making a difference inside and outside the courtroom.

Reem Alsalem, United Nations Special Rapporteur on Violence Against Women and Girls: thank you for your vital support and speaking up for me when I was silenced. I will always be grateful for your advocacy on behalf of mothers and children across the world.

Thank you to everyone at Latin American Women's Aid. It has been a privilege to represent the women you support, and I am in awe of the way you've gone above and beyond for them.

To those championing victims: your never-ending work drives essential change and saves women's and children's lives. Thank you.

Finally, to my family and friends, thank you for your love, support, and for always pushing me to keep going. I am endlessly grateful to my Mum, Aviv, Kathryn, Sarah, Heather, Freya, Christabel, Rachel, Elisabeth, Lera, Eve, Claire, Natalae, Tali, Anneka, Michelle, Christine – and, of course, to Ted, who remains my top priority. Your support has been the foundation upon which I build my work, and I am forever thankful.

Notes

Introduction

1   Tessier, A. (2023, September 6). 'What do we know about adults in private law proceedings?' Nuffield Family Justice Observatory. https://www.nuffieldfjo.org.uk/resource/what-do-we-know-about-adults-in-private-law-proceedings-spotlight-series.

2   Office for National Statistics (2023, November 24), 'Domestic abuse victim characteristics, England and Wales: year ending March 2023'. https://www.ons.gov.uk/peoplepopulationandcommunity/crimeand justice/articles/domesticabusevictimcharacteristicsenglandandwales/ yearendingmarch2023.

3   Ministry of Justice (2024, July 11), 'Diversity of the judiciary: Legal professions, new appointments and current post-holders – 2024 Statistics'. https://www.gov.uk/government/statistics/diversity-of-the-judiciary-2024-statistics/diversity-of-the-judiciary-legal-professions-new-appointments-and-current-post-holders-2024-statistics.

4   *X (A Child)* [2022] EWFC 177. [51, 96].

5   See *Griffiths v. Griffiths (Guidance on Contact Costs)* [2022] EWHC 113 (Fam) (20 January 2022) in which I represented Kate Kniveton MP (formerly Griffiths) https://www.bailii.org/ew/cases/EWHC/ Fam/2022/113.html.

6   Part 1, Section 3, 2(a) of the Domestic Abuse Act 2021 defines children as victims of domestic abuse when they see or hear or experience the effects of the abuse between parents (Domestic Abuse Act 2021). https://www.legislation.gov.uk/ukpga/2021/17/section/3/enacted.

7   'The weight of evidence from both research and submissions suggests that too often the voices of children go unheard in the court process or

are muted in various ways. The panel found that a significant number of children who have experienced domestic abuse are not consulted on their views and experiences during the court process.' Hunter, R., Burton, M., & Trinder, L. (2020). 'Assessing Risk of Harm to Children and Parents in Private Law Children Cases', p.67.

8 Women's Aid, 'Nineteen Child Homicides' (Bristol: Women's Aid, 2016) p.17. See also the case of Ellie Butler, a six-year-old murdered by her father after being returned to his custody: https://www.bbc.co.uk/news/uk-england-london-36587103; see 'Call for inquiry into abusive parents' access to children' (2019) at: https://www.bbc.co.uk/news/uk-48230618.

9 'Assessing Risk of Harm', p.51.

10 *Griffiths v. Griffiths (Guidance on Contact Costs)* [2022] EWHC 113 (Fam).

11 *Re Z (Disclosure to Social Work England: Findings of Domestic Abuse)* [2023] EWHC 447 (Fam) (2 March 2023).

12 *Re B-B (Domestic Abuse: Fact-Finding) (Rev1)* [2022] EWHC 108 (Fam).

13 *Re GB (Parental Alienation: Factual Findings)* [2024] EWFC 75 (B) (28 March 2024).

14 *Re H-N and Others (children) (domestic abuse: finding of fact hearings)* [2021] EWCA Civ 448.

15 *M v. S* [2023] RG21PO1079, *D v. R* [2023] EWHC 406 (Fam), *CM v. IP* [2022] EWHC 2755 (Fam), *B v. P* [2022] EWFC B18, *GK v. PR* [2021] EWFC 106, *K v. L and M* [2021] EWHC 3225 (Fam) and *A (Domestic abuse: incorrect principles applied)* [2021] EWFC B30.

16 *M (A Child: Private Law Children Proceedings: Case Management: Intimate Images)* [2022] EWHC 986 (Fam) (29 April 2022).

17 This was part of a group effort by leading NGOs and individual campaigners including: Payzee Malika, whose sister, Banaz Mahmod, was killed in a so-called 'honour killing'; Karma Nirvana, IKWRO, Forward, Girls Not Brides, Natasha Rattu, Baroness Liz Sugg, Pauline Latham MP.

18 Hall, R. (2024, October 8). 'Family court judges use victim-blaming language in domestic abuse cases, finds AI project'. The *Guardian*.

https://www.theguardian.com/law/2024/oct/08/family-court-judges-victim-blaming-language-domestic-abuse-cases-ai-project; Stavrou, A. (2024, August 16). '"It's not like you were beaten": The horrifying misogyny vulnerable women face from the judge's bench', the *Independent*. https://www.independent.co.uk/news/uk/home-news/family-court-judges-misogyny-domestic-abuse-b2595125.html.

19 'Assessing Risk of Harm to Children and Parents in Private Law Children Cases', p.47. Also see: Lens, Vicki. 'Judging the other: The intersection of race, gender, and class in family court.' *Family Court Review* 57.1 (2019): 72–87.

Chapter 1. 'Where Are You From?': Becoming a Barrister

1 McKinney, C. (2021, September 29). 'Competition for pupillage fiercer than ever, Bar Council report finds'. Legal Cheek. https://www.legalcheek.com/2021/09/competition-for-pupillage-fiercer-than-ever-bar-council-report-finds.

2 Bar Standards Board. (2023, September 20). 'Part 2: Code of conduct – Bar Standards Board'. https://www.barstandardsboard.org.uk/static/fod114af-9c5a-4be4-9dbffa9f8ob1e47f/8c50a665-79ee-4bfa-b36eb5c138798d72/Part-2-Code-of-Conduct18092019092228.pdf.

3 University and College Admissions Service. (n.d.). 'Keele University: Stats'. UCAS. https://www.ucas.com/explore/unis/5e07e833/keele-university/stats?studyYear=current ; Winton, A. (2021, May 26). 'Gender and Food Retailing'. Alliance Manchester Business School – AMBS. https://www.alliancembs.manchester.ac.uk/original-thinking-applied/original-thinkers/gender-and-food-retailing/.

4 Williams, M., & Pike, G. (2021, September). 'Barristers' Working lives 2021: A report for the Bar Council'. https://www.barcouncil.org.uk/static/26ee23c9-1e90-41e4-995806b353babb7e/Barristers-Working-Lives-report-2021.pdf.

5 Webber, A. (2019, May 15). 'Four in 10 female lawyers experience sexual harassment'. Personnel Today. https://www.personneltoday.com/hr/female-lawyers-sexual-harassment/; Simmons, R. (2018, March 1). 'Revealed: Biggest survey shows scale of sexual harassment in law'. The

Lawyer. https://www.thelawyer.com/metoo-lawyers-sexual-harassment-survey-2018-2/. Bullying, harassment and discrimination at the bar is a 'systemic' problem, the Bar Council said, with 44 per cent of barristers saying they have experienced or witnessed it in the past two years. The Bar Council. (2023, December 7). 'Bullying, harassment and discrimination at the bar 2023'. https://www.barcouncil.org.uk/resource/bullying-harassment-and-discrimination-at-the-bar-2023.html.

6 Ibid. p.18.

7 Rose, N. (2019, March 18). 'Barrister reprimanded and fined for "unwanted sexual conduct"'. Legal Futures. https://www.legalfutures.co.uk/latest-news/barrister-reprimanded-and-fined-for-unwanted-conduct.

8 Rose, N. (2021, January 28). 'Barrister who smacked colleague on bottom "thought she was consenting"'. Legal Futures. https://www.legalfutures.co.uk/latest-news/barrister-who-smacked-colleague-on-bottom-thought-she-was-consenting.

9 Bar Standards Board. (2023, July 19). 'Mr Robert Michael Kearney. Past disciplinary findings'. https://www.barstandardsboard.org.uk/disciplinary_finding/183646.html.

10 *Kearney v. Bar Standards Board* [2024] EWHC 924 (Admin) (29 February 2024).

11 Vine, S. (2015, September 10). 'SARAH VINE: If a man can't compliment a woman, the human race is in deep trouble'. *Daily Mail Online*. https://www.dailymail.co.uk/debate/article-3228538/SARAH-VINE-man-t-compliment-woman-human-race-deep-trouble.html.

12 Belam, M. (2015, September 11). 'A four hour window into the storm of abuse "feminazi lawyer" Charlotte Proudman faces on Twitter'. Medium. https://medium.com/@martinbelam/a-four-hour-window-into-the-storm-of-abuse-feminazi-lawyer-charlotte-proudman-faces-on-twitter-b654f5fa36ce.

13 Elgot, J. (2015, September 10). 'Barrister faces "career suicide" for exposing lawyer's sexist remark'. The *Guardian*. https://www.theguardian.com/law/2015/sep/10/barrister-career-suicide-exposing-lawyers-sexist-remark.

14 Weale, S. (2018, February 5). 'University of Cambridge admits

significant sexual misconduct problem'. The *Guardian*. https://www.
theguardian.com/education/2018/feb/05/university-of-cambridge-
significant-sexual-misconduct-problem.

15 Ailes, E., & Furst, J. (2019, May 15). 'Call for inquiry into abusive parents' access to children'. BBC News. https://www.bbc.co.uk/news/uk-48230618.

16 *JF v. MF* [2020] EWHC 86 (Fam) [37].

17 *C v. D* [2020] EWFC 83 (High Court Judges). [78–84].

18 Fouzder, M. (2020, February 6). '"Training is not enough": Family lawyers target Tolson over "outdated" views on consent'. *Law Gazette*. https://www.lawgazette.co.uk/news/training-is-not-enough-family-lawyers-target-tolson-over-outdated-views-on-consent/5103011.article.

Chapter 2. The Flip of a Coin: Meet the Judge

1 *Re H-N and Others (children) (domestic abuse: finding of fact hearings)* [2021] EWCA Civ 448. https://www.judiciary.uk/wp-content/uploads/2022/07/H-N-and-Others-children-judgment-1.pdf; [94–5].

2 Ibid. [68].

3 Ibid. [98].

4 Idem.

5 Ibid. [92].

6 *Re H-N and Others (children) (domestic abuse: finding of fact hearings)* [2021] EWCA Civ 448. [93]. 'The judge went on to ask with whom "the child" lives and was told that it was the mother. It was at this point that the judge said that "if this goes on the child will be taken into care and adopted". Unsurprisingly, the mother became deeply distressed and can be heard crying on the tape.'

7 Ibid. [96].

8 Ibid. [84], [110].

9 Ibid. [110].

10 Ibid. [82–3].

11 Hunter, R., Burton, M., & Trinder, L. (2020). 'Assessing Risk of Harm to Children and Parents in Private Law Children Cases', pp. 39–40. [Also published through the Ministry of Justice at https://assets.

publishing.service.gov.uk/media/5ef3dcade90e075c4e144bfd/assessing-risk-harm-children-parents-pl-childrens-cases-report.pdf.]

12 *Re H in Re H-N and Others (children) (domestic abuse: finding of fact hearings)* [2021] EWCA Civ 448. [119].

13 *Re L (Contact: Domestic Violence)*; *Re V (Contact: Domestic Violence)*; *Re M (Contact: Domestic Violence)*; *Re H (Contact: Domestic Violence)* [2000] 2 FCR 404; [2000] 2 FLR 334.

14 I was instructed to seek permission to appeal out of time in three of the mother's appeals in *Re H-N and Others (children) (domestic abuse: finding of fact hearings)* [2021] EWCA Civ 448. including *Re T*, *Re H*, *Re B-B*. At the substantive appeal hearing, I represented two mothers in the cases of *Re H* and *Re B-B*.

15 Cafcass, Rights of Women, Women's Aid, Welsh Women's Aid and Rape Crisis England & Wales, Families Need Fathers, and the Association of Lawyers for Children; Proudman, C. (2021). 'Analysis of the Historic Court of Appeal case on the Family Court and Violence against Women'. Centre for Women's Justice. https://www.centreforwomens justice.org.uk/analysis. Lady Justice King of her own motion said at a case-management hearing that FNF should be invited to intervene, presumably so the 'fathers' voices' could be heard in a domestic abuse case where *all* of the complainants and victims were mothers. Like other 'father's groups', FNF has also been accused of engaging in upsetting and targeted attacks of women.

16 *Re T in Re H-N and Others (children) (domestic abuse: finding of fact hearings)* [2021] EWCA Civ 448.

17 Ibid. [169].

18 Proudman, C. (2021, May 31). 'Modernising the Family Court on domestic abuse'. *COUNSEL.* https://www.counselmagazine.co.uk/articles/modernising-the-family-court-on-domestic-abuse.

19 The appeal in the individual case of *Re H-N* was allowed but the appeal in *Re T* was refused.

20 *Re H-N and Others* [51].

21 Mr Justice Cobb's judgment in Denise's case: *Re B-B (Domestic Abuse: Fact-Finding)* [2022] EWHC 108 (Fam).

22 Ibid. [50].

23 *Re B-B (Domestic Abuse: Fact-Finding)* [2022] EWHC 108 (Fam). [63], [64], [82]i.

24 Ibid. [65–66].

25 Ibid. [65].

26 Idem.

27 Ibid. [66].

28 Ibid. [95].

29 Ibid. [36].

30 Ibid. [66].

31 'Dr Proudman's use of the term "gaslighting" in the hearing to describe this conduct was in my judgment apposite; the father's conduct represented a form of insidious abuse designed to cause the mother to question her own mental well-being, indeed her sanity.' Idem.

32 Duignan, B. (2024, January 4). 'Gaslighting'. *Encyclopedia Britannica*. https://www.britannica.com/topic/gaslighting.

33 Ibid. [69].

34 Ibid. [65].

35 Ibid. [79–80].

36 Ibid. [78].

37 Ibid. [68], [90].

38 See Practice Direction 12 J; Reporting Watch Team. (2017, September 24). 'Domestic Abuse – revised guidance issued – what does it say?' The Transparency Project. https://transparencyproject.org.uk/domestic-abuse-revised-guidance-what-does-it-say/.

39 *Re B-B (Domestic Abuse: Fact-Finding)* [2022] EWHC 108 (Fam). [98].

40 Ehlers, A., & Clark, D. M. (2000). 'A cognitive model of posttraumatic stress disorder'. *Behaviour Research and Therapy*, 38(4), 319–45.

41 *Re B-B.* [42].

42 Ibid. [37].

43 Ibid. [82].

44 Ibid. [97].

45 The judge wrote: 'I am satisfied that she was truly intimidated by the family court process, and in all likelihood carried with her considerable distress from her earlier experience of a family court hearing (August

2019) in which the judge threatened the removal of her child, and whose utterances essentially founded her successful appeal to the Court of Appeal.' *Re B-B* [38].

46 Ministry of Justice. (2023, July 13). 'Diversity of the judiciary: Legal professions, new appointments and current post-holders – 2022 Statistics'. GOV.UK. https://www.gov.uk/government/statistics/diversity-of-the-judiciary-2022-statistics/diversity-of-the-judiciary-legal-professions-new-appointments-and-current-post-holders-2022-statistics#fn:27.

Chapter 3. Unsafe Spaces: Fighting Domestic Abuse

1 See *A (Domestic abuse: incorrect principles applied)* [2021] EWFC B30. *Re Z (Disclosure to Social Work England: Findings of Domestic Abuse)* [2023] EWHC 447 (Fam) (2 March 2023). *Re Z (Disclosure to Social Work England: Costs)* [2023] EWHC 982 (Fam).

2 *A (Domestic abuse: incorrect principles applied)* [2021] EWFC B30 [25].

3 Ibid. [11], [22].

4 Ibid. [15], [17].

5 Ibid. [21].

6 Domestic Abuse Act 2021, Section 1 (1).

7 Domestic Abuse Act 2021, Section 3.

8 I represented Women's Aid, Latin American Women's Aid (LAWA), Refuge, and was instructed by Rights of Women (ROW) in a landmark case introducing guidance to prevent service of court orders on women in refuges: *Re P (Service on Parent in a Refuge)* [2023] EWHC 471 (Fam).

9 *A (Domestic abuse: incorrect principles applied)* [2021] EWFC B30 [25].

10 Ibid.

11 See Rule 3A and Practice Direction 3AA, Family Procedure Rules.

12 *A (Domestic abuse: incorrect principles applied)* [2021] EWFC B30 [21].

13 Ibid. [22].

14 Ibid. [15–20].

15 Goodman, M. (2021, August 23). 'Agony of fighting for my child in

the courts . . . by a family lawyer: In a candid account, a lawyer reveals how – when she found herself in her clients' shoes – it almost destroyed her'. *Daily Mail*. https://www.dailymail.co.uk/femail/article-9916813/Agony-fighting-child-courts-family-lawyer.html.
16 *A (Domestic abuse: incorrect principles applied)* [2021]. [16].
17 Ibid. [18]. See *R (Children)* [2018] EWCA Civ 198 for source of HHJ Ahmed's statement at [18].
18 Ibid. [21].
19 Ibid. [9].
20 Ibid. [25].
21 Ibid. [22].
22 Ibid. [28].
23 *Re Z (Disclosure to Social Work England: Findings of Domestic Abuse)* [2023] EWHC 447 (Fam). [8].
24 Idem.
25 Ibid. [48].
26 Ibid. [49].
27 Ibid. [65].

Chapter 4. Abuse of Power: Griffiths v. Griffiths

1 'Mr Andrew Griffiths MP: Resolution letter: Letter from the Commissioner to Mr John Anderson, 3 September 2019'. https://www.parliament.uk/globalassets/documents/pcfs/not-upheld/andrew-griffiths-not-upheld.pdf.
2 World Health Organization. (2021, March 9). 'Devastatingly pervasive: 1 in 3 women globally experience violence'. https://www.who.int/news/item/09-03-2021-devastatingly-pervasive-1-in-3-women-globally-experience-violence.
3 'Call to action as VAWG epidemic deepens', National Police Chiefs' Council, 23 July 2024, via https://news.npcc.police.uk/.
4 *Griffiths v. Griffiths* [2020], Case NO: DEI900318. [4.4], [6.14].
5 Tickle, L. (2022). 'A finding of rape'. Tortoise. https://www.tortoise-media.com/audio/a-finding-of-rape/.
6 *Griffiths v. Griffiths* [2020]. [6.1].

7 Ibid. [6.14].

8 Ibid. [6.5], [6.8].

9 Ibid. [4.4], [6.8], [6.14].

10 Ibid. [6.14], [6.18].

11 Ibid. 'Schedule of findings', pp.17–21.

12 Ibid. [6.25].

13 Ibid. [6.5], [6.14], [6.34].

14 Ibid. [6.1].

15 See: *Griffiths v. Griffiths (Decision on Recusal)* [2021] EWHC 3600 (Fam); *Griffiths v. Griffiths (Guidance on Contact Costs)* [2022] EWHC 113 (Fam); *Griffiths v. Tickle* [2021] EWCA Civ 1882; *Tickle v. Griffiths* [2021] EWHC 3365 (Fam); *Griffiths v. Griffiths* [2020] DEI900318.

16 *Tickle v. Griffiths* [2021] EWHC 3365 (Fam).

17 Tickle, 'A finding of rape'.

18 *Tickle v. Griffiths* [2021] EWHC 3365 (Fam) [23].

19 Halliday, J. (2018). 'Tory MP who sexted women says he was having manic episode'. The *Guardian*. https://www.theguardian.com/politics/2018/nov/04/tory-mp-andrew-griffiths-who-sexted-women-says-he-was-having-manic-episode.

20 *Tickle v. Griffiths.* [25].

21 Ibid. [26].

22 Idem.

23 Ibid. [22].

24 Reed L. (2021), 'Griffiths v Tickle – a lawyer's view'. https://transparencyproject.org.uk/griffiths-v-tickle-a-lawyers-view/.

25 Ibid. [38], [45].

26 Ibid. [52].

27 Ibid. [21].

28 Ibid. [28].

29 *Griffiths v. Tickle* [2021] EWCA Civ 1882.

30 Tickle, 'A finding of rape'.

31 *Griffiths v. Griffiths (Guidance on Contact Costs)* [2022] EWHC 113 (Fam).

32 'Assessing Risk of Harm to Children and Parents', p.175.

33 *Griffiths v. Kniveton & Anor* [2024] EWHC 199 (Fam) [50].

34 Ibid. [47].

35 Ibid. [31]. 'The M gave evidence behind a screen and was very upset during parts of her evidence. I had no doubt that her emotions were entirely honest . . . She plainly found the whole process deeply upsetting, and indeed traumatising.'

36 Ibid. [63].

37 Ibid. [52].

38 McFarlane, A. (2023). 'The Transparency Reporting Pilot Guidance from the President of the Family Division'. https://www.judiciary.uk/wp-content/uploads/2023/01/The-Reporting-Pilot-Guidance-26-1-23.pdf.

39 Reporting Watch Team. (2024, January 12). 'Reporting pilot expanded across England'. The Transparency Project. https://transparencyproject.org.uk/reporting-pilot-expanded-across-england.

40 *Hannah Summers & Anor v. Kristoffer Paul Arthur White & Ors* [2024] EWFC 182. [7–9].

41 Ibid. [21].

42 Summers, H. (2024, September 14). 'Father who is convicted rapist stripped of parental responsibility for daughter'. The *Guardian*. https://www.theguardian.com/society/2024/sep/14/father-who-is-convicted-rapist-stripped-of-parental-responsibility-for-daughter.

43 Summers, H. (2023, August 31). 'Family Court Files: Mother "Devastated" After Rapist Father Granted Contact With Child'. The Bureau of Investigative Journalism. https://www.thebureauinvestigates.com/stories/2024-08-31/mother-devastated-after-family-court-granted-rapist-father-contact-with-child/.

Chapter 5. Double Standard: Rape and Sexual Violence

1 *X (A Child)* [2022] EWFC 177 [13], [93].

2 The Bar Council. (2023). 'Cab Rank Rule: Statement of the Four Bars'. https://www.barcouncil.org.uk/resource/cab-rank-rule-statement-of-the-four-bars.html.

3 *X (A Child)* [13], [89–90].

4 Ibid. [51].

5 Ibid. [44].

6 Ibid. [50].

7   Ibid. [51], [53].

8   Ibid. [54].

9   Ibid. [55].

10 Ibid. [44], [49].

11 Rape Crisis England & Wales. (2023, December). 'Rape, sexual assault and child sexual abuse statistics'. https://rapecrisis.org.uk/get-informed/statistics-sexual-violence/.

12 Crown Prosecution Service. (2021, May 21). 'Rape and Sexual Offences – Annex A: Tackling Rape Myths and Stereotypes'. https://www.cps.gov.uk/legal-guidance/rape-and-sexual-offences-chapter-4-tackling-rape-myths-and-stereotypes.

13 *X (A Child)* [2022] EWFC 177 (Fam) [57].

14 Ibid. [58].

15 Crown Prosecution Service, 'Rape and Sexual Offences – Annex A'.

16 Rape Crisis England & Wales. (2023, December). 'Rape, sexual assault and child sexual abuse statistics'. https://rapecrisis.org.uk/get-informed/statistics-sexual-violence/.

17 Ibid.

18 Ibid.

19 *X (A Child)* [2022] EWFC 177 (Fam) [70].

20 'Approximately 75% of women who are killed by their batterers are murdered when they attempt to leave or after they have left an abusive relationship.' Ganley, A. L. (n.d.). 'Domestic Violence'. Domestic Abuse Shelter, Inc. https://domesticabuseshelter.org/domestic-violence/.

21 *X (A Child)* [2022] EWFC 177.

22 Ibid. [96].

23 Crown Prosecution Service, 'Rape and Sexual Offences – Annex A'.

24 *X (A Child)* [2022] EWFC 177.

25 Ibid. [88].

26 Ibid. [87].

27 Crown Prosecution Service, 'Rape and Sexual Offences – Annex A'.

28 Ibid. [97], [103], [100], [112], [113], [118].

29 Ibid. [93].

30 Ibid. [79].

31 *A & Anor v. B & Ors* [2022] EWHC 3089 (Fam) (2 December 2022).

32 Ibid. [19].

33 Ibid. [26].

34 Ibid. [29].

35 Ibid. [124].

36 Ibid. [126].

37 Ibid. [123].

38 *JH v. MF* [2020] EWHC 86 (Fam), [36].

39 Levitt, A. (2013). 'Charging perverting the course of justice and wasting police time in cases involving allegedly false rape and domestic violence allegations'; Flatley, J. (2017). Crime in England and Wales: year ending June 2017. 'Crime against household and adult, also including data on crime experienced by children, and crime against businesses and society'; Lee, G. (2018, October 12). 'Factcheck: Men are more likely to be raped than be falsely accused of rape'. Channel 4 News. https://www.channel4.com/news/factcheck/factcheck-men-are-more-likely-to-be-raped-than-be-falsely-accused-of-rape.

Chapter 6. Pseudoscience: Parental Alienation and Unregulated Experts

1 *Florence v. F & Anor* [2021] EWHC 3846 (Fam). [2–4].

2 Barnett, A. (2020). A genealogy of hostility: parental alienation in England and Wales. *Journal of Social Welfare and Family Law*, 42 (1), 18–29.

3 World Health Organization. (2024). 'Parental alienation'. World Health Organization. https://www.who.int/standards/classifications/frequently-asked-questions/parental-alienation.

4 American Psychological Association. (2008). 'Statement on parental alienation syndrome'. American Psychological Association. https://www.apa.org/news/press/releases/2008/01/pas-syndrome.

5 Bowles, J. J., Christian, K. K., Drew, M. B., & Yetter, K. L. (2008). 'A judicial guide to child safety in custody cases'. Reno: National Council of Juvenile and Family Court Judges.

6 Doughty, J., Maxwell, N., & Slater, T. (2018). 'Review of research and case law on parental alienation'. Welsh Government.

7   *Florence v. F & Anor* [2021]. [6].

8   Ibid. [7].

9   Ibid. [8].

10 Ibid. [3].

11 Ibid. [4].

12 Ibid. [3].

13 Ibid. [5], [6].

14 Ibid. [16].

15 Ibid. [18], [20].

16 Ibid. [34].

17 *Re A and B (Parental Alienation: No.1)* [2020] EWHC 3366 (Fam).

18 *Re A and B (Children: 'Parental Alienation') (No.5)* [2023] EWHC 1864 (Fam).

19 *Re A and B (Parental Alienation: No.1)* [30; 46].

20 *Re A and B (Children: `Parental Alienation') (No.5)* [57], [95].

21 *Re A and B (Parental Alienation: No.1)* [8].

22 Ibid. [34].

23 Ibid. [29].

24 Ibid. [55].

25 *Re A and B (Parental Alienation: No.2)* [4], [5].

26 *Re A and B (Children: 'Parental Alienation') (No.5)* [7].

27 *Re B (Children: Police Investigation)* [2022] EWCA Civ 982 [3].

28 *Re B (Children: Police Investigation)* [16].

29 *Re A and B (Parental Alienation: No.1)* [8], [49].

30 *Re A and B (Children: 'Parental Alienation') (No.5)* [98].

31 *Re A and B (Parental Alienation: No.2)* [17].

32 *Re A and B (Parental Alienation: No.3)* [44].

33 *Re A and B (Children: 'Parental Alienation') (No.5)* [102].

34 Ibid. [20], [100], [103].

35 Macdonald, G. S. (2016). 'Domestic violence and private family court proceedings: Promoting child welfare or promoting contact?' *Violence Against Women*, 22(7), 832–52; Barnett, A. (2017). '"Greater than the mere sum of its parts": coercive control and the question of proof'.

36 Barnett, A. (2014). 'Contact at All Costs: Domestic Violence and

Children's Welfare'. *Child & Fam. LQ*, 26, 439.

37 Alsalem, R. (2023). 'Custody, violence against women and violence against children' (A/HRC/53/36). United Nations. https://www.ohchr.org/en/documents/thematic-reports/ahrc5336-custody-violence-against-women-and-violence-against-children.

38 Mercer, J., & Drew, M. (eds.). (2021). *Challenging Parental Alienation: New Directions for Professionals and Parents*. Routledge.

39 Thomas, R. M., & Richardson, J. T. (2015). 'Parental Alienation Syndrome: 30 Years On and Still Junk Science'. americanbar.org. https://www.americanbar.org/groups/judicial/publications/judges_journal/2015/summer/parental_alienation_syndrome_30_years_on_and_still_junk_science/.

40 Newspaper.com by Ancestry. (n.d.). 'Casualties of a custody war'. *Pittsburgh Post-Gazette*, Pittsburgh, Pennsylvania, p.10. Retrieved 26 January 2024, from https://www.newspapers.com/newspage/90837553/.

41 Press release (2022, February 6). 'Spain: UN experts denounce child custody decision that ignores evidence of sexual abuse'. United Nations Human Rights, Office of the High Commissioner. https://www.ohchr.org/en/press-releases/2022/02/spain-un-experts-denounce-child-custody-decision-ignores-evidence-sexual.

42 Alsalem, R. (2023). 'Custody, violence against women and violence against children' (A/HRC/53/36). United Nations. https://www.ohchr.org/en/documents/thematic-reports/ahrc5336-custody-violence-against-women-and-violence-against-children.

43 Ibid. p.3.

44 Family Justice Council (2024). 'Guidance on responding to a child's unexplained reluctance, resistance or refusal to spend time with a parent and allegations of alienating behaviour'. https://www.judiciary.uk/wp-content/uploads/2024/12/Family-Justice-Council-Guidance-on-responding-to-allegations-of-alienating-behaviour-2024-1-1.pdf

45 University of Manchester. (2023, September 4). 'Shocking impact of family courts on women's health exposed'. https://www.manchester.ac.uk/about/news/shocking-impact-of-family-courts-on-womens-health-exposed/.

46 E. Dalgarno, S. Ayeb-Karlsson, D. Bramwell, A. Barnett and A.

Verma. (2024, February 1). 'Health-related experiences of family court and domestic abuse in England: A looming public health crisis.' *Journal of Family Trauma, Child Custody & Child Development*, Volume 21, Issue 3, pp.277–305. https://www.tandfonline.com/doi/full/10.1080/26904586 .2024.2307609#abstract.

47 *Re C ('Parental Alienation'; Instruction of Expert)* [2023] EWHC 345 (Fam).

48 *Re C* [2023]. [36].

49 Ibid. [12].

50 Ibid. [12].

51 Ibid. [26].

52 *Re GB (Parental Alienation: Factual Findings)* [2024] EWFC 75 (B), His Honour Judge Middleton-Roy 3 April 2024 Schedule of Findings, [6].

53 University of Manchester (2023, 4 September). 'Shocking impact of family courts on women's health exposed'. https://www.manchester. ac.uk/about/news/shocking-impact-of-family-courts-on-womens-health-exposed/.

54 *Re GB*, EWFC 75 (B). [3], [24].

55 *Re GB (Part 25 Application: Parental Alienation)* [2023] EWFC 150. https://www.bailii.org/ew/cases/EWFC/HCJ/2023/150.html.

56 Ibid. [20].

57 *Re C (Parental Alienation: Instruction of Expert)* [2023] EWHC 345 (Fam) [103]. https://www.bailii.org/ew/cases/EWHC/Fam/2023/345. html.

58 *Re GB (Part 25 Application: Parental Alienation)* [2023] EWFC 150 [17]. https://www.bailii.org/ew/cases/EWFC/HCJ/2023/150.html.

59 Ibid. [21].

60 *Re GB*, EWFC 75 (B). [130].

61 Ibid. [42].

62 Ibid. [129].

63 Ibid. [116–17].

64 Ibid. [85].

65 Ibid. [98].

66 Ibid. [86].

67 Ibid. [97].

68 Ibid [79], [97–102].

69 Ibid. [86].

70 Ibid. [167–8].

71 Idem.

72 *Re GB (Parental Alienation: Welfare)* [2024] EWFC 168 (B).

73 *Re GB*, EWFC 75 (B). 'Costs' [15–16].

Chapter 7. Conditional: Abortion and Reproductive Coercion

1 'Reproductive control by others includes control or coercion over decisions about becoming pregnant and also about continuing or terminating a pregnancy. It can be carried out by intimate partners, the wider family, or as part of criminal behaviour.' Rowlands, S., & Walker, S. (2019). 'Reproductive control by others: means, perpetrators and effects'. *BMJ Sexual & Reproductive Health*, 45(1), 61–7.

2 This is in fact a common form of reproductive control associated with intimate partner violence. See: Moore, A. M., Frohwirth, L., & Miller, E. (2010). 'Male reproductive control of women who have experienced intimate partner violence in the United States'. *Social Science & Medicine*, 70(11), 1737–44.

3 García-Moreno, C., Jansen, H. A., Ellsberg, M., Heise, L., & Watts, C. (2005). 'WHO multi-country study on women's health and domestic violence against women'. World Health Organization.

4 Silverman, J. G., & Raj, A. (2014). 'Intimate partner violence and reproductive coercion: global barriers to women's reproductive control'. *PLOS Medicine*, 11(9), e1001723.

5 Taillieu, T. L., & Brownridge, D. A. (2010). 'Violence against pregnant women: Prevalence, patterns, risk factors, theories, and directions for future research'. *Aggression and Violent Behavior*, p.27.

6 *Carla Foster v. R* [2023] EWCA Crim 1196 [49].

7 Offences Against the Person Act 1861.

8 Grace, Karen Trister, and Jocelyn C. Anderson. 'Reproductive coercion: a systematic review.' *Trauma, Violence, & Abuse* 19.4 (2018): 371–90.

9   An Australian study notes: 'One of the issues raised by some participants was that when women reported reproductive coercion it had usually happened in the past, prior to separation, and magistrates may see it as "historic" and so not relevant to the current application'. Douglas, H., Sheeran, N., & Tarzia, L. (2020). 'Identifying and responding to reproductive coercion in a legal context: issues paper', p.10.

Chapter 8. Point of No Return: Child Abduction and the Hague Convention

1   De Ruiter, A. (2020). '40 Years of the Hague Convention on Child Abduction: Legal and Societal Changes in the Rights of a Child'. European Parliament, p.4.

2   Hale, 'Foreword' in Freeman M., Taylor N. (eds.), *Research Handbook on International Child Abduction: The 1980 Hague Convention*, Edward Elgar Publishing Limited, Cheltenham, 2023, p.xvii.

3   Convention of 25 October 1980 on the Civil Aspects of International Child Abduction. Hague Conference on Private International Law. (1980, October 25). https://www.hcch.net/en/instruments/conventions/full-text/?cid=24.

4   Article 13(b) defence under the Hague Convention.

5   Trimmings, K., & Momoh, O. (2021). 'Intersection between domestic violence and international parental child abduction: protection of abducting mothers in return proceedings'. *International Journal of Law, Policy and the Family*, 35(1), ebab001.

6   Edleson, J., & Lindhorst, T. (2012). 'Battered mothers seeking safety across international borders: Examining Hague Convention cases involving allegations of domestic violence'. *Judges' Newsletter on International Child Protection*, 18.

7   Masterton, G., Rathus, Z., Flood, J., & Tranter, K. (2022). 'Being "Hagued": How weaponising the Hague Convention harms women, family and domestic violence survivors'. QUT Centre for Justice Briefing Papers, (25).

8   'Multiple Perspectives on Battered Mothers and their Children Fleeing to the United States for Safety: A Study of Hague Convention Cases'

(ojp.gov), pp.154–5. https://www.ojp.gov/pdffiles1/nij/grants/232624. pdf.

9 Ibid., pp.157–8.

10 Ibid., p.158.

11 Ibid., pp.179–81.

12 Weiner, M. H. (2021). 'You can and you should: How judges can apply the Hague Abduction Convention to protect victims of domestic violence'. *UCLA Women's LJ*, 28, 223.

13 'Ensuring family safety in Australian Hague Convention cases'. (2022, December 12). Retrieved 2024, from https://ministers.ag.gov. au/media-centre/ensuring-family-safety-australian-hague-convention-cases-12-12-2022.

14 *Re TKJ (Abduction: Hague Convention (Italy))* [2024] EWHC 198 (Fam).

15 Ibid. [10.1].

16 Ibid. [10.2].

17 Ibid. [10.3].

18 Ibid. [10.5–10.7], [11].

19 Ibid. [53].

20 Ibid. [13].

21 Ibid. [26].

22 Ibid. [54.1].

23 Ibid. [57–8].

Chapter 9. Hostile Environment: Female Genital Mutilation

1 World Health Organization. (2023, January 31). 'Female genital mutilation'. https://www.who.int/news-room/fact-sheets/detail/female-genital-mutilation.

2 OHCHR, UNAIDS, UNDP, UNECA, UNESCO, UNFPA, UNHCR, UNICEF, UNIFEM, & WHO. (2008). 'Eliminating female genital mutilation: An interagency statement'. Sexual and Reproductive Health and Research. https://www.who.int/publications/i/item/9789241596442.

3 National FGM Centre. (n.d.) 'Female Genital Mutilation'. https://

nationalfgmcentre.org.uk/fgm/; UNICEF. (2023). Female genital mutilation (FGM) statistics. UNICEF DATA. https://data.unicef. org/topic/child-protection/female-genital-mutilation/?_gl=1*9b4eq6*_ga*OTQwODg4MDM3LjE3MDYwMzU5MjI.*_ga_ZEPV2PX-419*MTcwNjAzNTkyMS4xLjEuMTcwNjAzNjE1MC42MC4wLjA; World Health Organization. (2023, January 31). 'Health Risks of Female Genital Mutilation (FGM)'. https://www.who.int/teams/sexual-and-reproductive-health-and-research-(srh)/areas-of-work/female-genital-mutilation/health-risks-of-female-genital-mutilation.

4 Plan International UK. (2015, July 21). 'How "cutting season" keeps FGM hidden in the UK'. https://plan-uk.org/blogs/how-cutting-season-keeps-fgm-hidden-in-the-uk.

5 See Schedule 2 of the Female Genital Mutilation Act 2003 introduced through Part 5, Section 73 of the Serious Crime Act 2015.

6 Farouki, L., El-Dirani, Z., Abdulrahim, S., Akl, C., Akik, C., & McCall, S. J. (2022). 'The global prevalence of female genital mutilation/cutting: A systematic review and meta-analysis of national, regional, facility, and school-based studies'. *PLoS Medicine*, 19(9), e1004061; United Nations Children's Fund, & Gupta, G. R. (2013). 'Female Genital Mutilation/Cutting: a statistical overview and exploration of the dynamics of change'. *Reproductive Health Matters*, 21(42), 184–90. http://www.jstor.org/stable/43288321.

7 The Prohibition on Female Circumcision Act 1985, amended in 2003 and 2015.

8 Macfarlane, A. J., & Dorkenoo, E. (2015). 'Prevalence of female genital mutilation in England and Wales: National and local estimates'. City University London in association with Equality Now.

9 Proudman, C. (2022). *Female Genital Mutilation: When Culture and Law Clash*. Oxford University Press. p 65.

10 Countries with high levels of FGM prevalence included Somalia in 2020 (99.2 per cent), Guinea in 2018 (94.5 per cent), Djibouti in 2012 (94.4 per cent), Egypt in 2015 (87.2 per cent), Eritrea in 2010 (83 per cent), Mali in 2018 (88.6 per cent), Sudan in 2014 (86.6 per cent) and Sierra Leone in 2019 (83 per cent). (Unicef) UNICEF. 'Female genital mutilation (FGM) statistics'. UNICEF DATA. (2023). https://data.

unicef.org/topic/child-protection/female-genital-mutilation/.

11 See judgments, *Re A (A child) (Female Genital Mutilation Protection Order Application) (Rev 1)* [2020] EWHC 323. *Re A (A Child) (Rev 1)* [2020] EWCA Civ 731. *Re A (A Child: Female Genital Mutilation: Asylum* [2019] EWHC 2475.

12 *Re A (A Child) (Rev 1)* [2020] EWCA Civ 731; *Re A (A Child : Female Genital Mutilation : Asylum) (Rev 1)* [2019] EWHC 2475 (Fam).

13 *Re A (A child) (Female Genital Mutilation Protection Order Application)* [2020] EWHC 323 (Fam).

14 UNICEF (2023, December 16). 'Female Genital Mutilation in Sudan: Factsheet'. https://www.unicef.org/sudan/media/13281/file/FGM%20Factsheet%20in%20Sudan_Dec%202023.pdf.

15 *Re A (A Child : Female Genital Mutilation : Asylum) (Rev 1)* [2019] EWHC 2475 (Fam).

16 Ibid. [58].

17 Ibid. [44–54].

18 *Re A (A child) (Female Genital Mutilation Protection Order Application)* [2020] EWHC. 323 (Fam) [52].

Chapter 10. Reversal: Turning the Tide

1 *CM v. IP* [2022], EWHC 2755 (Fam). [20], [28].

2 *DG v. KB & Anor (Re EMP (A Child)* [2023], EWFC 180. [20, 502–16], [20, 519–26].

3 *CM v. IP* [12].

4 Ibid. [21–4].

5 Ibid. [30].

6 Ibid. [36].

7 *Re H-N and Others* [2021].

8 *Re H-N and Others* [2021]. [50–1].

9 *CM v. IP* [38, 42].

10 *DG v. KB* [2023], [21].

11 Ibid. [20, 392–8].

12 Ibid. [20, 393–401].

13 Ibid. [20, 563].

14 Ibid. [20, 6510], [20, 298], [20, 299].

15 Ibid. [41].

16 Ibid. [42].

17 Ibid. [37].

18 Ibid. [168].

19 Ibid. [169].

20 *CM v. IP* [28].

21 *DG v. KB* [2023]. [146].

22 Ibid. [175].

23 Ibid. [176].

24 Ibid. [175].

25 Ibid. [191–2].

26 Ibid. [226].

27 Ibid. [233].

28 Ibid. [236. j–k], [266. e].

29 Ibid. [266. a. 4].

30 Ibid. [266. a. 3].

31 Ibid. [266. d–f].

32 *DG v. KB & Anor (Re EMP (A Child))* [2024], EWFC 12 (B), [37].

33 *DG v. KB* [2023], [204].

34 Ibid. [175, g, xvii].

35 *DG v. KB* [2024], [26].

36 Ibid. [14].

37 Ibid. [15].

38 Ibid. [69].

39 Ibid. [103].

40 Ibid. [106].

41 Ibid. [68].

42 Ibid. [93, vi].

Chapter 11. Backlash: Complaints, Abuse and Threats

1 *Traharne v. Limb* [2022] EWFC 27.

2 Ibid. [99].

3 Ibid. [52–3].

4 Ibid. [21] iv.

5 Ibid. [31] ii–iii.

6 Ibid. [5].

7 Ibid. [31] ii–iii.

8 Ibid. [33].

9 Ibid. [32].

10 Ibid. [54].

11 'A barrister may therefore now express his or her personal opinion in the media, or make a public statement, even in relation to such anticipated or current proceedings.' p.1. The Ethics Committee. (2014). 'Expressing personal opinions about your cases to or in the media' [White paper]. The General Council of the Bar. https://www. barcouncilethics.co.uk/wp-content/uploads/2017/10/Expressing-personal-opinions-about-your-cases-to-or-in-the-media.pdf.

12 *Traharne v. Limb* [31] ii.

13 Ibid. [31] i.

14 Ibid. [31] iii.

15 Ibid. [31] iv.

16 Ibid. [32].

17 Idem.

18 Ibid. [49].

19 Ibid. [64].

20 Ibid. [95].

21 Human Rights Act 1998, Schedule 1, Part 1, Article 10.

22 *Traharne v. Limb* [53].

23 Bar Standards Board (2023, September 20). *The BSB Handbook.* The Bar Standards Board. https://www.barstandardsboard.org.uk/the-bsb-handbook.html?part=E3FF76D3-9538-4B97-94C02111664E5709&q=Guidance%2Bto%2BRules%2BC65.7-C68.

24 Bar Standards Board (2022, September 5). *Mr Anthony Daniel Bennett.* Past disciplinary findings. https://www.barstandardsboard.org.uk/disciplinary_finding/183624.html.

25 *Diggins v. BSB* [2020] EWHC 467 (Admin). [2].

26 Kirk. T (2023, August 11). 'Senior judge threatens to lock up defendants for "delaying justice" with late guilty pleas'. *Evening Standard.*

https://www.standard.co.uk/news/crime/judge-guilty-pleas-emptycourts-truro-plymouth-crown-court-threat-b1100088.html.

27 Sadiq, F (@FaiselSadiq), 'Hey Siri, please show me an example of unlawful conduct and abuse of power by a holder of judicial office.' (2023, August 10), X, https://x.com/FaiselSadiq/status/1689685179512627205.

28 The Cat From Greece (@acatfromgreece), 'This is (a) awful in itself; and (b) unfathomably stupid. Why, with a huge backlog, would any Judge want to encourage *more* trials?' (2023, August 10), X, https://x.com/acatfromgreece/status/1689615744630165504.

29 Sharma, R (@Raj_Sharma_UK), 'It should be remarkable that a member of the Judiciary thinks that they can get away with issuing such a policy. I imagine if the policy had been implemented but not committed to writing, no-one would have known.' (2023, August 10), https://x.com/Raj_Sharma_UK/status/1689666380079984640.

30 Siddique, H. (2024, September 9). 'Barrister applies for "boys' club" disciplinary case to be thrown out.' The Guardian. https://www.theguardian.com/uk-news/article/2024/sep/09/barrister-appeals-to-axe-boys-club-case-claiming-she-is-being-treated-unfairly.

31 Grierson, J. (2024, May 15). 'Barrister who fell asleep during inquest cleared of misconduct'. The Guardian. https://www.theguardian.com/society/article/2024/may/15/barrister-who-fell-asleep-during-inquest-cleared-of-misconduct.

32 Ibid. [141].

33 Dodd, V. (2023, January 26). 'Large rise in men referred to Prevent over women-hating incel ideology'. The Guardian. https://www.theguardian.com/uk-news/2023/jan/26/large-rise-in-men-referred-to-prevent-over-women-hating-incel-ideology.

34 Shropshire Star (2023) '"Men's rights activist" cleared of harassing barrister – but will receive restraining order'. https://www.shropshirestar.com/news/local-hubs/mid-wales/2023/11/28/mens-rights-activist-clearedof-harassing-barrister-but-will-receive-restraining-order-says-judge/; Martin, S. (2023, December 2). 'Exclusive: the "incel" ex-soldier behind Hate War on feminist lawyer: "Men's rights" activist who sent snap of himself with gun to barrister is found guilty of knife possession and told not to contact her'. Daily Mail Online. https://www.

dailymail.co.uk/news/article-12814993/Mens-rights-activist-sent-snap-gun-barrister-guilty-knife-possession.html.

35 David Mottershead on X: 'Court case on the in 3 weeks time. Not sure if Dr P will be there or not. Hoping she will be so my legal team can hold her to account for her violent, racist, sexist abuse of men and boys.' https://t.co/HZYZL5GbCX.

36 Martin, S. (2023, November 24). 'Veteran police inspector unmasked as a vile online troll who targeted women campaigning for justice for Sarah Everard has been sacked'. *Mail Online*. https://www.dailymail.co.uk/news/article-12788221/vile-troll-unmasked-police-inspector-targeted-women-campaigning-sarah-everard-sacked.html

37 Proudman, C. (2023, July 10). 'Speaking up: Charlotte Proudman'. *Counsel*. https://www.counselmagazine.co.uk/articles/speaking-up-charlotte-proudman.

38 Williams, M. and Pike, G. (2021). 'Barristers' Working Lives 2021: A report for The Bar Council', September 2021. https://www.barcouncil.org.uk/static/9a8ceb20-ba5e-44f8-9b3f765be564ea15/ a2be540b-666e-4ab8-aff e6ad74544812e/Barristers-Working-Lives-report-2021.pdf.

Chapter 12. Decision: Three Days in Court

1 Gentleman, A. (2024, April 15). 'High court judge removed from case in part due to his Garrick membership'. The *Guardian*. https://www.theguardian.com/uk-news/2024/apr/15/high-court-judge-jonathan-cohen-removed-from-case.

2 European Court of Human Rights Grand Chamber, Case of Morice v. France (Application no. 29369/10).

3 Ibid. [134].

4 Ibid. [139].

5 Ibid. [125], [131], [135].

6 *Diggins v. BSB* [2020].

7 *Adil v. GMC* [2023] EWHC 797 (Admin).

8 *Khan v. BSB* [2020] EWHC 2184 (Admin).

9 Cafcass (2024, October 9). 'Cafcass publishes new Domestic Abuse Practice Policy'. https://www.cafcass.gov.uk/cafcass-publishes-new-domestic-abuse-practice-policy.